POWER FREAKS

Dealing with Them in the Workplace or Anyplace

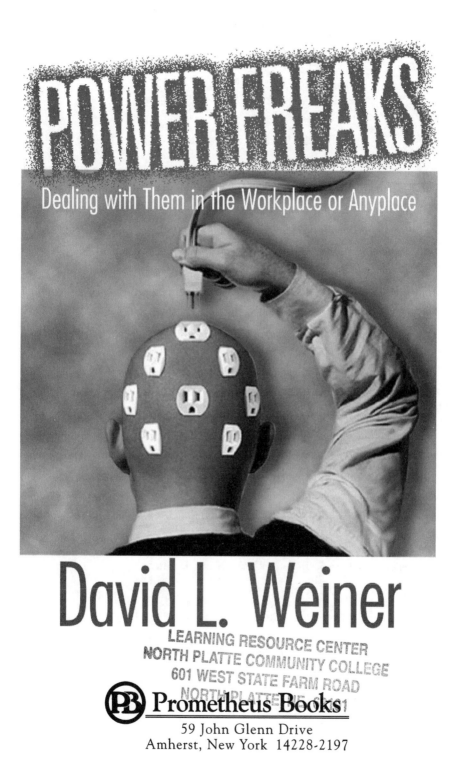

David L. Weiner

Prometheus Books

59 John Glenn Drive
Amherst, New York 14228-2197

Published 2002 by Prometheus Books

Inquiries should be addressed to
Prometheus Books
59 John Glenn Drive
Amherst, New York 14228–2197
VOICE: 716–691–0133, ext. 207
FAX: 716–564–2711
WWW.PROMETHEUSBOOKS.COM

06 05 04 03 02   5 4 3 2 1

Library of Congress Cataloging-in-Publication Data

Weiner, David L.
    Power freaks : dealing with them in the workplace or anyplace / David L. Weiner.
        p. cm.
    Includes bibliographical references and index.
    ISBN 1–59102–013–1 (alk. paper)
    1. Managing your boss. 2. Bullying in the workplace. 3. Office politics.
4. Psychology, Industrial. 5. Control (Psychology) I. Title.

HF5548.83 .W435 2002
650.1'3—dc21

                                                                2002068081

Printed in the United States of America on acid-free paper

To Barry, Andy, Robin, Myranda, and Kyle

POWER FREAKS

Contents

Acknowledgments

I am especially grateful to the University of Wisconsin Department of Psychology, in particular Charles T. Snowdon, professor and chair; Joe Newman, professor; Craig Berridge, professor; and Catherine Marler, associate professor, for assisting me in fact checking those chapters devoted to the workings of the mind as they relate to power freaks and the social dominance hierarchy in general. This outstanding department is consistently ranked in the top ten by U.S. News & World Report magazine, and is number two in clinical psychology. The department is number one in the nation in research funding received.

I am also grateful to the HealthEmotions Research Institute of the University of Wisconsin, which is led by Ned Kalin, chair of the university's department of psychiatry and Richard Davidson, professor of psychology and psychiatry. This is probably the world's leading research facility focusing on the biology of emotion and how emotions influence our health. My thanks to Steve Shelton, research psychiatrist with the Institute, who forwarded many papers to me dealing with the brain chemistry that works to create dominance and social hierarchies.

My thanks to Bob Lefton, CEO of Psychological Associates for writing the foreword to this book. Bob is one of the world's leading industrial psychologists and his firm is among the top three in the world, devoted to behavioral sciences in business. He has seen it all.

My thanks to Linda Regan, my editor at Prometheus, who was relentless in pushing this book along and who offered her criticisms in ways that didn't violate my own power program. My thanks also to Chris

Kramer, Katherine Deyell, Jacqueline Cooke, and Bruce Carle at Prometheus for their assistance, and to Jonathan Kurtz for his optimism and continuing encouragement.

My thanks also to Shirley Paolinelli, who served as my research assistant, to Carla Salinas for her help with the bibliography and to Suzy Chudzik for her help with the index. My thanks as well to Donna Czukla, Irene Bedzis, Lois Martyn, Frank Vallejo, Rick Asta, Kathy Parker, Lindsey Scheiblauer, Sarah Schutz, Dave Olsson, Scott Caras, Amy Bowne, Rebecca Levie, Fred Misher, Molly Dineen, Barry Berish, Bonnie Borgstrom, Joel Williams, Andy Weiner and Larry Dore for their assistance along the way.

Foreword
Robert E. Lefton

There is an apocryphal story about a CEO—let's call him Fred—who suffered from the typical shortcomings of an authoritarian personality. Fred had intense needs for esteem and autonomy. He loved being the center of attention, became ecstatic when others told him how great and effective he was, and placed great emphasis on making decisions with little or no input from others.

As you might expect, this fellow's behavior negated any possibility of honest, open communication. Consequently, he was totally deprived of any meaningful feedback and, thus, any use of his executives' intellectual capital.

Those who worked for him described Fred's management style as "operating out of the book of threats." They joked that he was a specialist in delegating blame. Fred had a particular fondness for pinning guilt on those who exhibited the most submissive, ingratiating behavior. He often repeated the quotation originally attributed to J. Paul Getty, "The meek may inherit the earth, but never the mineral rights."

That's why the vice president of human resources was so startled when Fred insisted on taking the battery of personality tests that were used by the company to select the people they hired. Soon after taking the tests, Fred was on the phone to the human resources head. "Get those tests scored and come up to my office and give me feedback."

You can imagine how panic stricken the VP of HR was. Nevertheless, after a lot of encouragement from his peers he was prepared to give Fred total, candid feedback, hoping that it would help modify the boss's troublesome behavior. "Sir," he proclaimed, "you are overly dominating, power hungry, overly controlling, and you micromanage your people. People find you intimidating. You are a very poor listener. You are very dogmatic. You are resistant to new ideas and bulldoze your decisions through. You are headstrong, unyielding, and inflexible."

The CEO listened intently and then said to the VP of HR, "That's very interesting. Was there anything bad?"

This story beautifully illustrates a point David Weiner makes in this wonderful book, *Power Freaks: Dealing with Them in the Workplace or Anyplace*. Power freaks rarely think in consequential terms. They lack insight into the impact their behavior and actions have on others. Furthermore, they almost immediately rationalize and explain away their behavior.

In my years working as a consultant, I have met many power freaks. Authoritarian personalities have a long history of flourishing and even being rewarded by their behaviors. Often those who are brilliant autocrats with integrity become extraordinarily effective CEOs.

About twenty years ago I worked with the CEO of a well-known railroad, who expressed many of the control aspects of the power freaks described in this book. He seemed not to care nor have any regard for the consequences his behavior had on his key executives. Whether under pressure or "relaxing" with others, he remained rigid and inflexible, rarely moving out of his authoritarian posture. He rarely received candid feedback from his executives, since they feared him and felt intimidated by him. People pretty much told him what they believed he wanted to hear or what would please him.

His people were so frightened by him no one dared leave work at night until the CEO went home. Distraught executives who had to live under these conditions found it impossible to attend any social events or even notify their spouses what time they would be home for dinner. Desperate, they persuaded the Security Department to record the precise time each day the CEO left, in hopes that they could establish his pattern of departure. After two months, they analyzed the data and found to their dismay that the CEO's exiting behavior was absolutely random, providing them no chance of anticipating their own time of arrival home. And so their suspenseful schedules continued.

Another CEO power freak was described to me by one of his direct reports as having a hammer mentality—he treated people like nails, always pounding on them verbally. During one particular meeting with a subordinate the CEO decreed, "You do the talking, I'll do the contradicting."

Then there was the authoritarian CEO who contracted me to do an employee morale survey. When the results were tabulated, it indicated a third of the employees were miserably unhappy due to the autocratic policies of the company. The company's head of human resources and I presented the results to the CEO, who sat silently, offering absolutely no response. The next evening at a social function, the CEO said to the HR guy, "What do you think of those damn survey results?" The HR guy responded, "It was a well-designed survey with good results. I think we need to act immediately to increase the morale of the employees." The CEO said, "I agree that we need to take immediate action. Fire the 33 percent unhappy employees and we'll have 100 percent satisfaction."

Perhaps the lesson to be learned here is that power freaks are everywhere and will always be with us. Sooner or later, each of us will be coping with one or more power freaks in our lives, if we are not dealing with them already. Fortunately, David Weiner has built a window into the mind of the power freak. He tells us why they behave the way they do and provides some great ideas on how to handle their authoritarian ways.

In the past, we used to lay the burden for this type of behavior in the laps of guilt-ridden parents. Today, as Weiner clearly describes it, the need to dominate and over-control is ostensibly built into our nervous system, a force we have been carrying around with us for thousands of years. Being a power freak results from a complex interaction of nature and nurture. The drive to dominate, intimidate and oppress others, to a large degree, appears to have its basis in an innate, instinctual, primitive need. Experts generally agree that the brain plays a key role here and whether our mothers were passive, dominant, overly nurturing, or smothering apparently can have much less influence than we've thought in these instances. Thank God!—Parents can breathe a sigh of relief.

David Weiner has created a book which is scholarly, educational, fun, and practical. It provides the reader with a greater understanding of how to diagnose authoritarian behaviors. More importantly, it provides prescriptions for effectively coexisting with such an intimidating menace. Incorporating these sound strategies will increase the probability that you can protect yourself against the power freaks in your life and *not* become the victim of their ruthless, remorseless behavior.

Power Freaks is a great read and an important book for any executive or professional. Even power freaks themselves will benefit from reading it. Perhaps it could serve as a form of bibliotherapy. I personally felt it helped me better understand behaviors I have observed over my forty-two years as a consulting psychologist to business. I'm sure it will help you be a better coach and counselor to your bosses, peers, subordinates, friends, and family.

St. Louis, Missouri
April 5, 2002

POWER FREAKS

Introduction

In 1973, David G. Winter, professor of psychology at the University of Michigan, wrote *The Power Motive*, a seminal book on the subject of power. He contends in the preface that power is a topic "about which everyone has strong, confused and of course uniquely correct ideas. . . . No one can hope to be unassailable when he writes or talks about power; it is a subject too close to us all, and our views are saturated with strong emotions and moral scruples."[1] He also observes that "the literature on power is full of discussion between power and other related concepts such as 'influence,' 'leadership,' 'authority,' dominance,' 'force,' and 'control.' From one writer to the next, different words are often used for the same concept and the same word is used for different concepts."[2]

This was obviously not an easy subject to cover then and it isn't today. Despite the fact that our propensity for power and status appears to be one of the major causes of the serious conflicts in our lives and in the world at large, it is a subject that is relatively understudied, which made the writing of this book much more difficult than I anticipated.

My objectives were threefold: First, to communicate what apparently is happening in the minds of power freaks that explains to some degree their twisted and distorted outlooks. Second, to define the many characteristics and viewpoints of power freaks so that there is no doubt in knowing one when we see one. And third, to enumerate the best ways to deal with them, particularly in the workplace, but with principles that may be applied anywhere.

It would appear that the drive some of us have to dominate, intimidate, and oppress others has its basis in an innate, instinctual, and primitive need. It is a need that we apparently share with both higher and lower animals. It is a vestige of the brain system that was most valuable to us when our ancestors lived in caves and on the African savannas and needed an alpha leader, the power freak of his time, to dominate and keep order. The experts agree that the brain has hardly changed at all in the past 100,000 years, and so it is apparent that we still carry this old system around with us.

For most of us, this primitive propensity to achieve and defend power and status is generally harmless. We either don't feel it enough—some of us actually "fear power"—or we have it under control. When this feeling does emerge, it is usually when we are facing a challenge. In a competitive athletic event, for example, some of us take on the primary characteristics of a power freak: becoming domineering, intimidating, ruthless, and remorseless. After the event is over and we've calmed down, we revert to our normal behavior.

Extreme power freaks apparently do not revert. They persist in domineering and intimidating everyone they consider fair game on any given day, which might include their children at breakfast, the people they supervise, a co-worker, the waiter at lunch, the vendors that call on them, a taxi driver, and their spouse, if they still have the strength to pick on them when they get home.

The bigger problem is that they are impervious to reason. You can't walk up and say, "Bob, you must know that you are acting like a big jerk. Everyone knows it. Why don't you get off of it?" Bob and others like him don't know it. Their thinking is distorted, the apparent reasons for which are described in chapters 2 and 3.

In fact, many extreme power freaks appear to exhibit psychopathic traits in combination with characteristics of other personality disorders and may be certifiably mentally disordered, as described in detail in chapter 5. And like most other people with mental disorders, they are free to live and work among us and may be our boss, a colleague down the hall who wants to walk all over us, a parent, a sibling, or someone else in our lives.

Still other extreme power freaks may not feel the dark urgings of psychopathy, but have become obsessed with their status, as described in chapter 6. Haughty, arrogant, and imperious, they can be just as miserable to deal with. When this condition is reinforced by a mental disorder, it's really time to duck.

Then there are those, as just noted, who become transformed only in specific situations: when they are challenged by a colleague for their job, for example, or when they are suddenly placed in a position of some power. Perhaps during the week they are a mild-mannered administrative assistant. But they own a sailboat and when they are on it, they turn into a veritable Captain Bligh, ordering crew and guests around as if they were king of the world. Or perhaps they become a bank teller and for the first time in their lives they are empowered. And so they may purposely keep us waiting in front of them while they pretend to shuffle paperwork as a means to exert their power. "Situational" and "directional" power freaks, two widely seen types among the power-crazed, are described in chapters 8 and 9.

How do we deal with all of them when reason won't work?

There are certain basics we need to know when dealing with a power freak boss or a colleague or another domineering individual, if we are unfortunate enough to have one or more of them in our lives. These basic strategies are spelled out in the last three chapters, but can be fully appreciated and properly executed only if you first read the chapters leading up to them.

How we ultimately deal with the power freaks in our lives depends in large part on how we *ourselves* rank on the power/status intensity scale. The higher we are, the more difficulties we will have. To find out how we might rank individually on the power/status intensity scale, I have inserted a simple test in chapter 10 for the reader to take at his or her leisure.

I can only say to you after being immersed in this subject matter for almost two years, that in your endeavors to co-exist with the power-crazed in your life, you have your work cut out for you. The answers don't come easy because there are no universal answers. The suggested strategies are basically a compilation of what I consider the best the experts have developed, along with my own recommendations based on many years of observation.

So here we go.

NOTES: Most names and circumstances have been changed where actual examples from my own experience have been used, with the pseudonyms shown initially in quotation marks.

If you are looking for a fast and easy read, there are a few technical bumps in chapters 2 through 6 that focus on the mental characteristics that drive power freaks into delusional thinking. But bear with it, the information is essential if you are to select the best strategies for dealing with the power freak(s) in your life. The book gets easier as you go along.

CHAPTER 1

Who Are These People?

I believe there is no one principle which predominates in human nature so much in every stage of life, from the cradle to the grave, in males and females, old and young, black and white, rich and poor, high and low, as this passion for superiority.

John Adams, second president of the United States[1]

Who is a power freak?

Was Michael Jordan one? After all, when he built his reputation playing for the Chicago Bulls basketball team, it was no secret that despite his smooth exterior, natural warmth, and charm, he would publicly put down teammates, create feuds, and have temper tantrums if he didn't get his way. And early in his professional career he trashed the team's coach when he didn't get the ball at the end of a game.[2] Is this enough to qualify him?

Or is a power freak the more obvious Bobby Knight, who was ultimately fired as coach of the Indiana University basketball team for physically and mentally abusing some of his players, demeaning many of his assistant coaches and intimidating others?[3]

Or is Leona Helmsley more the prototypical power freak, as the label resonates in our ears? For years she managed the Helmsley hotel chain and publicly humiliated or fired employees if they did the slightest thing to displease her.[4]

Or what about spiritual leaders like Marshall Applewhite, who in 1997 led thirty-seven Heaven's Gate cultists to mass suicide? Applewhite's dominance over the group's thought processes and its activities was so powerful that he convinced them that after their self-inflicted deaths, their spirits would reside safely on a spaceship hidden behind the Hale-Bopp comet.

Or what about military leaders such as Douglas MacArthur, who fought courageously in World War I, exposing himself to enemy fire, did the same during the recapture of the Philippines in World War II, and led the postwar Japanese government? Despite these achivements, MacArthur was described by Pulitzer-prize winning author and historian Herbert P. Bix as "Extremely egotistical, sometimes pompous and arrogant . . . [who] believed that all credit and acclaim . . . should accrue to himself alone," and he always viewed failures as the consequence of inadequate support or machination from above.[5]

Or what about people outside the limelight, the people you and I deal with on a daily basis? For instance, consider middle managers like "William Sundahl," an executive I knew, who after his appointment as a manager of purchasing, called together his staff, many of whom had been working for the company for twenty or more years, and threatened them with immediate termination unless, from that point on, they did exactly as he said, without question.

Or "Hilda Chamberlain" (pages 143–46), a manager at a consulting company, who sabotaged the presentation of a subordinate, because she thought he was after her job?

Or "Marvin Axel" (page 131), an office administrator who would put down his subordinates, if, among other things, they didn't place paper clips precisely one-half inch from the left-hand border of their documents?

It turns out that they all would probably fall within the broad parameters that characterize a power freak. Power freaks can project a wide range of exterior personalities, ranging from the warm and innocent to the obviously brash and despotic. What defines and separates power freaks from the rest of us appears to be an instinctual, automatic need to do whatever is necessary, frequently without regard to morals, ethics, civility, or common decency, to achieve greater levels of dominance and status.

The short list of characteristics would include some of those that define a psychopath, whose traits are echoed by power freaks in the business world and elsewhere:

❧ **Glibness/superficial charm:** When needed most power freaks can turn it on, to the point they can knock you off your seat with their repartee. Others lack any form of charm. "Me Tarzan, you Jane," might be their typical statement.

❧ **Grandiose sense of self-worth:** They think no one else is as smart or innovative as they are.

❧ **Lack of empathy for other human beings:** They can get a "high" from watching others suffer under their direction. It can make their day.

❧ **Lack of remorse or guilt:** Long after the outburst or episode demeaning others is over, they still feel no remorse or guilt. Nobody is there.

❧ **Cunning, callous, and manipulative:** They will do whatever it takes to reach their objectives. Misrepresentation and cunning are mother's milk to them.

❧ **Won't take responsibility for their own actions:** Nothing is ever their fault. They will always find ways to blame others for any failure.

❧ **Exploitive attitude toward others:** They perceive you as beneath them on their imagined scale of social hierarchy, and so feel free to exploit and demean you.

❧ **Question the loyalty or trustworthiness of friends or associates:** When you're with them, you frequently feel that you've done something wrong when you haven't.

Many power freaks exhibit these traits as a normal part of their daily lives, as mentioned earlier, from the moment they wake up, barking at a spouse or their children, through their day at work, where it's their way or the highway, and then in the evening at a restaurant where they demean their waiter; in short, whenever they come in contact with people they perceive as beneath them: almost everyone.

An excellent description of a power freak was offered in the book *Cain & Abel at Work: How to Overcome Office Politics and the People Who Stand between You and Success*, by Gerry Lange, a veteran of the political wars, and Todd Domke, media consultant. The authors use the euphemism "Cain" as their descriptor of a power freak:

Cain is so driven by ambition that he'll do almost anything to satisfy his lust for success. To get his way, he will use and manipulate others; he will stab an innocent colleague in the back, with no remorse; he will not only mislead those he works with, he will abuse them and make their lives miserable—and he will take pride in doing so. . . . [He] needs to prove to himself that he is superior in power and status.[6]

Power freaks, as we noted in the Introduction, may also be *situational* or *directional*. The character traits only emerge when they are in a competition, on a basketball court or in a court of law, for example; or when they are challenged by a new hire who has told them they are out for their job and who promptly begins to undercut them. When the challenge has been resolved, when the competition ends, they revert to their normal behavior. As we shall see, there are a wide variety of power freak types, differing in combinations and intensities and exhibiting themselves in different ways and varying circumstances.

In the business world the general rule of thumb is that power freaks, especially those who are extreme (they are classified as mild, moderate, and extreme, as will be detailed later), will eventually self destruct, unless they have such enormous talent and intelligence that their character flaws are overlooked and tolerated. Most of the best CEOs and other managers in the business world are those who cultivate climates of teamwork and innovation among their employees. These CEOs work to submerge their own roles, which, oddly enough, gives them even greater power.

There is a significant difference between a management leader, at whatever level of the business world, who is relentless in the pursuit of excellence for the sake of excellence, and one who pursues excellence for the sake of self-glorification, as does the extreme power freak. Employees immediately know the difference and given other characteristics of leadership, will almost always work harder for the former than the latter, even though the pressure from the former is not coercive.

The incongruity is that at the beginning of a career, many of the characteristics of an extreme power freak might be perceived by superiors as reflecting the type of aggressiveness and ambition that the company seeks in its young employees. And so these employees may be promoted and given ever greater responsibilities, in the belief that their overbearing attitudes toward their peers and subordinates are just what the doctor ordered. However, unless they reach a point where they become indispensable to a corporation because of specific talents and unless others above and below them are willing to accommodate, their increasing visibility and the unmasking of their true nature will usually result, eventually, in their downfall.

Power freaks, of course, also exist outside of the business world of which professional sports are a part. They can encompass neighbors who freak out if you cross their lawns, because in their minds, you are threatening their domain, their area of authority. They can include parents who threaten the referees of their kids' organized sports leagues with bodily harm because the decisions those referees made are perceived as a challenge to the status of their children and by extension to themselves. Then there is the fellow in the car in back of you who incessantly honks his horn at you because you inadvertently cut into his lane on the highway. He is under the perception that you have challenged his status. That lane, in his mind, is his turf, his domain.

The world of power freaks even extends to academics who should know better. How many times have we read how one academic has tried to sabotage or demean the studies of another so that his paper is the first in print, giving him dominance over his rival, whose status is then diminished among his colleagues? How many of us watched in amazement at the bitter rivalry that existed in the quest to sequence the human genome between the privately owned Celera and the publicly funded Human Genome Project? Bitter charges and countercharges flew between them, each believing that the other was threatening their status. And yet this is considered by many scientists to be the most important study ever conducted, because it will ultimately reveal how the human genome works to create the human form and the causes of more than 3,000 inherited diseases.

Power freakishness at some level has also been known to infect mothers, the most hallowed persons in our collective lives. Sara Roosevelt, mother of Franklin Delano, our thirty-second president, made it a point to humiliate and exert dominance over Franklin's wife, Eleanor, in front of the family with enough frequency that they had to have a separate house built for Eleanor on the family's Hyde Park estate.[7] Think of mothers and also fathers you have known who have never been able to give up control of their children no matter how old they grow to be.

There is undoubtedly a bit of the power freak in most of us, which is not all bad in limited quantity. But as we shall see, when it is at high levels it can make us unbalanced and distort how we see reality. Unless we live as hermits, a distorted view of reality is not good for ourselves or those around us.

In the meantime, those of us who come within the power freaks' sphere of influence must learn how to deal with them. And that begins with understanding how they really think, which, as we shall see in the next chapter, is quite possibly a contradiction in terms.

CHAPTER 2

How Does a Power Freak Think?

A design engineer working for a Fortune 500 company brought a document to his supervisor for review. Later in the day, the supervisor walked into his office and began "zinging" page after page at his head, shouting repeatedly that this was an "obvious error that should have never been overlooked." As the engineer related the story: "It turned out that he was upset that I forgot to change the color of one cell in an Excel spreadsheet and so he was literally ripping the pages off the stack I had given him and whizzing them at me like a frisbee." His supervisor was a mechanical engineer with a degree from Harvard.[1]

How does a power freak think?

That's the whole point. They don't think. At least not in the way we commonly use the word.

You can't walk up to an extreme power freak and say, "Please, stop what you're doing. You're upsetting people with your power plays, your put-downs, your pomposity, your backbiting, your abrasiveness, your favoritism, and your temper tantrums. You know that how you act is wrong. It is not only causing stress in everyone around you, but it is also hurting your career, I can assure you. You can see that clearly can't you?"

"No, I can't see that clearly," the extreme power freak might say in reply. "And by the way, you're fired."

The moment that we try to change the thinking of a power freak, we are engaged in a futile gesture. It would be just as useless to walk up to someone we know is addicted to drugs or alcohol with a rational plea to get them to stop. "Now you know that stuff is no good for you," we might say. "It is ruining your health and can end up killing you before your time. Down deep you know that. Everyone knows that. So please, get some treatment and stop it right now."

"I am not addicted to alcohol," the person might reply. "I am in complete control, I drink simply to relax. There is a problem with my stomach, however, that part I know. It isn't absorbing the alcohol properly, too much is remaining in my stomach overnight. Regarding treatment, I just can't do it. I know I am not an alcoholic and going into treatment will only embarrass my family."

Most of us apparently understand the difficulties of getting people who are addicted to admit to the addiction and begin the painful process of withdrawal. According to neuroscientists, as will be pointed out in more detail shortly, we can become victims of an addiction when the reward or pleasure mechanism of our brain feels a "high." Some of us feel these highs more than others and some of us are more capable of overriding them than others if they become habituating.

Many young people become addicted to drugs like cocaine because they believe they have the will power, the rational strength to prevent any future addiction. The virtual inevitability of addiction is rarely apparent before they begin. "It won't happen to me, I'll be able to stop at any time," they think. Some can, many can't. In the field of psychology, every characteristic is measured in levels of intensity. And each of us has each characteristic in varying levels of intensity, which is why we are all so different and why we all react so differently to new influences in our lives. No two human brains are alike, even among identical twins. Since our minds, which house our thought processes, our ability to reason, our creative capacities, outlooks, memory, system of emotions and our sense of consciousness, reside in our brains, there are no two minds that are alike.

An addiction, in the parlance of psychology, is an "extreme attachment." There is a whole body of academic work relating to the field of attachment. It appears the brain/mind has a propensity to attach to all sorts of things from love interests, to religions, to our children, to substances, to philosophical ideas, to a far-reaching variety of physical and metaphysical phenomena, including exercise and masochism. John Bowlby is known as the father of attachment theory and developed one fascinating subtheory, which might be paraphrased as follows: Once we become intensely attached or addicted to an authority figure, we will subsequently become attached or addicted to his or her ideas, no matter how peculiar they may be.[2]

What then frequently follows when we become addicted to something, be it a substance, an activity, a person, a group, an idea, or a belief is that *our thinking can become more or less distorted within the subject range of the addiction*. Thus the distorted thinking of an alcoholic whose problem is obvious to the rest of us is evident in his denial that he has a problem. Marshall Applewhite likely believed there was a new life for his Heaven's Gate group on the spaceship behind the Comet Hale-Bopp. Adolf Hitler actually believed that the Aryan race, as he called it, was superior to all others and worth purifying through murdering others. Fundamentalist religionists may disdain or even spit on women walking down the street whom they believe are not properly clothed. The compulsive shopper actually believes that the money spent on needless things is worth the thrills or highs the activity gives them, even when they begin to face bankruptcy. An active member of the Ku Klux Klan actually believes that all African Americans are inferior, even though the Klan member may be unemployed and homeless and the African American he is thinking about is a member of the U.S. Supreme Court. These are all examples of thinking that the more balanced of us would agree are more or less distorted. And yet in other ways, these people might be perfectly normal. They might wake up in the morning, say hello to a neighbor as they pick up their newspaper on the porch, have a pleasant breakfast with the kids, kiss their spouse goodbye, and meet an old friend for lunch—all perfectly normal things. You would look at them, talk to them under these conditions, and never know that in the area of their addictions, and they may have several, that their thinking is distorted.

To make matters worse, as we've noted, it is extremely difficult and often impossible to alter the thinking of these people through rational argument.

As family therapist Craig Nakken points out in his book *The Addictive Personality*, "Slowly over time, addictive logic develops into a belief system—a delusion system from which the addicted person's life will be directed. The person will fight this and delay it as long as possible, but eventually the delusion system . . . take[s] control."[3] Craig Berridge, professor of psychology at the University of Wisconsin-Madison, added in a note to me that the addict may be aware in some cases that his actions are self-destructive, and yet "the addict cannot control his compulsion."

What does this all have to do with power freaks, particularly extreme power freaks? As we'll soon learn, it is apparent that they are addicted to power and status, and that they are capable of feeling the same type of highs when they demean and intimidate people that addicted drug users feel when they imbibe substances. These highs all appear to emanate from the reward or pleasure system that is wired into the mental software of our brains, and which for many of us may be flawed, as will be described in chapter 4. Thus the thinking of the power freak within the area of the addiction, the need for power, may be distorted, even though he may appear logical and reasonable in his rationalizations. If we are to deal with extreme power freaks, we need a closer understanding of this phenomenon.

It was psychoanalyst Sigmund Freud who suggested that human behavior is largely driven by unconscious and nonrational drives, and then is rationalized and justified in terms of logic and reason.[4] We have since learned that what Freud and other early thinkers called our unconscious is a system of instincts, motives, etched memories, and emotional reactions that are controlled by a subset of brain structures that operate in parallel and frequently in opposition to our own rationality and intellect.

This parallel system has been given many labels: the limbic brain, the dinosaur brain, the primitive brain, the inner mind, the inner child, the inner grown-up, the inner voice, the inner dummy, the id, the instinctive brain, the unconscious, the subconscious, the reptilian brain, and the emotional brain, among others. It is partially instinctual, containing what scientists call appetitive drives, some of which are readily recognizable, such as those that regulate hunger, sex, kinship, status, and our need to nurture the young. It also includes our reactive emotions and feelings, what scientists call "affect," which can be rewarding or punishing, or in a nutshell, makes us happy or sad.

In a paper titled "Appetitive Pleasure States," clinical psychiatry professor Norman Doidge of the University of Toronto described this system as our "lower instinctual-affective processes,"[5] which strikes me as being highly descriptive. "Lower" refers to the lower part of the brain, where these older brain structures reside. "Instinctual" can be said to refer to our autonomous, or to use the less academic term, "automatic" responses . . . we come across an alligator in the park who is about to lunge at us and we sense fear even though we see it is on a chain. "Affective" refers to our reactive feelings and emotions such as fear, depression, elation, happiness, disgust, and anger. "Processes" refers to the brain chemicals and connections that create the system and make it work. For the purposes of this book and to make the descriptor clearer, we'll use the metaphor the "instinctual-emotional system."

The term "instinctual" appears more appropriate than the term "instinctive," which implies a natural, genetic tendency. In fact, our natural instincts are molded over time by events, particularly traumatic events that take place in our lives. Thus, we may have a low natural power drive, but in late adolescence, our father tells us "you will never amount to anything." If at the time we are vulnerable to such a statement by an authority figure we respect, it may ratchet up our power drive and innately change us. On the other hand, it could depress us, depending on the nature of our vulnerability at the time, and put us in a long-term funk. This is why many psychologists prefer not to refer to instincts in their vernacular of the mental components that drive us, preferring the term "motive."

The term "instinctual-emotional" will thus be used in this book in the context of a system that is vulnerable to varying forms of traumatic change and synonymous with psychology's interpretation of the term "motive." In other words, the system reacts automatically to what it senses, but its settings can be changed by trauma. One day we get on an elevator and feel no fear at all. But there is an accident, the elevator suddenly drops ten floors and we are injured. If we are vulnerable to a trauma of this kind—some of us would not be, we'd crawl off, get ourselves medical attention and forget about it—the experience will nonetheless change our instinctual settings. The next time we get on an elevator, instead of feeling calm, we automatically become deathly afraid.

While the instinctual-emotional side of our minds does many nice things for us, such as reminding us when we're hungry and giving us the feeling of love, it is also capable, due to its primitive nature, of virtually infecting our rationality with twisted views that appear perfectly logical and reasonable to those so infected.

Thus, a schizophrenic lawyer may be able to argue beautifully in a courtroom, but believe that he is Jesus Christ reincarnated and give us very convincing arguments structured in a logical and reasonable sequence, attempting to prove that he is. A fanatic Muslim extremist can offer similar logic and reason in attempting to prove to us that Western civilization is satanic and must be destroyed, including women, children, the whole lot. This vulnerability of the rational mind among many of us, to the infection of twisted realities generated by the primitive drives of the instinctual-emotional side of our minds, is perhaps the human race's greatest weakness.

Freud also made an invaluable observation that the id, which was his metaphor for the instinctual-emotional system, *has no sense of logic, time, or awareness*. By this he meant that this side of our mind is not only capable of becoming addicted, or using the more common term, fanaticized, to a distorted outlook or attitude, but once it does, it is not immediately open to rational persuasion, no matter how logical or compelling.

For example, if twenty years ago, you were on an airplane that had an inordinately bumpy flight and you were forced to make an unscheduled landing, which made you extremely nervous and anxious, you may still feel skittish about getting on planes altogether and may refuse to ride in them at all. Your best friends could line up dozens of Boeing officials and flight safety experts to take you through one presentation after another, showing you why today's planes are safe, including the fact that more people are killed worldwide by donkeys than by planes, but it simply wouldn't register. Think of anxieties, mild fears, phobias, and compulsions you have been trying to change for years without success. Then think about the problems psychiatrists and psychologists must have in getting through to people with distorted outlooks that are ensconced behind the walls of this primitive, instinctual-emotional, brain/mind system. "Yes, your father does love you. Here are dozens of letters that say so." "No, you are not disliked by everyone. You were elected by your class as most likely to succeed." "No, it is not necessary to have everyone's approval, you can still function normally in life if some people disapprove of what you are doing." "No, you are not too fat, you weigh only eighty pounds." If pure rationality was the answer, if we could talk people out of these outlooks with simple reason across the dinner table, then professional therapists would be out of business.

Many people, however, believe that this is all hogwash. A well trained and disciplined mind, they contend, can see reality at all times. Such a mind knows what is right and wrong and acts accordingly.

But think for a moment of what happens to your thinking when you become extremely angry. Anger is part of the arsenal of reactions that is mediated by the primitive, instinctual-emotional system. And associated with anger is the mechanism that creates a drive for vengeance. That is apparently why when many of us become angry, we begin to lash out with a stream of invectives that is meant to hurt the offending party. Later, when we calm down, we might wonder what we were thinking to say all those terrible things. Our thinking, in a nutshell, had become distorted as we were held captive for the moment by our instinctual-emotional system, which as we shall see, has an array of punishing emotions that can work to defeat our rationality and distort our outlooks. Some of us are more vulnerable to the phenomenon than others, but all of us are vulnerable under certain circumstances.

Think of times in your life when your thinking became distorted. Perhaps it was when you were fired from a job through no fault of your own, because of a general layoff, for example. You might have begun to think that what happened to you was your fault, that there was definitely something you could have done, even though you also knew rationally that you were simply a victim of circumstance. Nonetheless, you might have found that your self-esteem and self-worth dropped, perhaps making you want to hide, even though you remained the same person you were the week before.

Or perhaps there was a time in your life when your sex drive was strong enough to overcome your rationality and you ended up throwing caution to the wind. Or perhaps you became romantically attached to a person you knew rationally was wrong for you, that everyone you knew told you was wrong for you, but you ended up in a relationship and marriage anyway, wondering after the inevitable divorce what you had been thinking during that time.

"What were they thinking?" is the question that many of us first ask when we are confronted with apparently normal people who did something totally out of whack, something stupid, whether for a few minutes or a longer length of time. A better question might be, "Did you know that what you did was irrational?" If the answer is "yes," the next question should be, "Then tell us about the conflict in your mind at the time and why you think the wrong side won."

If we agree that this last question is a sensible one, then we may innately understand that there are two sides of our minds, one of which, when we're under pressure, we can frequently sense is instinctual and might be driving us in a direction that later in a rational and calm moment we realize was not in our best interests. How many times have we heard, "My mind tells me one thing, but my gut tells me something else"? Or, "my head tells me one thing, but my heart tells me differently"? Or, "I feel this in my blood (or my bones or my soul)"? Or, "I feel this deep down"? Or, "I don't know why I'm so hard on myself"? These are all metaphors of our own making to explain what we are feeling instinctually, the workings of this second operating system in our brain/minds. The physiology of the mental side of our brain is rarely covered in our formal education and so most of us explain away the irrationalities we might observe in others based on what we know from experience and what we are told by others. E. O. Wilson, the Harvard sociobiologist and author of *Concilience*, says, "People know more about their automobiles than they do their minds,"[6] and this is obviously true, even for those who of us rarely peek under our auto's hood.

For example, most of us are unaware that our minds are totally located in our brains and that the process of thinking and feeling emotion is ultimately all biological. The brain in its entirety has been described as the most complex object in the known universe. Everything that we think and feel is the result of chemistry and cell connections that create a form of mental software that is extremely complex and it is all located in our brains. There is no mental software in our gut, heart, blood, or bones, although the emotional side of our brain may issue commands to other parts of our body. An adrenalin rush, for example, may make us believe that the feelings emanate from those parts affected. In fact, they are simply reactive. There is a whole body of science devoted to the physiology of the mental side of the brain, which has found that the brain is very much like a computer, with its nerve cells or neurons filling the same role that transistors do on our computer chips. These neuron cells are turned on or off through a complex system of chemistry, which, among other things, generates about five volts of electricity. The pattern in which the neurons are turned on or off controls what we are thinking cognitively, feeling emotionally, and recalling from our memory at any given point in time. As Donald W. Black, professor of psychiatry at the University of Iowa College of Medicine, notes in his book *Bad Boys, Bad Men: Confronting Antisocial Personality Disorder*, the chemistry of our brain/minds is based on fifty neurotransmitters identified to date, and chemical substances such as serotonin and dopamine that "provide the chemical basis for every thought, emotion and memory we experience."[7] Of course these processes are far more elaborate than those we'll discuss here.

The field of study having to do with the *biology of emotions* is called "Affective Neuroscience." Among the brain structures involved in driving this system are those previously mentioned in the description of Freud's theories. They are located beneath our cerebral cortex and form what is commonly called the limbic system. The cerebral cortex covers the surface of the brain and is the brain structure that is visible to us in photographs. It controls, among other things, our basic intelligence, rational memory, and creativity, which it blends into our consciousness in ways still largely unknown to neuroscience. Unbelievably, the cerebral cortex with its wrap-around folds, if spread out, would only be about the size and depth of a linen table napkin.[8]

The limbic organs that are a primary focus of the field of affective neuroscience and the biology of emotions are located under the cerebral cortex and, as will shortly be pointed out, house the basic foundation of the instinctual-emotional side of our mind which interacts with the cortex.

It would be hard to explain to an extreme power freak whose outlook has been distorted that all of his arrogance and pomposity has to do with brain cells whose creation at the very least, he had nothing to do with— he was not alive as yet the night of the fateful sexual intercourse that created the basic structure and nature of his body and brain. For example, would he be seven feet tall, athletic, and capable of slam dunking a basketball, or five-foot-two, an athletic dolt, and retarded? Further, his intellectual powers over which he thinks he has so much control, takes up no more space than a linen table napkin. This is not an argument that would have sat well with Adolf Hitler. "What are you talking about?" he might have replied. "Certainly my intelligence is larger than a table napkin." Not so, Adolf. Just as significant is the fact that the brain as a whole weighs only about three pounds and it has to control everything physical about us as well, including the rate of our heartbeat, eye-hand coordination, and other functions, the list of which could fill hundreds of pages.

Some scientists, most notably Dr. Paul McLean, who formerly headed the National Institute of Mental Health, have claimed that the human brain evolved along with our body shapes during the long course of human evolution. They claim that it was the reptilian and limbic sections of our mind which were developed first and the napkin-sized cortex evolved over it later.[9]

Through the study of affective neuroscience and related fields, scientists have learned that these are the structures which house the basis of our instinctual-emotional system, and that we share them in an almost identical design with other higher animals, including chimpanzees. It turns out that we share 98.7 percent of our genetics, our DNA, with chimpanzees,[10] including the basis for the design of the instinctual-emotional side of our brains, which was apparently developed first, before we grew much of a cerebral cortex, to allow us to survive better in the earliest of primitive times, when we lived in caves and on the savannas of Africa with little linguistic ability.

The bewilderment that most of us feel when confronted with this subject matter is apparently due to the strength of our reasoning and creative powers, which have allowed us to develop great civilizations, philosophies, and technologies and which have given us an innate arrogance that works to mask the fact that our old instinctual side continues to inhabit our heads. Yet we also know innately that it is there. The "dark side of human nature," we might call it, or our "evil side," our "demons within," our "human frailties." This is how we explain away how more than 90 million people were killed in twentieth-century warfare alone and tens of millions more because of other mayhem, the perpetration of which the vast majority of humans would agree doesn't make good sense.

Most of us would agree that a life of peace, harmony, and opportunity for all is a better alternative to wars. Yet we continue to have wars and so it would appear that the main battle of our individual and collective lives is not us versus whoever we perceive our adversaries to be. Rather, it appears to be between our cerebral reasoning power and this old instinctual-emotional system, whose workings and processes, its basic software, hasn't changed in hundreds of thousands of years. Science writer L. Sprague de Camp describes this landscape well in the title of his book *The Ape-Man Within*.[11] Yet the beauty of the brain is that we never can know for certain how it might continue to evolve or what technological advances might speed this evolution along. That is why we are probably quite correct in assuming that there may be hope for positive change.

The key to this hypothesis is that while the brain physically functions much like a computer, it is far more malleable, particularly in the early stages of our lives. To begin with, while our brain is created genetically at the rate of 250,000 neuron cells per minute in the womb, the mental software it comes with is designed to absorb knowledge and behavior from the environment in which we are born. And so if we are born in Lithuania, the software is designed to absorb the Lithuanian language, the culture of our surroundings, and the behavioral patterns we observe and are being taught by those raising us.

However, the malleability of the behavioral side of the brain gradually begins to harden for most of us as we reach early adolescence. Our personalities and behavioral patterns become relatively fixed. From that point on, most of our personality changes for the better or the worse, are caused by traumas, including traumatic epiphanies or insights, some of them seemingly trivial at the time. A vulnerably shy and ungainly male teenager might overhear a degrading remark as he passes a group of schoolmates and become traumatized to the point that his self-esteem drops on the spot and he turns antisocial in his relationships with the opposite sex. His personality changes in this respect almost immediately; alterations that may last for years to come. Others of us passing the same group and hearing a similar degrading remark might not be affected at all. As with many personality characteristics studied in the field of psychology, the degree of our vulnerability or resilience to specific types of traumatic events at given times in our lives are measured on metaphoric scales of intensity. On a scale of one to five, ones would be the least vulnerable to specific types of events at any given time; threes would be moderately vulnerable, and fives highly vulnerable to specific traumas at given times, including the person whose father told him, "you'll never amount to anything." In that case, the trauma worked to strengthen him.

With young children, traumas are greatly magnified. A scolding or beating from a parent can be traumatic enough to change a behavioral pattern. The Victorian rules of upbringing focused on "not sparing the rod." Use of the rod by parents and teachers in caning children was thought to be the only true way to mold behavior. In a sense, these authority figures were acting as lion tamers, attempting to tame the instincts and emotional reactions of their wards. Although they didn't know it, because the science hadn't evolved sufficiently at the time, their efforts were aimed not so much at the reasoning power of the children, but at their instinctual-emotional system that may be subject, depending on our vulnerabilities, to traumatic change, as we've observed.

How many old English movies have we seen set in boarding schools, where a chief character is a boy who is caned and punished week after week, but remains arrogant and unruly, while his brother, afraid of the punishment, remains meek and attentive? The first brother, who is obviously a level one in terms of vulnerability to early traumas, is an odds-on favorite to become an aggressive, hard-bitten adult. His brother, who might as an adult devote his life to the church, could have been a level four in terms of early trauma vulnerability. But the vicissitudes of the brain are such that the opposite might actually happen. The young, unruly boy, somewhere along the line might have a trauma that suddenly changes him, perhaps an epiphany, a coming to religion that puts him on the road to becoming a church minister. The mild, meek boy might somehow be recruited into a gang of toughs, who act on him in the manner of drill sergeants in the U.S. Marines and eventually turn him into an extreme power freak of the first order. For many of us, our entire lives can be shaped by these unexpected traumatic events, particularly in our early years.

The physiology of traumatic events that causes personality change has become an academic field of its own and there is a body of work that describes it. What apparently happens is that the memory of a traumatic event, the frightening ride in an airplane, for example, is shunted directly to our instinctual-emotional system, where it becomes encoded and imprinted on specific primitive or limbic brain structures. The traumatic event becomes what neuroscientists call an "emotional memory,"[12] whose characteristics make it impervious to change through rational thought, argument, or persuasion.

The memory of the traumatic event sits there buried in this system, which apparently forms a significant part of our subconscious mind, and is only triggered when something in our lives occurs that alerts the system that the original trauma is about to be repeated. When such an alert is sensed, the system responds with strong emotional reactions, including anxieties, phobic feelings, blood rushes, and other physical alarms designed to guide us into activity, including fleeing to what the system perceives as safety.

Our friend who was traumatized by the rocky airplane flight thus has the memory of the event imprinted on the brain structures of his instinctual-emotional system. The memory inhabits its subconscious space without effect, until the boss or someone else says, "Okay, you've got to fly to Dallas tomorrow." In other words, the emotional memory of that airplane flight doesn't distort his thinking until it is alerted, as per the boss's statement. Then a strong phobic response kicks in and he is overwhelmed with the fear of airplane travel. Since the cause of this response is an emotional memory, there is nothing the boss or anyone else can tell him that will make him feel any better at the moment.

The same holds true for the bulimic fifteen-year-old described in the book *Battling the Inner Dummy: The Craziness of Apparently Normal People*, who weighed eighty pounds but thought she was fat. Previously, when she weighed only ninety-five pounds, she was told by a friend innocently enough that she "was beginning to look fat." Since she was apparently vulnerable at the time, the statement traumatized her, imprinting an emotional memory. She began to avoid food and when she did eat, she later tried to force herself to vomit. When she dropped to eighty pounds, she was hospitalized in a room with a large mirror. Although she was put in front of the mirror by her mother and placed on a scale that showed that she weighed only eighty pounds, she still believed she was fat. She could see she weighed only eighty pounds, but her emotional memory continued to drive the obsessive thought that she was either still fat or on the cusp of it. And there is no amount of rational logic that could quickly convince her, or others like her, otherwise.[13]

The same thing happened to rock star Karen Carpenter. One day somebody made the simple statement to her, "Karen, on television you look thirty pounds overweight." From that point on she became anorexic and literally tried to stop eating. She was hospitalized several times and eventually died from the disorder.[14]

As formerly noted, psychotherapists understand that the instinctual-emotional system is capable of infecting or capturing our rationality sometimes to the point that we become victims of it. There are many, on the other hand, who believe that this hypothesis is only a "cop-out." They believe we are masters of our own destiny at all times and can be in control of ourselves if we just will it.

The problem is that it is difficult to show these nonbelievers any physical proof of the instinctual-emotional side of the mind taking over and overwhelming rational thought. There are people who will look at someone quaking and in a panic attack at the thought of boarding an airplane and say, "Come on, you're not fooling anybody, snap out of it, you can get on that plane without this big act you're doing." They would rephrase the statement for the bulimic girl and Karen Carpenter, but the point would be the same: They are mistaken. The instinctual-emotional system is not capable of rational thought. It does not think, it drives and reacts.

Yet these same people would probably agree that a catatonic schizophrenic who remains frozen in a single position for the day has been captured by the disorder, primarily because there is physical proof. The person won't move, even if slapped about repeatedly. And yet if the schizophrenic were merely delusional, thinking that he was the king of Galena, Illinois, they would say, "Come on, snap out of it, everyone knows you're not the king of Galena, Illinois. Galena doesn't have a king. You're just putting on an act to get attention." And so if these skeptics have problems with schizophrenics faking it, you can understand their reluctance to accept the abductions of the rational mind that lead to milder distorted outlooks, such as, "I know I am not the king of Galena, but I am the king of this office and you had better believe it." Believe it, because these kings of the office believe it.

Bolstering the skepticism of some concerning mind disorders or even psychosis is that there is little if any physical proof to be presented. There are no X-rays or CAT scans as yet that can be taken to prove definitively that we have post-traumatic syndrome, even though as one of the few survivors of the Oklahoma City bombing, we might be so depressed, phobic, and delusional it is difficult to get through the day. There are no X-rays or blood tests that show we have an obsessive-compulsive disorder or that we are seriously antisocial, or psychopathic in any way.[15] Furthermore, psychiatric diagnosis of mood and personality disorders in particular remains as much an art as science. In fact it may be a bit more art than science. A professional psychotherapist must deduce the disorder, not from X-rays or a physical examination or a wide array of blood and other tests, but from discussions with the disturbed person and colleagues, and perhaps with the help of some oral or written tests. The results, however, are influenced by the subjectivity of the psychotherapist. Consequently, we see renowned psychiatrists with credentials a mile long disagreeing with each other in court cases hinging on the alleged mental disorder of a defendant.

And so the problem of determining a "capturing line" or a threshold remains evasive. At what point are we captured to the extent that our outlooks have become distorted and our rational will power is not strong enough to keep us in balance? Most of us can understand that we, individually, might become "captured" (Daniel Goleman in his book *Emotional Intelligence* uses the term "hijacked"[16]) in a fit of temper, or in a passionate sexual encounter, or when we gobble food we have rationally resolved not to eat for a diet or other purposes, or when we spend more for a home or other object we've become attached to than we can afford, but some of us find it difficult to recognize this phenomenon in others. Everything can be handled through self-control, they say.

These readers must take it as a "leap of faith," that there are such things as mental disorders which overwhelm our reason by whatever physiology the disorders produce. If you can do that, you might be able to affirm the possibility that we can also be captured by extremely intense instinctual drives that propel us into irrationality and by emotional memories that can fill us with phobic feelings and precipitate panic attacks if the threat of a trauma similar to that which caused the emotional memory is about to repeat itself. Whether or not we are culpable for dangerous or hurtful acts under these conditions is one of the greatest unresolved questions of our time, primarily because we can't hold up an X-ray and show that a line has been crossed.

But setting culpability aside, if you are totally unconvinced of any of this, then it is time to close this book and find members of families who have had to live with people who have had mental disorders and discuss the phenomenon with them or read their books. There are plenty of them.

So again, what does all of this have to do with power freaks and particularly extreme power freaks?

It has everything to do with them because extreme power freaks look at their need for domination and status with distorted outlooks that are buried within the walls of their instinctual-emotional systems and are therefore impervious to rational argument or persuasion. As we shall see in chapter 5, they may be suffering from the psychopathic traits of a psychiatric disorder called antisocial personality disorder. One of the purposes of this book is to help you to imagine looking beneath the scalps of the extreme power freaks that confront you and actually imagine the brain organs that make up their instinctual-emotional system in order to understand what is causing the phenomenon.

The recommendations on how to deal with them listed later in this book can only be well implemented with a firm understanding of their thought processes.

CHAPTER 3

The Power Freak as Caveman

"The supervisor of our brokerage firm managed by intimidation. He was a couple of steps removed from the cave. He would come out on the last day of every production month with a Louisville Slugger bat, and he'd go from office to office, from desk to desk. He'd have the brokers put their hands on the edge of their desks, and then he'd take that baseball bat . . . and swing as hard as he could near the edge of your desk."[1]

It appears that we continue to retain vestiges of our ancestors' mentality. A relatively new and somewhat controversial body of academic study called evolutionary psychology concerns itself with tracing our instinctual drives or motives and emotional reactions derived from our biological roots. Moreover, some investigate how these primitive roots can cause havoc in our twenty-first century lives.

In a sense, evolutionary psychology is the study of the original instinctual-emotional side of our brain described in the last chapter. This primitive brain that nature bestowed on us appears designed to give us the greatest odds for surviving long enough in tribal groups so that we could mate and pass our genes along to the next generation.

For example, one of the hypotheses of evolutionary psychology is that male sexual jealousy—which wells up when a male suspects his female mate is attracted to another male—is a neurobiological design of nature, intended to assure via "fits of jealousy," outbursts and threats, that the female remains loyal to him. This loyalty would ensure that only his genes—not those of another male—would be passed on to the next generation.[2]

The tension that frequently exists between a stepfather and the children of his previously divorced spouse is theorized as arising from the resentment the stepfather innately feels toward those children for carrying the genes of another man. The same instinctual, limbic brain structures that trigger this resentment also exist in other higher animals, including lions, whose resentment is not at all moderated by a power of reason. When a lion is successful in separating another lion from his new mate and her offspring, the first thing he does is kill the offspring. His instinctual-emotional brain, according to this theory, is intent on having only his genes passed along to his new mate.

Charles T. Snowdon, chair of the department of psychology at the University of Wisconsin and one of the world's leading primatologists, adds the following:

> In addition to lions, there are many examples of infant killing closer to home: it has been described in male chimpanzees and gorillas, our closest relatives. But in the family-living marmosets that I study, females will kill their sister's infants if they both give birth about the same time. Helpers are essential for infant survival and the more dominant sister will literally kill her niece or nephew to assure that her own children have helpers available.[3]

The inner mind can work with deadly intent.

Women also get jealous when they think their mates have a wayward eye, because they don't want the male's nurturing and supportive capability to be spread thin, or so the theory goes. Women innately want their mate's attention focused exclusively on them and their respective offspring. In the primitive wilds, for which this design was apparently developed, protection against predators and an abundance of food were never a given.[4]

And speaking of food, we are frequently driven to overeat, according to the theories of evolutionary psychology, because in our primitive lives, we were never sure that we would have a next meal or that it would be abundant. And so when we did have food, our appetites went on overdrive and we would eat until we were unable to squeeze down another morsel.[5] This is one reason why many of us are overweight and find it so difficult to lose weight. (What a marvelous excuse.) Our instinctual-emotional system, impervious to logic or time, is unaware that we now live in a civilized world in which many cultures offer status to thin people, but instead remains calibrated with fat-seeking caveman eating habits. That many of us are able to moderate our eating habits by filtering out and overriding our natural appetites shows that we don't always have to be victims of this primitive brain/mind system, despite the strength of its drives.

Many young children who have never seen a snake before become frightened of snakes because they are dangerous and it was easy in our primitive lives to mistake one for a fallen branch or log. Our general dislike for snakes may thus be partially innate, according to the theory of evolutionary psychology.[6]

We are driven to fear strangers, the theory contends, because in the caves, we never knew if the tribe over the next hill was friendly or not.[7] Nature in its design of the instinctual mindset apparently didn't want us to take chances. At the first sign of an alien on our "turf," this mindset was triggered, driving us not only to become fearful and suspicious, but perhaps aggressive, hateful, and vengeful as well.

This portion of the theory as well makes a great deal of sense. Many of the darker skinned African Americans, including students at Harvard Law School, can attest to the tension they arouse in strange neighborhoods and to the harassment they receive from police forces.[8] The lighter of their race and other lighter-skinned minorities—Hispanics, Asians, Jews, and Arabs with light skins who do not dress differently—are generally not harassed indiscriminately on the streets. However, they are still somewhat discriminated against, according to the theories of evolutionary psychology, because those who have in general refused to assimilate, keeping to themselves in groups, remain aliens to the instinctual-emotional mind of the dominant culture and are suspect. In general, if we perceive others as not members of "our group" (read "our tribe"), we ostensibly have an innate drive to discriminate against them until they agree to assimilate with us, and we allow them to do so. Then the natural bonds of nurturance may begin to emerge over time.

The fact that many of us since the civil rights movements of the 1960s have come so far in accepting the presence of minorities within our midst indicates again that we do not always have to be victims of the instinctual-emotional mind. Over time, through education, observation, insight, and most important, the emergence of new generations who associate with diverse groups, these old group prejudices, vestiges of a primitive outlook, can be diluted and changed.

Evolutionary psychology has been called Darwinian because the purpose of the instinctual drives and emotional reactions produced autonomously by this part of our minds have been ascribed to keeping us alive long enough to reproduce and fulfill the biological imperative of perpetuating life. And so in the caves such drives were the foundation of the struggle for the "survival of the fittest," the evolutionary theme of natural selection.

In today's world, we are told, these old instincts and emotions have become "adaptive," in that they refocus on twenty-first-century phenomena and in a sense become masked. This appears to be why stepfathers who feel tension or anger with their stepchildren for no apparent reason can't figure out why they feel this way and neither can their wives. Or why many husbands and wives who get into a close conversation with someone of the opposite sex at a social gathering create irrational jealousies in their spouses who spy them across the room. The instinctual-emotional mind reacts automatically to what it sees, perceiving the interaction as a threat to the continued support and nurturance of the couple's offspring, even if they have no offspring. No mental software upgrades have been issued from heaven to modify these designs for twenty-first-century living, where we have concepts such as marriage, commitment, honesty, virtue, and morality. We are left to our own intellectual devices to deal with these primitive vestiges and some of us are better at controlling or disciplining them than others.

The instincts and emotions that make up the power freak are also adaptive, as we soon shall see. The primitive brain mechanism drives us into creating hierarchies, an essential for primitive tribal organization and survival. It confers on some of us today an innate need to dominate others in situations where we might also understand rationally that cooperation would make better sense than domination. Or it can drive us to dominate in everything we do. "I didn't want to be president of the PTA, I really don't have the time, I don't like all the conflicts, it is taking time away from my business and my children, but yet I did everything possible to fight for the job. Why I did that I can't tell you."

Sound familiar?

The theory of evolutionary psychology makes great common sense and provides answers to many of the questions about the continuing irrationalities of the human species, but, as previously noted, it is also controversial. While a great body of academic work has been generated on the subject, led by Oxford's Richard Dawkins, author of *The Selfish Gene*; Harvard's E. O. Wilson; and many others, there are academics who disagree with it, most notably author and evolutionary theorist Stephen Jay Gould, who passed away in 2002. Gould believed that there has been considerable modification in our baser emotions. There was even a book published in 2000 titled *Alas, Poor Darwin: Arguments against Evolutionary Psychology*, a compendium of opposing viewpoints authored by highly credentialed academics. Their arguments focus on the theory that behavior is considerably more nurture than it is nature. Aggressiveness, many of the adversaries of evolutionary psychology contend, is caused more by children watching it take place on television than by our natural instincts. There are also feminists who disagree with the handful of academics who have thrown rape into the primitive instincts category under the label of "Male Deprivation Hypothesis."[9] We should also take note of the fact that there are controversies applying to the entire field of psychology, which is based primarily on empirical observation and not on what some scientists call "real science."

"Real science" would include such fields as chemistry, where mathematics can "prove the work." "Proving the work" is the operative term. The problem with psychology, the study of our behavior and our thought processes, as Nobel Prize–winner Francis Crick, co-discoverer of the DNA helix, and others have pointed out, is that *we can't experiment with live human brains*.[10] We can't put a live person on a table in a laboratory and talk to him as we probe about in his brain studying the mental circuitry, or take cuttings of his brain before an emotion is generated and afterwards, to determine how the circuitry changed. PET scans and functional magnetic resonance imaging do allow scientists to see on-going brain activity in humans while they are lying on a table thinking about something, but the images created are not as yet strong enough to trace changes in specific circuitry caused by specific emotional reactions. Researchers in the field are compelled to use animals for the "real science" aspect of their work, but the real science advocates believe that what they have proved in animals may not relate to humans.

They believe this despite the fact that the two studies of the human genome, the privately funded Celera study and the publicly funded Human Genome Project, have found that humans have only a little more than twice as many genes as the fruitfly, 30,000 versus 13,000, and only five times as many as yeast.[11] We've already noted that the differences in the genetic code between a human and a chimpanzee—the mammal considered closest in physiology to a human—is only 1.3 percent.

Obviously, the coding for our advanced cerebral cortex does not appear to take up as much space on our string of DNA as would make the more arrogant of us feel comfortable, at least, compared to the cortex of the chimpanzee, which is estimated at maturity to provide an average intelligence of a three-year-old human for the brightest of chimpanzees.

These findings of the genome studies are bad news for those who oppose any form of anthropomorphism— the label that ascribes human characteristics to a nonhuman animal—believing that humans are uniquely human and refusing to concede that nonhuman animals have any human attributes at all. There are many others, however, who agree with the findings of psychiatrists and other academics such as Jeffrey Masson, psychoanalyst and author of *Dogs Never Lie about Love*, that dogs, like many other higher animals, have a full range of humanlike emotion.

In the midst of this debate and as a brief aside is the philosophic argument about why we even need the more negative of these old instinctual emotions in today's world. Mightn't we as humans be better off without the chemical reactions in our brains that produce feelings of extreme aggression, jealousy, envy, depression, grief, suspicion, and so forth? Hindu gurus, who have spent years staring at a mountainside and who have succeeded in transcending these "earthly negative emotions," report great feelings of peace and harmony.

Of course, there are many people who would respond, "Hey, don't take my depression and hatred away from me. They are all I have left."

With all that said, let's assume that the results of the studies related to affective neuroscience and evolutionary psychology deserve the credibility that those academics who support it assign to it. Even if you don't agree with them, their theories can serve metaphorically as the reasons why certain parts of the mental software of our brains continue to drive us instinctually, to react emotionally as if we were still living in the caves.

This is the brain chemistry that can produce an extreme power freak. And it leads us to how this side of our brain is programmed.

If you were working for a leading software company today and had the engineering capability of a god and his crew or an amorphous creative force, and were asked to design the mental software for the instinctual side of a human brain that did not yet possess language skills and whose general intelligence level was low, as the brain was about 3 million years ago, what programs would you include in the core design? In all probability you would come up with the programs that were actually generated and which have been called our five basic psychological drives or motives.[12] Each of these drives varies in intensity in each of us, and in the descriptions that follow, we've applied a one-to-ten scale in classifying the intensity levels. The following is a quick summary of these drives.

POWER/STATUS

Power/status is the drive that is the focus of this book and which can propel us into the realm of power freakishness. David G. Winter, professor of psychology at the University of Michigan, observes that "What a particular writer thinks of as 'good' power is usually described as 'leadership,' 'guidance,' or perhaps 'authority'; while 'bad' power is called 'authoritarian dominance' or 'coercion.'"[13] We shall soon see how the brain chemistry that forms the basis of our instinctual-emotional minds may spell the difference between the two.

Anthropologists and others have found an innate ranking system, a social hierarchy among every primitive tribe they were capable of studying in depth, including those that still exist today. The Greek alphabet has traditionally been used to describe the ranking levels. The alpha male is the leader, who in primitive societies needed physical prowess to fight his way up the ranks and defend himself against all challengers. Next in line is the beta male, frequently the alpha male's chief lieutenant, then down the ranks to the gamma, delta, and at the bottom, the omegas. The same ranking system exists among tribal females. When it comes to the drive for power and status, there is apparently no gender difference. I for one have dealt with alpha females who could be every bit as terrifying as alpha males.

Sociobiologists describe how the ranking of a tribe takes place through the motivating force of "status tension." This tension to move up the ranks or defend one's position apparently exists innately within our instinctual-emotional minds and is activated when we sense an opportunity for advancement or we receive a challenge from someone attempting to displace us from our rank and move us down.

The status tension of ranking is most obvious in hens, where hen "A" pecks and intimidates hen "B," who pecks and intimidates hen "C" and on down the line into what we know as the "pecking order."

In his book *Evolutionary Psychology*, David M. Buss, professor of psychology at the University of Texas, describes an experiment involving fifty-nine three-person groups of individuals who had been previously unknown to each other. Within one minute a clear hierarchy emerged in 50 percent of the groups. A clear hierarchy emerged within the first five minutes in the other 50 percent.[14]

In the one of the few books written that focus on the subject of human status and ranking, *Social Hierarchies: Essays toward a Sociophysiological Perspective*, one of the essays describes a research study timing the ranking systems of rhesus monkeys and of humans. It reports a compelling fact: *Humans form themselves into ranked hierarchies faster than the monkeys.*[15]

Does this surprise us?

When we begin work for a new company, one of the first things we might say is, "Okay, what's the pecking order around here?" We understand innately the concept of human ranking and social hierarchy. In the military, our rank is so formalized that it is displayed on our uniforms and hand salutes are required to make sure that we understand the ranking system, as if to say, "Yes, I understand that you are a lieutenant and I am a mere corporal." Neighborhood gangs, which are a regression to our primitive roots, also organize by rank and defend their status as a group with territorial markings, signs of greeting, and varying rituals.

In general society, ranking is displayed at the upper end by large estates, country clubs, and societal groups that restrict membership. The accumulation of great amounts of money doesn't automatically gain you entrance to groups who think of newly monied people as the "nouveau riche" and not worthy of advancement to their status, even though two or three generations ago, their own families may have been immigrant peasants. The middle class also displays its rank by how and where they live and with whom they associate, among other things. Even people living in public housing projects manage to find someone or some group of people upon whom to look down. In India, the caste system includes the "Untouchables," who even in the more liberal parts of India are not allowed to use the same wells as the so-called upper classes, nor are they allowed to touch members of the upper classes, sit with them, or be with them in any meaningful way and they are relegated to the worst possible jobs, such as cleaning latrines.

And so we go along with this innately based ranking nonsense throughout the world at large, including the business world, where many among top management who display characteristics of a power freak view their subordinates in terms of rank. They socialize only with their "inner circle," who have displayed submissiveness and loyalty. We describe the nature of the power/status program in more detail in chapter 6. There is little doubt that nature provided us with an innate mechanism to organize ourselves by rank so that we could live with relative peace and harmony in the caves and on the savannas. And so each of us apparently has a propensity to seek and defend status, with an intensity level ranging from a metaphorical "one," who is at the lowest rank and merely wants enough status to stand unabused in a check-out line, to the "five," who likes the feeling of power and status, but refuses to achieve it by intimidation and walking over others ("good power"), to the "ten," who has traits of psychopathy, narcissism, and status obsession as described in later chapters. He wants nothing but more power and greater omnipotence, regardless of how much he already has, and will do practically anything to gain it ("bad power").

There is a considerable difference in the significance of our innate power/status-seeking drive between primitive tribes and the modern business world in that a mere striving for power by a strong and fearless person is no longer what solely counts. As we shall see, our enlarged cerebral cortex has come into play and there are many large organizations run today by "nerds," the omegas as they would have been classified in primitive times, who rise to the top because of their intelligence, talent, and managerial ability; who eschew formalized structures, creating only as much as is needed to manage efficiently; and who may be self-effacing to the point of choosing an office that is no larger or better than those of other managers.[16] The power freak, it would appear, is coming closer to being out of step in a society where intellectual, creative, and organizational capacities are becoming paramount. Hope is wonderful, isn't it?

TERRITORIAL

It is much easier for most of us to recognize our innate drive toward territoriality because it involves something physical, be it land, space, or possessions. We know how comforting it feels to come back to our own home or apartment. If we have a home with a backyard, we know how upset we might become if strangers started tramping through while we're out there reading our newspaper on a Sunday morning. If someone cuts in front of us in a supermarket checkout line, we also become upset because that's "our space," right there in front of us. We also understand innately the Western movies about ranchers who, no matter how many square miles of ranch land they owned, always wanted more, threatening neighboring ranchers with harm unless they sold out. Their voracious appetite for more land never shocked us.

Our instinctive territorial program was even popularized in the 1966 book *The Territorial Imperative: A Personal Inquiry into the Animal Origins of Property and Nations* by Robert Ardrey, which became a bestseller then and was reissued in paperback in 1997. Ardrey asserts that man can be just as territorial as a pack of wolves, who mark the far reaches of the territory they have established for themselves with urine. Other wolf packs who enter this territory know they will be in for a fight, sometimes to the death.[17]

In primitive times, according to the theory of evolutionary psychology, human territorialism was a drive aimed at staking out and protecting a preserve where hunting and gathering could take place; this way there would be minimal confusion between groups of tribes as to who occupied which space. Rituals of permission were required to enter another tribe's space, even if they knew you were friendly. An unauthorized intrusion to steal goods or females (a frequent occurrence), would mean killings if the perpetrators were caught. There might be a war between tribes if one had outgrown its territory and invaded that of another tribe to increase its holdings.

Today, our territorial drive, which can meld with our drive for power and status, has been adapted to twenty-first-century living. Those high on the territorial scale, the "eights," "nines," and "tens," now want big homes on a lot of land, apartments with the right addresses, and large corner offices laden with status symbols. They will rarely be satisfied with anything they have for very long. Wars to gain another's territory still exist, but with more than spears and clubs. As of this writing, there are more than ninety border wars taking place in the world.

Land and possessions are like mother's milk to a power freak. They reflect power and status and so they will always want more. Nothing will ever be enough. The continuing accumulation of homes and apartments in various parts of the world, or the relentless collection of works of art, are natural for the "eights" and up. Those in the middle of the territorial scale, the great majority of us, who have more modest drives, have learned to tame or harness our acquisitive natures. We are among those who won't grossly overspend on a home simply because we "feel in our gut" that we must have it. Those lowest on the territorial scale would hardly feel the drive. "Just give me a sleeping bag and a toothbrush and I'm at home anywhere," they might say.

Extreme power freaks are high on the territorial scale. They envision your space as their space; you occupy it at their pleasure.

NURTURANCE/ATTACHMENT

In the general field of psychology, nurturance is covered by the broader term "attachment." Apparently we are instinctually inclined to attach to others in nurturing relationships. Those of us who are parents know the immediate feelings of attachment and nurturance that are triggered when we first hold our new baby in our arms. We can understand that this is instinctual, an involuntary response. We see the same feelings of nurturance when our dog has puppies or our cat has kittens.

This instinctual response is obvious among humans and the higher animals, where the newborn have to be nurtured and raised, unlike minnows, where the babies just swim away. The infants, human or higher animal, emerge from the womb, chemicals adjust in our brain/minds, and love is exuded.

"Chemicals?" you might ask. "You mean that love for a child is chemical?"

"Yes," we reply. "As a matter of fact all love, including romantic love—commonly called in psychology our biosocial attachment process mechanism—is basically a function of brain chemistry and neuronal connections. It is part of the psychopharmacology of everyday life."

"Oh . . . of course."

In this sense, the nurturance/attachment program is complicated somewhat by the fact that it appears to exist in four separate areas, sometimes called compartments by academics: parent-child attachments; romantic-spouse attachments; attachments among co-workers, family, and kin; and stranger attachment.

Our propensity to nurture or attach might be different for each compartment. Thus, while we may love our child, we might do everything we can to avoid developing new relationships with strangers. Some of us go to cocktail parties where we don't know anyone and have a ball. Others of us lurk in a corner. Basically, the higher we are on the metaphorical "one" to "ten" nurturance/attachment scale, the more nurturing we would tend to be in all four compartments. Thus, level tens might be psychopathic in their need for nurturing. Both family and strangers are fair game for intense attachment. If tens had their way, they would probably never want anyone they're attached to out of their sight.

But unlike power or territoriality, there may be psychopathic personality traits at the other end of this scale. These traits, at a level one, would include little or no capacity for nurturance, nor for remorse, guilt, shame, or empathy. Combine low nurturance with a high power drive and you have the characters we often see personified in action motion pictures as the villain. The villain's adversary walks in the room while the villain is eating breakfast. Pretending to reach for a piece of toast, the villain pulls a gun, shoots him, and then without so much as a blink of an eye, picks up the piece of toast and munches on it, ignoring the bloodied body in front of him. Fortunately, most of us are in the midrange of this scale. We are intensely attached to our children and we are in the normal range in our propensity to feel attachment to a spouse, family, kin, and, if we are not inordinately shy, even to some strangers.

Most power freaks would probably rank at the lowest levels of the general nurturance/attachment scale. In terms of evolutionary psychology, this would make perfect sense. True alpha males as leaders of primitive tribes would need to be remorseless in leading attacks against other tribes, killing or enslaving women and children with impunity. They would also need this capacity for putting down challengers within their tribes, feeling no remorse whatsoever as they clubbed them over the head. Showing sensitivity to others might be taken as a sign of weakness by others, specifically the beta male, the lieutenant standing in the wings, licking his chops, waiting for an opportunity to move up to alpha rank and take over the tribe. Thus, some powerful CEOs are able to fire tens of thousands of employees, thinking more about the enhanced shareholder values they have achieved than the suffering of the employees.

It is possible, under the theory of nurturance/attachment compartmentalization, to order the deaths of tens of thousands of people in a war of aggression and still go home at night and hug your wife and kids. Slobodan Milosevic, the Yugoslavian leader generally recognized as the person behind the genocides that took place in Kosovo and Bosnia in the late 1990s, was known to call his wife, Mirjana, "dumpling." Adolf Hitler was known to have loved his dogs, and Leona Helmsley was passionate about her husband, Harry.

It is thus possible to love your child and no one else. Or your family as a whole and no one else. Or your sister and no one else. Or your pet and no one else. In political elections, we appear to suspect innately that this type of nurturing compartmentalization exists. When a politician drags his wife and kids on stage, all of whom beam or say wonderful things about him, deep down we wonder if it's staged and how nurturing he will be with the rest of us. The point is that just because an extreme power freak shows off the loving relationship he has with his wife or kids, it doesn't mean that in a clinch, he wouldn't be willing to throw you or them off a cliff, if it came down to it. Nice stuff, huh?

SURVIVAL/FEAR

The survival/fear drive of the instinctual-emotional system is familiar to all of us as the "self-preservation" or "survival" instinct. It is the strongest of all our drives under the theory of evolutionary psychology, because if we didn't survive long enough to produce offspring in our days in the caves and on the savannas, then we would be definitely behind the eight ball. Children were necessary to spread the workload to assure there was enough to eat for the family, not to mention again, the innate biological imperative of getting our genes into the next generation to perpetuate the species.

The strength of our "survival instinct" appears to be based on the level of fear we feel when challenged. Level tens on this metaphorical scale would be extremely fearful, victims of paranoid personality disorder or worse, to the point that they would never want to leave the house, touch another human, or even open a window. The billionaire Howard Hughes, who owned TWA airlines, motion picture studios, and a large industrial conglomerate, was probably a level ten just before he died. He refused to leave his room, or even to talk in person to his trusted lieutenants. They conversed exclusively by phone. When he was moved, it was by ambulance or ambulance plane.

An eight on this scale would also be fearful. In the classical psychological dilemma of "fight or flight," when confronted with a challenge, the eights, in all probability, would take flight. The mid-range of this scale, the fours, fives, and sixes, includes most of us. We can feel healthy doses of fear at times, but we have learned how to deal rationally with most of them, we hope.

The level ones on the scale would be practically fearless; they are the bungee jumpers among us, or the parachutists who leap from cliffs. They, however, can be as psychopathic as the tens. In any "fight or flight" situation, they will almost always "fight." The prototypical, extreme power freak would thus, in all probability, be at this level on the scale. In terms of the design of the alpha male, this behavior makes perfect sense. The leader of a primitive tribe must not only be insensitive, free of guilt or remorse, but also fearless. Any challenger within the tribe must be taken on without a flinch or second thought. In wars against neighboring tribes, the alpha male leader must be savage in leading attacks. When successful the "savage warrior" not only maintains his status, but enhances it considerably. Tribal sacrifices are often made in his honor. Even today, this phenomenon continues. Our successful warriors, particularly the generals and others deemed heroes, have been honored when they return home with ticker-tape parades, keys to cities, and streets and schools named after them. General William Wainwright fought gallantly in World War II. But when he was running out of food and ammunition, he surrendered Bataan in the Philippines. He was shunned after his release from prison camp at the end of the war. Douglas MacArthur, whose lack of foresight led to the surrender, but who escaped from Bataan and later went on to lead the victory in the Pacific, was accorded every honor, including a New York City ticker-tape parade, when he finally returned home.

There is one idiosyncracy in this program, however, that bears noting. There is such a thing as a "limbic spike," a single phobia or a cluster of phobias that might infect the most fearless of alphas. John Madden, for example, a former football tackle, coach of the Oakland Raiders, famed for his toughness on the football field and later a football broadcast commentator, is phobic about airplanes. He travels coast to coast by bus.[18] Former President Richard Nixon was known for his cold manner in dealing with foreign adversaries, faced death on three foreign expeditions, and was ruthless in ordering bombings and sending thousands to their deaths during the latter stages of the Vietnam war. Yet he appeared to suffer from a variety of social phobias. He would spend hours alone in a private office in the Executive Office Building attached to the White House, had to "steel" himself to attend his cabinet meetings, trusted only a few close lieutenants, and was paranoid about a whole host of people, to the point that he ordered illegal wiretaps on many of them, including his own brother, Don.[19]

There are other strong and fearless men who may be afraid of mice or the dark. Textbooks about phobias and anxieties are full of these "limbic spikes" that may belie a low ranking on the metaphorical survival/fear scale. It is thus dangerous to deduce that an extreme power freak may be less than ruthless because he or she doesn't like to ride on elevators or has other relatively meaningless phobias, which he may broadcast to help camouflage his true self.

SEXUAL

It is apparent from the world's growing population that the drive to have sex hasn't changed significantly from the earliest days of our evolution. The metaphorical scale that measures the pressure of the sex drive is similar to the other psychological drives. Level ones would be asexual and couldn't care less if they never had sex at all. The mid-range would be like most of us with normal sex drives. The level tens would be sexual psychopaths who would kill for sex if they had to, if they thought they could get away with it.

The correlation of the sex drive to power freaks has to do with the evolutionary psychology theory that the alpha male not only had a high power drive, but a high sexual drive as well. Being the strongest in the tribe, he was thus impelled to impregnate as many females as possible, providing multiple chances to pass his strong genes on to the next generation, which would give those genes a much better chance of being passed on further.

We see this same combination of high power and sex drives among many of the higher animals, including the horse. In documentaries about wild herds of horses, we watch as the alpha stallion chases off all would-be male suitors of the females in the herd. These betas or lower go elsewhere or linger just outside of the herd's moving territorial boundaries, watching the females in much the same way that a luckless and horny man might eye a pretty girl in a singles bar. The alpha stallion wants all those females to himself and to carry out that task a high sex drive is apparently a biological imperative. Thus, it is no wonder that many high-powered people who have climbed their way to the top of their professions have gotten themselves in trouble with extracurricular sexual encounters, including Bill Clinton, Jesse Jackson, Newt Gingrich, Gary Hart, Henry Hyde, countless professional athletes, professors, and undoubtedly hundreds of thousands in the corporate world who either never got caught, were divorced because of it, or whose spouses either forgave their infidelities or accepted them as the price of being married to someone of power.

Female infidelity, evolutionary psychology theorizes, is aimed at finding a male whose genes are stronger than those of her existing mate or spouse, someone who she feels intuitively will create a stronger and healthier offspring. Thus, there are some females, according to this theory, who are driven to have sex with the wealthy and powerful. This might account for the actions of "groupies," the highly visible females who stalk professional athletes, motion picture stars, and rock groups. It was Monica Lewinsky who opened her trench coat to reveal her underwear to Bill Clinton, who was apparently high on both the power and sexual scales, while relatively low on will power, obviously. For Bill, who was probably near a level nine on the sexual scale, after Monica revealed herself, it was all over. Jimmy Carter, one of Clinton's presidential predecessors, would talk about "lust in his heart," thus implying a high sex drive, perhaps in the Bill Clinton range. But either Carter had a high level of intellectually willed control, or he was afraid of his wife Rosalyn, who probably upon hearing Jimmy's public pronouncements of his lust, or simply knowing her man, always tried to be around him, even in White House staff meetings.

The point of this all is that it should come as no surprise to us that people with a high power drive may also have a high sex drive that can get them in trouble in the workplace, or anyplace. There are now laws to help protect victims against sexual harrassment, fortunately.

BELIEFS/MISSIONS/OBSESSIONS

There is a sixth psychological drive that we *don't* share with other higher animals. While we share with them emotional memories—traumatic incidents that have become imprinted in the structures of instinctual-emotional minds and shape our future behavior—"emotional beliefs," it would appear, are exclusively endemic to humans.

There is a great deal of difference between an emotional belief, as we might call a religious belief, and an intellectual belief. For example, an intellectual belief might be one in which we believe, while our spouse is at our side, that the shopping center we are driving to is "absolutely" six blocks west and four blocks to the right of the street we're on. When our spouse tells us, "No, it is five blocks to the west and six blocks to the left," we might react with anger. "Don't tell me, I know where I'm going." But when we make our right turn and find out we are wrong, we might get angry again, but we turn around and go in the opposite direction, admitting to ourselves that we were wrong. Thus, an intellectual belief can be changed when we see irrefutable evidence.

An emotional belief, like the previously described emotional memory, apparently gets imprinted on one or more of our limbic-cortical brain structures and thus becomes highly resistant to rationality, just as would a phobia or compulsion. As described in the last chapter, if the belief becomes addictive, we become fanaticized by it. The result is that we cannot walk up to a religious evangelist, trying to convert the rest of the world to his belief, and say, "Come on, loosen up. There are approximately 10,000 distinct religions in the world, counting all the tribal beliefs in the Amazon, Malaysia, the outback and so on.[20] Each one of these beliefs, in particular the rituals and methods of prayer, differs from every other to a greater or lesser extent. This would tell a rational person that we know nothing for sure, but it's possible that any one belief could be the truth. So if your religion makes you comfortable, go on and keep believing in it, but please, leave me alone."

Such an argument to an evangelist, or others like him, would fall on deaf ears, just as would the pleas to a bulimic child to believe that she is not fat. An addictive, emotional belief, good or bad for us or those around us, is held tightly by our instinctual-emotional system. Only a trauma or a traumatic insight is likely to change it. A very close friend of mine became a born-again Hindu after a nasty divorce. What he learned in studying the tenets of Hinduism became for him an "emotional belief." There was no arguing him out of his Hindu beliefs by his parents and other relatives. Many years later he contracted a sickness that brought him close to death. The trauma changed him, as he described it, "from a Hindu to an undo," although he continued with his meditation and other therapeutic and health-related practices he had learned from his years as a Hindu. This is not to say that there is anything wrong with Hinduism, but to exemplify that an emotional belief associated with any closely held religion may change relatively quickly if we experience an intense traumatic event—the death of a child after long suffering, for example—that may corrode our belief in the power of the religion.

In the corporate world, we find many power freaks who become addicted to or fanaticized by a mission or obsession as an emotional belief. Once the imprinting takes place, there is no changing it through rational persuasion. Thus, the power freak who believes that his or her vision is the only goal in the world that counts may chop down both friend and foe in his zeal to pursue that vision, whether it is rational or not. He may lose families and friends in the process; divorce is endemic to such people. You can send them to therapists and other counselors when their fanatical beliefs are patently irrational, yet nothing that can be said to them will change their minds. You can even say to them, "Look, as humans, we don't even know where we are. The Earth is basically lost in space. It would take 7,000 years traveling at 400,000 miles an hour to reach the nearest star, 1.2 trillion years to reach the next galaxy and there are 50 billion galaxies beyond that. Don't you see? We're lost, we're basically insignificant, so loosen up." Again, such arguments would fall on deaf ears. It takes a trauma before they'll finally see the light and begin thinking with some rationality.

Power freaks, unfortunately, are beset with emotional beliefs. As we'll later see, presenting them with irrefutable evidence to the contrary may set them into a rage.

CHAPTER 4

The Power Freak Factor in All of Us

"All year my boss promised me a 'really nice bonus' if I worked very hard. So work hard I did. Many nights I slumped home feeling like overcooked linguini. Here it is December and I walk into the boss's office with great hopes and expectations. I envision a new pool, a week in the Caribbean, a case of Dom Perignon. I impatiently tear open the envelope containing notice of my hard-earned reward. It's an invitation to dine with the boss at Taco Delight."[1]

Me a power freak? No way, any one of us might say.

But how would most of us react if we were sitting at our desk, eating our lunch, when someone we didn't know walked by, and without a word, took the sandwich from our mouth and walked away eating it? Even the meeker among us would temporarily become a power freak, driven to get even with that person, thinking of ways to threaten him.

Or what if a new co-worker is hired by your firm and after studying the situation for a week or two, he walks up to you and says, "Look, I've seen how you are fooling everyone with the work you pretend to do. But you don't fool me. I'm going to tell you right now that I am going to do my best to see that your section is absorbed in mine. If you don't want that to happen, you do exactly as I say."

Even the more balanced of us of might become a "challenged power freak," described in chapter 7, doing and saying things from that point on in defense of our position and working against the new peer, in the hope that he will be recognized for what he is and fired. When the situation is resolved—he's fired or transferred—or we are transferred or leave, we will

---

go back to being who we were, albeit perhaps a bit more defensive because of the "emotional memory" left by the incident.

Almost all of us react to a challenge. The intensity level of our power drive, to which we'll assign the metaphor "power freak factor," will probably determine the strength of our reaction. For example, think of the person lounging in his backyard on a Sunday morning, when a group of loud teenagers bursts through the bushes, lays down a blanket, and begins smoking cigarettes and eating fast food. If our power freak factor is low, a level two, we probably would feel some discomfort and politely ask them to leave as soon as they had finished. If we are a level five, we would probably become angry and ask the teenagers in firm tones to leave now. If we are an eight, we would probably shout threats and call the police. If we are a level ten and had a gun in the house, we might get it, aim it at the teenagers, threaten to use it, and maybe even fire a shot in the air.

What determines our power freak factor at any given moment? There are apparently both "push" and "pull" elements that help create our intensity levels, as described below.

THE "PUSH" OF OUTCOME EXPECTANCIES

There have been several terms used to describe the "push" side of our instinctive, motivational system. William McDougall, one of the earliest psychologists to study human motivation, including instincts, describes them as "propensities." He described the power drive as a "Self-assertive propensity, to domineer, to lead, to assert oneself over, or display oneself before one's fellows."[2] Other "push" terms I've come across in various references include cravings, strivings, and impulses.

Jack Panksepp, professor of psychobiology at Bowling Green State University and author of *Affective Neuroscience*, points out that there have been diverse labels given to the system over the years, including the "foraging/expectancy system," and the "behavioral/activation system." He prefers the term "Appetitive Motivational/Seeking System."[3]

So there is obviously some confusion about what this push side should be called. For purposes of this book, we'll use the simpler term "outcome expectancies" because it is easier on the ear. Stanford professor of psychology Albert Bandura, who coined the term, describes outcome expectancies as "expectations about whether the desired reward or reinforcement will be forthcoming if the person behaves appropriately."[4]

Simple enough.

Outcome expectancies can be conscious and rational. For example, if we work hard we will expect to make more money. But they also appear to work subconsciously as a motivational force for all of our core psychological drives: power/status, territorial, nurturance/attachment, survival/fear, and sexual. All appear to have their own "outcome expectancies," with the intensity of those expectancies correlating to the intensity of the drives at any given moment in our lives.

Thus, someone with a power freak factor of eight would have much stronger outcome expectancies than a level two. When we meet those expectancies, our instinctual-emotional system literally rewards us with positive emotions. We'll feel happiness, elation, delight, joy. If our expectations are not met, the system punishes us, literally, with feelings of sadness, depression, irritation, disappointment, and frustration, even if the matter is relatively trivial.

We drive into our garage one day prepared to park in our reserved parking space. Our "expectancy" is that this space will be ready for us. We see another car has taken our space. The expectancy is thus unmet and we will be punished with feelings of anger, frustration, and vindictiveness. Or, someone steps in front of us at a checkout counter line in a supermarket. Our expectancy is that the space in front of us is ours. Again we are punished with the same emotions.

Are our reactive emotions to a met or unmet outcome expectation really that automatic?

Apparently, they are. Our reward/punishment system, which Freud called the "pleasure-unpleasure principle" (usually abridged to the "pleasure principle"), is also covered in a separate body of academic work.[5] Again, if we imagine ourselves as the god figure or creative force in charge of developing this primitive section of the brain, when we were in caves and on the savannas, with little or no communication skills, we would have probably developed a similar system. When we are successful in leading a great hunt or gaining the territory of the tribe over the hill, the system rewards us with joy and elation. When we fail, we are punished with depression and frustration. When we gain a sexual conquest, we are joyful and elated. When we lose, we are frustrated and depressed.

The system remains with us today and so our motivation becomes not only the rewards of our endeavors, the money we earn from winning a contest, for example, but the highs we feel because we won the contest.

Let's assume that professional basketball player Michael Jordan has a power freak factor of nine when he is on a basketball court during a game. The expectancy at a level nine is an intense need to win. When Jordan was a member of the Chicago Bulls and they lost an important game, you could see in postgame interviews that he was punished with feelings of sadness, disappointment, and frustration. When his team won, he was joyful, elated, exuberant. When he played in the league championships for the first time and lost to Detroit, he was beyond sad and unhappy, he was practically inconsolable. When he won his first league championship against the Los Angeles Lakers, he was so happy he cried and clung to the team trophy for hours. Our outcome expectancies apparently rise in accordance with the importance of the challenge and the rewards and punishments we feel as a result of the outcome intensify accordingly.

Thus, when we are at work and eating a sandwich for lunch, our outcome expectancy is that we will finish it. If somebody walks up and takes it from us, we are saddened, irritated, and vengeful. But the intensity of these punishing emotions isn't as great as when the new peer walks up to us and tells us that he is out to get us fired. The challenge to us is much greater in the latter case than the stolen sandwich and so our reactions are more intense.

The point is that these punishing emotions, or the threat of their being unleashed if we lose a challenge, are capable of driving us into a *"power freak mode,"* which we might define as being in a state when our brain/mind chemicals are driving us with great intensity to defend or enhance our level of dominance or status over others. Even Adolf Hitler, who might be described as the prototypical extreme power freak of all time, was not always in a power freak mode, we might presume. We see him in documentaries, romping about his Bavarian getaway in Berchtesgaden, making jokes, nuzzling his dog, and playing the gracious host. Traudl Junge, who was Hitler's secretary from January 1943 until his death, in her recent book *To the Last Hour*, describes Hitler as a gentle soul in his working relationship to her. She quotes him as saying, "How are you, my child? Have you had some rest? I want to dictate something." The "something" was his last will and testament.[6]

In hospitals while visiting the wounded, he appears thankful and humble, patting injured German soldiers on the head. But we might also visualize him at night getting a message he doesn't like or walking into his office in the morning and being instantly transformed into his power freak mode, ordering the continuing murder of innocent women and children.

Michael Jordan, who apparently has the characteristics of a "competitive power freak," described in chapter 7, is probably in a power freak mode more often than those of us who are less competitive. He wants to win on the golf course, in the gambling casinos, in card games with his friends, in earning more money than his peers, in the business world, anywhere. He went into a funk when he thought the coaches of the Bulls weren't correctly scoring a *practice* game, in the Bulls' practice facility.[7]

It is apparent that whenever Jordan's instinctual-emotional system senses that he is in a competitive activity of whatever endeavor, be it a practice, a pick-up game in a gym, or a card game, it transforms him into a power freak mode. When he is in this condition, he is capable of intimidating teammates, coaches, his opponents, anyone who poses a threat to his outcome expectancies, without the slightest guilt or remorse at the time. On the other hand, when he was with the Chicago Bulls, he was frequently left in tears after weekly visits with dying children from the Make-a-Wish-Foundation, an activity he insisted on doing.[8]

Then there is John McEnroe, once a star on the main professional tennis circuit and more recently a television commentator for major tennis events. On the air he can be charming, jocular, and delightful. But he still plays on the seniors tennis circuit and apparently transforms into his power freak mode as soon as he steps on the court. The first call by a linesman that he thinks is wrong causes him to erupt in a tirade, particularly if he is losing. The linesman can be young, old, female or male, a grandmother, a grandfather, it doesn't matter. McEnroe will be intimidating. The outcome expectancy of his power/status program is that he will win on a tennis court and anything that puts a roadblock in front of this expectancy, such as a line call he thinks is bad, will cause his reward/punishment system to punish him with vengeful feelings that apparently overcome his rational capacity for containing them.

In the summer of the year 2000, McEnroe became so enraged at a call that he accidentally hit a young boy in the stands with a near-empty water bottle during an argument with the chair umpire. Later, when he was out of his "mode," he did what he could to make it up to the boy.[9]

I was at that match, sitting near the front row of the portable stadium erected in Chicago's Grant Park, and heard him later mutter to someone else in the stands that he behaves like this to "get myself going."

We might presume that two other high level tennis players, Andre Agassi and Pete Sampras, also have high competitive power freak factors and they, like McEnroe, begin to transform into their modes just before the start of their tennis matches. We might also presume that they also are inflicted with punishing emotions of depression and vengeance when they perceive a wrong line call has been made—when their outcome expectancies are roadblocked. But they are also capable of holding the feelings within themselves, perhaps harnessing them internally in an attempt to ratchet up their game. How each of us reacts when we are in a power freak mode can differ significantly, but one fact is probably true for all of us: We are not as rational in the power freak mode as we are in nonanxious moments of relative peace and quiet.

There appear to be three basic types of power freaks, to be described in subsequent chapters. "Extreme power freaks" whose characteristics are described in the next two chapters are presumably in the mode almost constantly when they are interacting with others. They do not revert back to "rational" behavior after being challenged in a competition, as do Michael Jordan and John McEnroe. This *is* their normal behavior. They are in a constant state of challenge. At work, outside of their trusted inner circle, we can expect them to be invariably intimidating and domineering when interacting with others, particularly when their expectancies are not being met, even though those expectancies may be irrational, impossible to achieve. In restaurants we can expect them to demand the best table and insult the waiters for the slightest problem with the food or the service. At home it is usually their way or the highway with a long-suffering spouse and children who try to hide from them. In the car they consider the road their own right of way. They are usually rude to tradesmen working in their homes, car attendants delivering their cars, or anyone they perceive to be beneath them in status, which is just about everyone. To interpolate Justice Stewart Potter's famous 1964 quote about hard-core pornography to help define an extreme power freak, most of us "know one when we see one."

"Situational power freaks," described in chapter 7, are transformed into the mode under only specific circumstances, as we've formerly noted. Someone is hired at work who threatens their job and their expectancy of security. They begin playing on a basketball court, hockey rink or tennis court and they are immediately out for blood. They board their sailboat and they immediately become the tyrannical Captain Bligh. Once their situation is resolved or they are off the field of battle, their expectancies are no longer under challenge and they can become sweet and charming.

"Directional power freaks," described in chapter 8, transform into the power freak mode when they are absorbed with specific outlooks. They might be "perfectionist power freaks" to the point of irrationality. Their expectancy is that everything they do must be beyond perfect, but they might be great company for dinner . . . as long as the silverware is precisely placed, of course. Or they might be "control power freaks" in that they expect to be in charge of absolutely anything they are engaged in, including creating the schedule for their weeknight poker club. Or they might be "prejudicial power freaks," intimidating and domineering only toward specific social or ethnic groups they view as beneath them. Or, they might be "symbol-laden power freaks," their outlooks driving them into going overboard with what they perceive as status symbols, from a body covered with tattoos to homes full of artwork they never have a chance to view. We might envision the extreme power freak per se as incorporating all or most of the traits of the situational and directional power freaks.

We might envision the "push," or pressure underlying our power freak factor as a piston that operates under hydraulic pressure, much like a car lift in an automotive repair facility. The higher our power freak factor as it relates to situations or outlooks, the higher the hydraulic pressure of our outcome expectancies and the more intense the rewarding and punishing (pleasurable and unpleasureable, as some academics and clinicians put it) emotions that are released based on whether or not what is happening at the moment is meeting those expectancies.

Thus we have all seen many alpha males and females with extremely high outcome expectancies working day and night, tired and stressed out and berating and intimidating others, to meet the needs of those expectancies and avoid the punishing emotions that would be released if they failed.

Maybe a better mental system evolved on another planet.

THE SENSELESS "PULLS" OF FLAWED PLEASURE SYSTEMS

There is apparently a second aspect to the triggering device that transforms us into a power freak mode and may account for the meanness and ruthlessness that can infect people with a high power freak factor. This has to do with an apparent flaw some of us have in the chemistry of our reward or pleasure system, of which the pleasure center is a part.[10]

Recall that this system was apparently designed for primitive life in the wilderness, giving us feelings of elation or "highs" when we met the outcome expectancies of our core instinctual drives. Thus a caveman who never tasted an alcoholic drink before and came across a bottle of Dewar's Scotch in the forest, dropped by a mythical time machine, who took a swig, may have felt a "high," because alcohol tends to lower our level of fear and raise our sense of power. "Oh, oh, this is good stuff," his pleasure center signals him, and he takes another drink and another until he finishes the bottle. If he finds additional bottles, he will finish them as well. There are no clinicians and academics around as yet to tell this caveman that alcohol in this quantity is bad for his health.

The same sequence would apply if our caveman friend finds a pound of pure cocaine. After chewing it, his pleasure center would mimic the same type of high he would feel after winning a fight against the tribe over the hill or killing a large beast. This would motivate him to continue taking the substance because he is getting a high on the cheap, so to speak.

The image of these substances as we are taking them and the memory of how they make us feel can become imprinted as an *emotional memory*, which can lead to an addiction. Remember that in our earliest days as humans in the wilderness we were primarily at the mercy of our instinctual-emotional system, and it must have been much easier for more of us to become addicted to substances and processes that rewarded us. Good-tasting, fat-laden foods and sex, for example, were positive addictions. For many, they still are. The instinctual-emotional mind, of which the pleasure system is a part, doesn't know the difference between good and bad. It only knows what feels good or bad and drives us accordingly.

But today, even though we live in advanced cultures and have the cerebral intelligence to know rationally the difference between what is good or bad for us, we can still become addicted to substances that are unhealthy, such as alcohol and cocaine. Most of us also know today that over time it takes ever increasing levels of these substances to reach our initial highs, levels that we all know may ultimately destroy our health. And yet, many of us are helpless to stop without intensive treatment. Once an addiction of any sort is anchored—and each of us has varying levels of vulnerability to addiction, whether to substances, beliefs, or processes, it buries itself behind the walls of the instinctual-emotional system and can become impervious to ordinary logic. Again, it takes a traumatic event or very hard work to control or end addictions and for some of us, neither may be possible.

And so the flaw in the pleasure system is not so much in its original design, which made sense in its day, but because many of the highs it continues to generate have become inappropriate given what we know today about the body: what it takes to remain healthy, what we have learned about the origins of life and the universe, and what we have learned about the nature of the pleasure system itself.

In a recent article in the "Science Times" section of the *New York Times*, "Scientists Examine How 'Social Rewards' Can Hijack the Brain's Circuits," Dr. Hans Breiter, a Harvard neuroscientist, was reported as observing that in our brain the neurotransmitter dopamine is primarily responsible for mediating our reward or pleasure system.

> Some people seem to be born with vulnerable dopamine systems that get hijacked by social rewards. The same neural circuitry involved in the highs and lows of abusing drugs is activated by winning or losing money, anticipating a good meal or seeking beautiful faces to look at. . . .
>
> . . . Compulsive gamblers seem to have vulnerable dopamine systems. . . . The first time they win, they get a huge dopamine rush that gets embedded in their memory [read "emotional memory"]. They keep gambling and the occasional dopamine rush of winning overrides their conscious knowledge that they will lose in the long run.[11]

In the same article, Dr. P. Read Montague, a neuroscientist at Baylor College of Medicine in Houston, "estimates that 90 percent of what people do every day is carried out by this kind of automatic, unconscious system that evolved to help creatures survive."[12]

It bears repeating that the pleasure system, like the instinctual-emotional system of which it is a part, is impervious to logic and cannot sense what is rationally good or bad for us. It knows only what makes us feel good and then drives us to want more of it. In the conflict between nature and nurture it is nature in the raw. The nurturing aspect of the dilemma is the foundation of the statement "Just say no," intended to convince us to be rational early on to avoid substances and processes that may prove addictive. This would follow the model of learning early to look right and left at traffic intersections.

As has been pointed out, it is as easy to become addicted to a belief, good or bad, as it is to a substance, and the belief addiction can lead to distorted outlooks. In his paper "Hatred as Pleasure," Otto F. Kernberg, professor of psychiatry and former president of the International Psychoanalytic Association, writes, "It is, of course, well known that hatred, a derivative of rage, may give rise to highly pleasurable aggressive behaviors, sadistic enjoyment in causing pain, humiliation, and suffering and the glee derived from devaluating others."[13] In other words, some of us have distorted outlooks that give us a high when we devalue, intimidate, or harass others. This may be one consequence of the system of dominance hierarchy described previously in this book. In establishing ourselves in the pecking order, the "status tension" drives us in a natural state to look down upon those beneath us. "Human A pecks Human B, who pecks Human C," and so forth. There is a photo I recall seeing in a primatologist's book that shows a female gorilla at the very bottom of the pecking order of her group, an omega, who has a look of terror on her face. There is no one who is not harassing her. It reminds one of the child in the school yard who is harassed by everyone and stands alone in sorrow and fear.

And so we might assume that the high some of us feel when intimidating others is a rewarding emotion of our pleasure system, a shot of dopamine, for meeting an outcome expectancy of maintaining or advancing ourselves in a pecking order.

Even the meekest of us might sometimes feel a high when intimidating others. I recall several movie plots where a meek husband who is put down daily by his wife and boss one day has had enough and releases a torrent of words in a temper tantrum that surprises and shocks everyone. The camera closes in on the character's face and we see a glimmer of satisfaction that he was able to do it.

In high school shootings, most of the perpetrators have had a history of being teased and bullied in the schoolyard, according to psychologist Judith Harris, author of *The Nurture Assumption: Why Children Turn Out the Way They Do*. This can be intensely traumatic and in many cases beyond the help of caring parents.[14] Does the satisfaction the teenage shooters receive from their intimidating bloody rampages constitute a high? Are high levels of dopamine being excreted? Perhaps so, even for those who thereafter shoot themselves.

Presumably, like most everything else in psychology, the highs we feel when intimidating others can be placed on a metaphoric scale, say one to ten, with the level ones barely feeling such a high—for them intimidation of others might be more of an embarrassment—to the tens, who might get a natural high from intimidating others. The tens are the people who presumably look around addictively for anyone they can intimidate, just as the alcoholic seeks out a bottle of liquor.

There is a separate body of academic work on the subject of "bullying" or "mobbing," as it is also called academically. Weaving throughout the literature is the concept that some people "will derive satisfaction from the harassment of somebody else."[15] In the field of psychiatry the condition has been known as sadistic personality disorder, which is described in the next chapter.

The disorder can start early in life. The boy on the block with a high power freak factor and a low level of nurturance/attachment who succeeds initially in bullying your son or daughter may find that he gets a natural high from the experience and begins repeating it until he eventually becomes addicted to the process. He may actually be encouraged in this process by a father who as an adult, continues to act in the same way. Or he may be more fortunate in having parents or other authority figures who recognize what he is doing and begin to intervene. (An excellent book on this subject is *Bullies and Victims: Helping Your Child*

Survive the Schoolyard Battlefield.[16]) The torment that the young bully may spread among his more vulnerable victims can be indescribable. The traumatic experiences imprinted as emotional memories can alter personalities for the worse for a lifetime.

It is apparent that an addiction to bullying, like the addiction to a drug, can begin at practically any age. Many of us have seen people who have had little authority all their lives, suddenly thrust into a position of power, or even a position with a modicum of power, become domineering, if not tyrannical, in their treatment of others. The waitress, for example, who is promoted to maitre d' and now thinks she is the queen of England, not only in the restaurant, but everywhere she goes. The bank clerk who becomes a teller and who takes forever to call the next person in line. The airport screener who insists on practically strip searching you, even if you are eighty-five and a grandmother. The bus driver who passes you by with a half-empty bus in freezing weather, because you are standing one foot past the bus stop boundary line. We might call them closet eights, nines, or tens. For the first time in their lives they are in a position where they can control and intimidate others, and so feel the natural highs that they might have had years ago, if the opportunity for dominance presented itself.

Many years ago I was helping a manufacturer establish its distribution strategies. In the midst of the project, the president and owner of the company passed away. His estate passed his stock to the widow, who instead of selling to the competent group of managers her husband had hired, decided to run the company herself. This woman was mild and pleasant during the time that I knew her while her husband was alive. But from the moment she sat in her dead husband's chair, she was transformed into an extreme power freak, actually enjoying the tyranny she was spreading. You could literally see the happiness in her face as she belittled the managers who had held the company together for years. She told me over lunch one day, "You know, Rex (a pseudonym for her deceased husband) really didn't know a damned thing about business. He was too nice. But I didn't want to say anything, I didn't want to be a nagging wife. But now that I'm here, things will change. And to tell you the truth, I never knew business could be so much fun." When we drove back to her office, she screamed at a security guard at the gate, "Goddamn it, you get rid of those suspenders. You're supposed to be wearing a belt. Suspenders are the wrong image for this company. It makes us look old fashioned, out of touch. If I see you wearing suspenders again you're fired, do you understand me?" As we drove on, I could see a smug little smile on her face. She was feeling her high.

I also knew a president of a relatively large company, whom I was commiserating with one day because he had to lay off about twenty middle managers, who told me confidentially that the process was actually giving him a high. Writer Joel Stein, in a *Time* magazine article about "Bosses from Hell," reported that Al Dunlap when he was CEO at Scott Paper terminated 11,000 employees and later when he worked at Sunbeam terminated 6,000 employees and "crowed about it." Nicknamed "Chainsaw Al," he was apparently experiencing a high when these events occurred.[17] Leona Helmsley might also have felt a high when she browbeat employees for perceived miscues that were not apparent to others present at the time. According to the same *Time* article, she fired employees at a whim, including "one for taking an apple from the kitchen while working through lunch." She was nicknamed the "Queen of Mean," Stein's article reports.

There is one other theory covering the "pull" side of the power freak factor that is worth noting because it applies to how each of our reward levels is set and may explain why some of us feel a "high" when intimidating others while most of us do not. In a paper he wrote entitled "Appetitive Pleasure States," clinical psychiatry professor Norman Doidge of the University of Toronto describes what he calls the "pleasure threshold."[18]

In the simplest of terms this means that if we have a low pleasure threshold, it is easier for us to feel buoyant and euphoric. People with a low pleasure threshold require less out of life to make them happy, they are more consistently enthusiastic and optimistic. However, if we are at the extreme low end of the pleasure threshold, we may suffer from hypomania, we become so euphoric that we are disordered, spending money we don't have on shopping sprees, for example. People who are high on the threshold require great efforts for them to feel pleasure and may be consistently saddened and pessimistic. If we are at the extreme high end of the threshold, we may be unable to feel any pleasure at all, a condition that psychiatry calls "Anhedonia." Most of us, fortunately, are some-where in the middle of the pleasure threshold.

The point has been made that the higher our pleasure threshold, the harder it is to achieve a natural high, the feeling most of us get when we win at something. And so, the theory goes, they need to seek out abnormal experiences or attach to abnormal beliefs or processes or imbibe stimulating substances to achieve their highs.

We might thus conjecture that the extreme power freak has a high pleasure threshold and finds in the intimidation, tormenting, and domi-neering of others the feelings of contentment and gratification that most of the rest of us would achieve by catching the train on time.

In his book *Eyewitness to Power: The Essence of Leadership*, journalist David Gergen describes in detail his experiences working for four U.S. presidents, including Richard Nixon and Ronald Reagan. We might pre-sume from Richard Nixon's general countenance and reactions that he had a relatively high pleasure threshold. The day after he won the elec-tion for his second term in office in a landslide, for example, he should have been enjoying a natural high. Instead, he called in his White House staff, who thought the meeting was to praise their efforts, and asked for their resignations. In all, it turned out, more than 1,000 of his appointees were asked to submit letters of resignation, not the act of a happy, buoyant, optimistic man.

Ronald Reagan, on the other hand, presumably had a low pleasure threshold. It was apparent to the world that he was naturally optimistic and enthusiastic, and Gergen confirms that he was the same way in pri-vate. Whereas Nixon was often surly and demeaning of others in private, Gergen said, Reagan was genial and gracious and hated the thought of firing anybody.[19] We can presume that he woke up most days feeling in good spirits.

The overall theory is interesting because it would account for some of the brain chemistry and circuitry that creates the distorted, self-deceiving thoughts and actions of all varieties of power freaks. Holding back the opportunity for extreme power freaks to intimidate others, according to this theory, would be akin to hiding a liquor bottle from an alcoholic. Sooner or later they'll find a substitute—and if it's us, we need to know how to prepare ourselves and divert the onslaughts.

As we shall see in the next chapter, the imbalances that produce pleasure from intimidating and taunting others are found in some of the traits exhibited by psychopaths, sadists, narcissists, and paranoids. In other words, it is quite probable that the extreme power freak in your life is, at the very least, mentally disordered.

The Power Freak as Mentally Disordered

Jim, a manager, thought he was moving along well on the project assigned to his department. Then one day his supervisor . . . stopped in front of Jim's desk and without a warning, shouted: ". . . You're an idiot, a moron, you're completely incompetent and an embarrassment to the human race! You must be a genetic mistake. You've been working on this for two weeks and you're already three weeks behind. I won't listen to any more of your excuses. Pay attention, because this is what you are going to do. . . ." Out of the corner of his eye, Jim could see that everyone else in the office had either run for cover or stood frozen, paralyzed with fear. [The supervisor] barked out his orders . . . and then moved off, leaving Jim sitting amid the rubble of his best efforts and good intentions.[1]

It appears that when the power freak factor in any of us is at a high enough level, we may have one or more *psychiatric personality disorders*, which have been partially defined as enduring, twisted patterns of personality that cause significant impairment and distress. The distress, unfortunately, is also generously endowed on the people around them.

These disorders have been described by some as extreme personality variations or quirks, but they are far more than that because they result in distorted outlooks, attitudes, and beliefs. In those with borderline personality disorder, for example, which belies its name, there is a constant pattern of changes in outlooks, moods, and attitudes. They are up one day and down the next. Personal relationships are turbulent; one day they love you, the next day they hate you. You rarely know where you stand with them. They are deceitful, impulsive, and remorseless and frequently engage in self-mutilation, such as cutting their arms or wrists or burning themselves with cigarettes. A quirk? I don't think so.

There are ten personality disorders listed in the *The Diagnostic and Statistical Manual of Mental Disorders* (DSM-IV), the Bible of psychiatry, and others that remain under study. Extreme power freaks appear to have many of the characteristics of antisocial personality disorder or psychopathy. They also appear to have selected characteristics of narcissistic personality disorder, paranoid personality disorder, and sadistic personality disorder.

In short, these people have severe personality problems.

It is estimated that between 10 and 13 percent of us are afflicted with a personality disorder, and it is not uncommon for some of us to suffer simultaneously from the traits of more than one of them.[2] Further, some of the traits of one disorder can be found in the characteristics of another, as we soon shall see.

One of the purposes of this book is to attempt to define the primary characteristics of an extreme power freak, to give us the understanding we need to deal with him or her. It would appear that most of the characteristics are found in these personality disorders. We'll start with antisocial personality disorder.

PSYCHOPATHIC OR ANTISOCIAL PERSONALITY DISORDER

In chapter 3 we defined the prototypical alpha male in terms of evolutionary psychology, and the characteristics that he needed to lead tribes in the caves and on the African savannas. He must, we noted, have had an intense drive to achieve power and dominance and to protect and enlarge the tribe's territory as necessary. Accompanying this must have been a low level of nurturance . . . little or no guilt, remorse, shame, or empathy for others. He must have been able to punish challengers without hesitation or regret. He must also have had a low level of fear; the threat of physical punishment or defeat must not have deterred him as he took on all challengers or led the tribe in battle against another.

Perhaps we don't have to go back to the caves of primitive times to define the traits of the prototypical alpha. Maybe they are manifested just as clearly in the modern-day warlords inhabiting underdeveloped nations such as Afghanistan and Somalia, who remind us that we can quickly regress to our primitive ways when there is no law and order to keep our adverse instinctual drives under control. Unfortunately, these modern-day alpha warlords today have access to machine guns, tanks, artillery, missiles, and potentially, weapons of mass destruction.

Or maybe the modern-day alpha is equally defined as the intimidating, domineering, and demeaning boss, the extreme power freak who doesn't need guns to make you miserable.

Whether early primitives or modern-day primitives, compare the description of the prototypical alpha with those of psychopaths, as described incisively in the *Oxford Textbook of Psychopathology* in an article by Robert D. Hare, a professor of psychology at the University of British Columbia and one of the leading authorities on the subject:

> Interpersonally, psychopaths are grandiose, arrogant, callous, superficial and manipulative; affectively, they are short tempered, unable to form strong emotional bonds with others, and lacking in guilt or anxiety; and behaviorally, they are irresponsible, impulsive and prone to delinquency and criminality. [However,] it is important to recognize that psychopathy is not synonymous with criminality or violence; not all psychopaths engage in criminal activities and not all criminals are psychopaths.[3]

As a matter of fact, there is a classification of psychopath known as the business psychopath, which we will soon cover.

Park Dietz, a forensic psychiatrist, professor of psychiatry at the UCLA School of Medicine, and a recognized expert on psychopathy, including business psychopaths, estimates that there are 5 million psychopaths in North America. He points out that only 2 million of them are in prison.[4]

Dietz's estimates appear close to the mark. Remi J. Cadoret, professor of psychiatry at the University of Iowa, estimates that between 2 percent and 3 percent of the population is antisocial or psychopathic and indicates there is a difference between males and females.[5] According to the reference text *Abnormal Psychology*, the gender split is 1 percent of the female population and 3 percent of the male population.[6] For females in the United States and Canada as of December 2001, that would amount to 1.26 million psychopaths. For males that would amount to 3.9 million psychopaths, a total of just over 5 million.

It is quite possible that one of those 3 million psychopaths on the loose might be down the hall in another office or at the family dinner table.

There appears to be a confusion in terms today between "psychopath," "sociopath," and "antisocial personality," and we should attempt to clear this up before we go further.

The term "psychopath" was first used in 1891 to describe a whole range of personality disorders. The term was narrowed during the years that followed, and was fully defined in 1941 by Harvey Cleckley in his seminal book on psychopaths, *The Mask of Sanity*, which was reissued in updated editions through 1988.

The term "sociopath" was introduced in 1968 because it was thought at the time that "psychopath" disproportionately reflected biological and genetic origins. "Sociopath," it was then believed, would reflect many of the social forces and early experiences in one's upbringing that might create the personality previously described as psychopathic.

That same year, the American Psychiatric Association introduced the term "personality disorder, antisocial," and subsequently antisocial personality disorder was listed in the DSM.

As Cleckley pointed out in his book, the three terms, "psychopath," "sociopath," and "antisocial personality" can today be "used as . . . synonym[s] to designate patients with this specific pattern of disorder."[7] Hare, in his book *Without Conscience: The Disturbing World of Psychopaths Among Us*, said, "The same individual therefore could be diagnosed as a sociopath by one expert and as a psychopath by another."[8] In other words, we would just be splitting hairs in attempting to define the three terms as other than synonymous.

However, certain segments of the academic and clinical world prefer one term over the other. In general, it appears that the term "psychopath" is preferred by most psychologists, "sociopath" is preferred by most sociologists and criminologists, and "antisocial personality" is preferred by most psychiatrists.

For purposes of this book, we will focus on the term "psychopathic," since along with "antisocial personality," it is the term used in much of the psychological and psychiatric reference work that exists.

As just noted, most psychopaths are not in prison, but are sprinkled among us. Hare said the following:

> [M]any psychopaths never go to prison or any other facility. They appear to function reasonably well—as lawyers, doctors, psychiatrists, academics, mercenaries, police officers, cult leaders, military personnel, businesspeople, writers, artists, entertainers, and so forth—without breaking the law, or at least without being caught and convicted. . . . [T]heir intelligence, family background, social skills, and circumstances permit them to construct a facade of normalcy and to get what they want with relative impunity.[9]

Thus, those mean and ruthless police detectives or military officers or other so-called good guys we see in the movies may be just as psychopathic as the bad guys. However, they have constructed enough of a "facade of normalcy" to function as a so-called good guy.

The following is a list of the characteristics that appear to define the *business psychopath*, which combines the pertinent characteristics detailed in Cleckley's *Mask of Sanity* and the "Psychopathy Checklist" developed by Robert Hare, some of which were listed in chapter 1:

- **Superficial charm and good "intelligence":** When you are first with this type of person, you may not notice anything disagreeable about them. They appear to be professional and can have high levels of intelligence. They can be professors, mathematicians, bankers, doctors, and so on, possessing superb credentials.
- **Grandiose sense of self-worth:** They have an exaggerated sense of entitlement, feeling that the ordinary rules of life don't apply to them. They believe that the whole world revolves around them and the views of others are irrelevant.
- **Need for stimulation/proneness to boredom:** Business psychopaths need excitement in their lives. Cleckley describes a psychopathic psychiatrist who was unable to tolerate self-containment for long and went on periodic binges, usually on weekends, that included degrading and insulting women in his company.[10]
- **Frequently impulsive:** They will not sit back at their desks and endlessly weigh the pros and cons of an issue. On the contrary, they fre-

quently make decisions on a whim, leaving those about them puzzled. "He can't really mean this," we might think. Yes, he can.

* **Lack of empathy for other human beings:** They have no concern for the feelings of others. They don't need approval. Other people are there just to be used; they are pawns in his life. Psychopaths find it extremely difficult to feel any kind of love.

* **Lack of remorse, guilt, or shame:** They have no social conscience. They will do whatever they deem necessary to make others suffer and feel no regret. This is one of the outstanding features of a psychopath. Many of us who lash out at others when angered may feel no remorse or guilt at the time, but later, when we calm down, we regret our actions. The psychopath has no room for regret.

* **Cunning, callous, and manipulative:** Psychopaths will do anything it takes to reach their objectives. They may make promises this week that they break next week. Any strategy at all is fair play. They are usually pathological liars (don't trust their resumes) and predisposed to take what they want and do as they please, with little or no feelings of anxiety or fear. They are almost totally uninhibited.

* **Poor behavioral controls:** Hare pointed out that such people take offense easily and can become angry and aggressive over trivialities. But their outbursts, extreme as they might be, are generally short-lived and they quickly resume acting as if nothing ever happened.[11]

* **Absence of delusions and other irrational thinking:** A psychopath doesn't hear voices and doesn't have genuine delusions. In other words, he doesn't think he is the King of England. As Cleckley said, "he is likely to be judged a man of warm human responses, capable of full devotion and loyalty."[12]

* **Won't take responsibility for own actions:** Nothing is ever the psychopath's fault. No matter what happens, no matter if it was their idea or how much they were involved, if it goes wrong, they will always find a way to blame others.

* **Sexually promiscuous:** We know what that means.

Might we presume that people with psychopathic traits were purposely sprinkled among us by genetic design so that in primitive times they could rise quickly to lead our early tribes? It would appear that a psychopathic leader in caveman times might have been just what the doctor ordered, when it came to physically enforcing order in the tribes and fearlessly engaging in hunts and battles against rival tribes. If nature imbued us with psychopaths at the rate of 3 percent of the adult male population, there would be enough of them to lead a tribe of thirty-three adults and many more with children.

Certainly we have had our share of psychopathic monarchs and other leaders over time. Some of the more famous might include Caligula, Genghis Kahn, Attila the Hun, Benito Mussolini, Joseph Stalin, Pol Pot, Mao Tse-tung, Idi Amin, and Adolf Hitler. A list of those of lesser known could probably fill libraries across the country. But whether a purposeful genetic design or not, the fact is that these psychopathic people continue to live within our midst and many of them may end up being our boss; that is, if they have enough intelligence to satisfy the needs of the job. They also, unfortunately, may end up being either our mother, father, a sibling, or all three.

One of the hallmarks of psychopaths or antisocials, as noted, is that they are perfectly capable of performing in the workplace or at home. In other words, when they need to do so, they can wear a mask of civility that disguises a significantly unbalanced instinctual-emotional system. Cleckley, in his description of "The Psychopath as Businessman," says, "He is pleasant and affable during his normal phases, which make up the greater part of his time. . . . For perhaps 80 to 90 percent of his existence he has been a prosperous and respected member of his community and outwardly is not unlike other men of the same position."[13]

John Wayne Gacy, the serial killer who murdered thirty-two young men, is an extreme example of how this mask of civility can be worn. If Gacy can present a normal exterior, how difficult can it be for our boss or co-worker down the hall to do so?

In his earlier years in Waterloo, Iowa, Gacy managed a string of Kentucky Fried Chicken restaurants, was chaplain of the local Junior Chamber of Commerce, and organizer of the group's first communitywide prayer breakfast. He volunteered to shop for Christmas presents for underprivileged children and joined the Merchant's Patrol, a volunteer group that helped to police area businesses. He was married, had a seemingly normal home life, inviting neighbors over for barbeques. But he began having sex with teenage boys and was soon imprisoned.

After his release from prison, he moved to Des Plaines, Illinois, where he quickly became a respected trade contractor and was named a Junior Chamber of Commerce "Man of the Year." He entertained children at numerous civic and other events as "Pogo the Clown." People who knew him, by and large, genuinely liked him. He was glib and entertaining, which helped him attract young men in bars whom he lured to his home. He then forced sex on them and murdered them, something he hadn't done in Waterloo. He buried them, thirty-two in all, in his basement crawl space.[14]

Talk about what can lurk under the mask of sanity.

Another example of the ability to create a mask of civility is Adolf Hitler, who could be a poster boy for psychopathy. An elderly woman in a television documentary about Hitler's early days in power said, "He was presented to us originally as a very kindly man. We always saw photos of him hugging children and presenting flowers to women. We could see that he loved his dogs and so we formed this kindly impression of him."[15] Hitler was also described as one of the most popular leaders in Europe during the early 1930s, and we noted earlier his concern for his secretary.

Aaron T. Beck, one of the founders of behavior modification (cognitive) therapy points out in *Cognitive Therapy of Personality Disorders* "that a patient with antisocial personality disorder [Beck notes that "psychopathy," "sociopathy," and "antisocial personality disorder" are often used interchangeably] typically holds a number of self-serving beliefs," including but not necessarily limited to the following:

1. Justification—"Wanting something or wanting to avoid something justifies my actions."
2. Thinking is believing—"My thoughts and feelings are completely accurate, simply because they occur to me."
3. Personal infallibility—"I always make good choices."
4. Feelings make facts—"I know I am right because I feel right about what I do."
5. The impotence of others—"The views of others are irrelevant to my decisions, unless they directly control my immediate consequences."
6. Low-impact consequences—"Undesirable consequences will not occur or will not matter to me."[16]

Bobby Knight, the former Indiana basketball coach, comes across in personal television interviews as a calm and rational man. In one interview I watched, he denied that he had any serious problem with his temperament, even after watching tapes of his explosiveness on the basketball court.[17] Bobby Knight may not be a psychopath, but he can frequently display psychopathic traits, including those previously listed above, and particularly, "My thoughts and feelings are completely accurate, simply because they occur to me."

To make matters worse, power freaks exhibiting psychopathic traits are practically immune to therapeutic treatment, particularly as younger adults. The primary problem, as all the experts in the field affirm, is that they don't believe that anything is wrong with them. When confronted, they perceive that you are in the wrong, not them, or that you don't understand or accept them, or that you are trying to limit their freedom.

Beck points out the only real hope for improvement in these individuals is if they finally recognize that they do have a problem, which is a key factor for any kind of therapeutic intervention. One industrial psychologist reported to me that improvement is only possible for such people in management when they finally come to believe that their behavior, although justified in their mind, is being so poorly perceived by others that it will damage their careers.

Robert Hare pointed out at a meeting of the American Neuropsychiatric Association that the treatment of psychopaths is likely to make them worse.[18] "What do you treat?" he asked. "They have no subjective distress; they don't have low self-esteem; they are not dissatisfied with their behavior. Do you treat personality traits that they don't want to change?"

If people like Dr. Hare have trouble working with these people, what about the rest of us who experience that person as our boss or a co-worker in the next cubicle? This all alludes to the points made in chapter 2 about how a power freak thinks. The fact that the best cognitive therapists in the business may not be able to get through to the psychopath's sense of reason indicates the strength of the outer walls of the instinctual-emotional system. As previously noted, once beliefs and outlooks are imprinted on the appropriate structures of this system, they are beyond rationality. Only a traumatic event can change them, and it still may even be for the worse. For example, during the latter part of World War II,

Hitler survived the explosion of a bomb hidden in a briefcase under a conference table at a meeting. Instead of bringing him to his senses, grateful to be alive, the attack made him even more vindictive and remorseless.

Psychiatry, for the most part, measures the severity of disorders on scales, frequently using the terms "mild," "moderate" and "severe."[19] Or it might describe the severity of a disorder as being in the "lower ranges," "middle ranges" and "upper ranges." Additional terms have been developed to measure the severity of psychopathy, including business psychopaths and their ability to create a veneer or mask of civility. One term refers to someone who is "high functioning," according to Donald W. Black, professor of psychiatry at the University of Iowa College of Medicine: "Their disorder seems to have limited impact on their ability to get by in the world. . . . It reflects the fact that in our society, money and status can effectively disguise ugly and destructive behaviors."[20]

Cleckley uses the term "partial psychopath" to allude to the mild or moderate case. He also uses the term "primary psychopath" to describe a psychopath with absolutely no guilt or remorse, and no sense of conscience, and "secondary psychopath" to describe those who can be just as exploitive, but report some feelings of guilt.

Finally, a paper titled "Ten Subtypes of Psychopathy," written by Theodore Millon and Roger B. Davis, both associated with the Institute for Advanced Studies in Personology and Psychopatholgy in Coral Gables, Florida, describes fascinating variations of persons with psychopathic traits. The categorizations Millon and Davis have developed may seem like splitting hairs, but they are interesting, nonetheless, in reinforcing descriptions of people who exhibit psychopathic traits. The following are four of the more pertinent, though each of the names of these categories may sound redundant:

    ❧ **The unprincipled psychopath:** "These psychopaths display an indifference to truth that, if brought to their attention is likely to elicit an attitude of nonchalant indifference. They are . . . adept in deceiving others with charm and glibness. Lacking any deep feelings of loyalty, they may successfully scheme beneath a veneer of politeness and civility. Their principal orientation is that of outwitting others—'Do unto others before they do unto you.'"

❀ **The disingenuous psychopath:** "A flagrant deceitfulness is a principal prototypal characteristic of this variant of psychopathy. These individuals are more willful and insincere in their relationships, doing everything necessary to obtain what they need and want from others."

❀ **The explosive psychopath:** "In contrast to (some) other psychopaths, explosive individuals do not move about in a surly and truculent manner. Rather, their rages burst out uncontrollably, often with no apparent provocation. In periods of explosive range, they may unleash a torrent of abuse and storm about defiantly, voicing bitter contempt for all. . . . Many are hypersensitive to feelings of betrayal."

❀ **The abrasive psychopath:** "To the abrasive psychopath, everything and everyone is an object available for nagging and assaulting, a sounding board for discharging inner irritabilities, or even a target for litigious action. More than merely angry in a general way, these persons are intentionally abrasive and antagonistic. . . . They may have few qualms and little conscience or remorse about demeaning even their most intimate associates."[21]

Anyone here you know?

ADD TRAITS OF SADISTIC PERSONALITY DISORDER

The authors of the paper "Psychopathy and Sadistic Personality Disorder," succinctly describe the sadistic personality disorder (SPD) as follows:

> SPD is underpinned by a cruel, demeaning and aggressive approach to interactions with other people. As with all other personality disorders, it starts early in life, it is long lasting, and it pervades most of the individual's interactions with others at school, work, socially and within family relationships. . . . Sadists share many of the critical features of the psychopath: they lack remorse for their controlling and exploitative behavior, they do not experience shame or guilt, and they are unable to empathize with their victims. They are cold-hearted.[22]

It would appear that some of the characteristics of the disorder as defined in DSM-III (the previous edition of the Diagnostic and Statistical Manual of Mental Disorders),[23] would indeed help build a definition of the extreme power freak. They are as follows:

- Humiliates or demeans people in the presence of others
- Has treated or disciplined someone under his or her control unusually harshly
- Is amused by, or takes pleasure in, the psychological or physical suffering of others (including animals)
- Has lied for the purpose of harming or inflicting pain on others (not merely to achieve some other goal)
- Gets others to do what he or she wants by frightening them
- Restricts the autonomy of people with whom he or she has a close relationship, e.g., will not let spouse leave the home unaccompanied or permit teenage daughter to attend social functions
- Is fascinated by violence, weapons, martial arts, injury, or torture[24]

Haven't most of us known people along the way who have exhibited many of these traits? Now we have a name to apply to them, other than world-class jerks.

NOW ADD NARCISSISM

One of the traits of the psychopath is "grandiose sense of self-worth." This is also a trait of another personality disorder called narcissistic personality disorder. According to a table in the book *Abnormal Psychology*, 55.6 percent of all people afflicted with antisocial personality disorder or psychopathy also have traits associated with narcissistic personality disorder.

The same book also offers a succinct description of this disorder:

People with narcissistic personality disorder have an unreasonable sense of self-importance and are so preoccupied with themselves that they lack sensitivity and compassion for other people. They aren't comfortable unless someone is admiring them. The exaggerated feelings and fantasies of greatness or "grandiosity" create in these people a number of negative attributes. They require and expect a great deal of special attention from other people—the best table in the restaurant, the illegal parking space in front of the movie theater. They also tend to use or exploit other people for their own interests and show little empathy for others. When confronted with other successful people, they can be extremely envious and arrogant.[25]

Robert D. Hare and Stephen T. Hart, in a paper titled "Association between Psychopathy and Narcissism," suggest that "narcissism is a basic factor underlying half of all psychopathic symptoms," and that it is possible that "all psychopathic individuals are narcissistic."[26] Other authors have suggested that psychopathy is actually a sub-set of narcissism.

Following are the characteristics of narcissistic personality disorder, from the DSM-IV:

- Has a grandiose sense of self-importance (e.g., exaggerates achievements and talents, expects to be recognized as superior without commensurate achievement)
- Is preoccupied with fantasies of unlimited success, power, brilliance, beauty, or ideal love
- Believes that he or she is "special" and unique and can only be understood by, or should associate with, other special or high-status people
- Requires excessive admiration
- Has a sense of entitlement, i.e., unreasonable expectations especially of favorable treatment or automatic compliance with his or her expectations
- Is interpersonally exploitive, i.e., takes advantage of others to achieve his or her own ends
- Lacks empathy; is unwilling to recognize or identify with the feelings and needs of others
- Is often envious of others or believes that others are envious of him or her
- Shows arrogant, haughty behaviors or attitudes[27]

The second trait, preoccupation with fantasies of unlimited success and power, helps clarify a conversation I had with Joseph P. Newman, professor of psychology at the University of Wisconsin and another leading expert on psychopathy. He told me that psychopaths don't necessarily have an innate drive for power and status. Having a "grandiose sense of self-worth" apparently doesn't always include the need to wield power over another. However, if the traits of narcissism are added, particularly "a preoccupation with fantasies of unlimited success and power," we might have a clearer picture of the business psychopath in particular.

In his book *Disorders of Personality, DSM IV and Beyond,* Theodore Millon describes those who have the combined traits of psychopathy and narcissism as "Unprincipled Narcissists," with the following traits:

- Evidences a rash willingness to risk harm and is notably fearless in the face of threats and punitive action
- Vengeful gratification is often obtained by humiliating and dominating others
- Lacking a genuine sense of guilt and possessing little social conscience, they are opportunists and charlatans who enjoy the process of swindling others
- Relationships are dropped with no thought to the anguish they may cause as a consequence of the narcissist's careless and irresponsible behavior
- Displays an indifference to truth that, if brought to their attention, is likely to elicit an attitude of nonchalant indifference
- Capable of feigning an air of justified innocence, and adept in deceiving others with charm and glibness
- Lacking any deep feelings of loyalty, they may successfully scheme beneath a veneer of politeness and civility
- Their principal orientation is that of outwitting others, getting power, and exploiting them "before they do it to you."

Millon then adds this interesting point: "A number of these narcissists attempt to present an image of cool strength, acting tough, arrogant and fearless. To prove their courage, they may invite danger and punishment. . . . Rather than having a deterrent effect, it [a negative outcome] only reinforces their exploitive and unprincipled behavior."[28]

Any questions?

MIX IN A DASH OF PARANOIA

It would seem odd that after all we've read about psychopaths and narcissists, particularly "unprincipled narcissists" who have low levels of fear, that paranoia should be included in the list of traits that help define an extreme power freak.

Nonetheless, the *Abnormal Psychology* table on personality disorders states that 27.8 percent of those with antisocial personality disorder or psychopathy may also have traits of paranoid personality disorder. However, it would appear that most extreme power freaks would have some, if not all of the characteristics of this disorder, which are listed in the DSM-IV as follows. See if you agree:

* Suspects without sufficient basis that others are exploiting, harming, or deceiving him or her
* Is preoccupied with unjustified doubts about the loyalty or trustworthiness of friends or associates
* Is reluctant to confide in others because of unwarranted fear that the information will be used maliciously against him or her
* Reads hidden or demeaning or threatening meanings into benign remarks or events
* Persistently bears grudges, i.e., is unforgiving of insults, injuries, or slights
* Perceives attacks on his or her character or reputation that are not apparent to others and is quick to react angrily or to counter-attack
* Has recurrent suspicions, without justification, regarding fidelity of spouse or sexual partner[29]

We might make the presumption that the prototypical alpha male while showing little or no fear in taking on all challengers and leading his tribe in battle might also have a natural proclivity to feel suspicious about members of other tribes who have joined his tribe forcefully or voluntarily, and whom they don't know. As pointed out previously, part of our instinctual territorial program is to react with suspicion, dislike, and aggression toward aliens who have invaded our turf. Even among chimpanzees, those who come from one group to join another and are eventually accepted, remain as outcasts long after they have made the new group their home.

Is it possible that extreme power freaks perceive instinctually that all but their inner circle, whom they know and trust, are aliens and objects of suspicion? Perhaps this is one reason why CEOs in the business world and other managers, including those involved in the world of professional sports, and who exhibit traits of an extreme power freak, want to bring in "their own people" when they take on a new job. I have seen many competent people replaced for no reason by a new CEO, other than the fact that he wanted his own people around him, many of whom did a pitiful job.

ABOUT THE ISSUE OF SELF-ESTEEM

Many of the psychologists and psychiatrists I talked to about this book before I began writing it almost universally told me that people who dominate, intimidate, and demean others do so because they are coming from a position of low self-esteem; these acts of domination help them build their esteem. As I was writing this chapter, it occurred to me that people afflicted with antisocial personality disorder or psychopathy, and/or narcissistic personality disorder don't appear to have low self-esteem at all. If anything, they appear to have high self-esteem.

This perception was reinforced by Roy Baumeister, professor of psychology at Case Western Reserve University, in an article written for *Scientific American*. He points to research indicating that the concept of low self-esteem among aggressive and intimidating people appears to be false; that, in fact, people who are overtly aggressive and narcissistic have *high* levels of self-esteem. If one looks again at the design of the prototypical alpha male, a predisposition toward higher levels of self-esteem would appear to be essential. You don't want to feel self-doubt when the unfriendly tribe over the next hill is invading your territory to steal your women and your food.

Baumeister said, "Psychology is not yet adept at measuring hidden aspects of personality, especially ones that a person may not be willing to admit even to himself or herself. But at present there is no empirical evidence or theoretical reason that aggressors have a hidden core of self-doubt."[30]

In an article titled "The Trouble with Self-Esteem," in the *New York Times Magazine*, psychologist Lauren Slater quotes another researcher on self-esteem, Nicholas Emler of the London School of Economics, who observes, "The fact is . . . we've put antisocial men through every self-esteem test we have and there's *no* [his emphasis] evidence for the old psychodynamic concept that they secretly feel bad about themselves. These men are racist or violent because they don't feel bad *enough* about themselves."[31]

So there you go.

The Power Freak as Status-Obsessed

Benito Mussolini had an office whose desk was about two hundred feet from the entrance. The floor was marble so that visitors would make loud and embarrassing clicking sounds as they ran up to Mussolini, who would sit behind his desk, not noticing them until they stood at attention before him. The "general rules for interviews [were] that people should run all the way to the Duce's [Mussolini's] desk and then run out at the double, stopping to salute at the door." This included supreme court justices.[1]

Another category of power freaks may be delineated—those who are status-obsessed. They believe that how their status or rank is perceived in their worlds of business, family, and community is critical in their lives. In their drive to achieve or maintain this ranking, they can make others in their lives whom they perceive as beneath them feel miserable.

Obsessive status seekers at some point in their lives begin to harbor the assumption that they are better than the rest of us. The thought dominates their lives, and may correlate to some characteristics of narcissism. It would appear, however, that they don't bully just for the sake of doing so, to fulfill some underlying pathological urging. They expect you to know your place and can be autocratic, domineering, and nasty if you attempt to be their equal, and in so acting, they are capable of mimicking certain traits of psychopathic behavior.

The academic field of work devoted to studying status-seeking is called "social dominance." It rests on the theory that the status-seeking drive is an innate predisposition of the animal world that allows the strongest and most fearless to fight their way up the ranks to become the leaders, who then work to create order.

The key to the system are challenges followed by submission or capitulation. Among the higher animals, including chimpanzees, gorillas, orangutans, and baboons, Jane Goodall and other primatologists have noted in detail the constant struggle for dominance and status among the members of the colonies they observed and studied. The fact that "human beings share the general primate tendency to seek high social rank," is an assumption that is "uncontroversial," asserts Jerome H. Barkow, professor of anthropology at Dalhousie University in the book *The Adapted Mind: Evolutionary Psychology and the Generation of Culture*. He also contends, "From the pre-school years onward . . . we are much concerned with our relative standing and generally seek to improve it in various ways and to communicate to others that our rank is higher than our rivals might generally concede."[2]

If we are not comatose, we can all see that we share this drive for social dominance with the animal world, even though humans might display it in a different way.

In their book *Shadows of Forgotten Ancestors*, Carl Sagan and Ann Druyan describe the following:

> In crocodiles, dominance is established by slapping the head into the water, roaring, lunging, chasing and biting, pretend or real. When interrupted in his mating embrace, a male frog croaks; the deeper his croak, the greater his implied size when disengaged, and the more diffident is the would be intruder. A toothless, brightly colored Central American frog, genus Dendroates, intimidates intruders by performing a vigorous sequence of push-ups. . . . When hermit crabs introduce themselves, they devote a few seconds to taking each other's measure—by stroking one another with their antennae; the smaller then promptly submits to the larger.[3]

By contrast, the authors state, in the history of human warfare, in which one group seeks to dominate another, "The alphas—generally old men—sequester themselves in safety, often where the young women are, and dispatch the subordinates—generally young men—out to fight and die. In no other species have alpha males gotten away with such cushy arrangements for themselves."[4]

The point is that in the modern human world, we have the ability to use our intelligence and creativity to push our way upwards in the ranks if we choose to do so. We don't necessarily need the physical skills of the caveman, although looks and stature, when combined with intelligence, can provide an edge in some endeavors. However, like nonhumans, there appears to be a biological reason why our attitudes become distorted and power freakish when we begin to view others as beneath us.

David M. Buss, professor of psychology at the University of Texas, says that *in the battle for status, our behavior actually changes when we gain or lose status.* "If a cricket tends to win a lot of fights," he said, "it becomes more aggressive in subsequent fights. On the other hand, if it loses a lot of fights, it will become submissive."[5]

The physical manifestations of winning or losing apparently shows up most vividly in crayfish. Buss states:

> More than one male crayfish cannot inhabit the same territory without determining who is the boss. The crayfish circle each other cautiously, sizing up their rivals. Then they plunge into a violent fray, trying to tear each other apart. The crayfish who emerges victorious becomes dominant, *strutting* [emphasis added] around "his" territory. The loser *slinks* [emphasis added] away to the periphery, avoiding further contact with the dominant male.[6]

We know innately that behavior changes when status changes, because we've seen it happen. However, we might not have known that *this behavioral change is an instinctual, autonomous, or automatic reaction.* For the purposes of this book I have given this phenomenon the designation "The Crayfish Effect." Okay . . . you may not like it, but the point is, if we come out on the winning side of the crayfish effect, the arrogance we *automatically* feel may transform us into a status-obsessed power freak.

At a 2001 symposium on the biology of emotions sponsored by the Health/Emotions Research Institute of the University of Wisconsin, Huda Akil, professor of Neurosciences, Department of Psychiatry at the University of Michigan, showed one slide that took my breath away when I was able to comprehend it. It showed an actual change in the neurons of a higher animal after a "social defeat." One half of the slide showed a brain structure called the amygdala in relative repose. The other half showed an amygdala immediately after the animal suffered a social defeat. The neurons appeared to be firing in every direction. Here was the biology of defeat. There is little difference in physical make-up between the amygdala of the Sprague-Dawley rat I saw on the screen and the one in our human brains (well . . . we actually all have two amygdalas, one in each hemisphere of the brain).

The amygdala in humans is an almond-sized structure within the instinctual-emotional brain system that is associated with the control of fear and depression, among other things. It apparently is not involved in the elation we feel after a social victory.

Interestingly enough, Dr. Akil also mentioned that social defeats in mice not only induce submissive behavior, but activate drug taking behavior: The mice are more apt to imbibe stimulating intoxicants after a loss. This reminded me of a local softball team that would quickly migrate to the nearest bar after a loss and drink twice as much as the winning team, reflecting an old, apocryphal saying that "alcohol medicates depression."

Professional sports team coaches probably recognize and understand innately the neuronal behavior that changes our attitudes after victories and defeats more than most of us. If their team loses a series of games, the confidence of the players on the team in general is lowered, their amygdalas apparently punishing them big time. They begin to act like losers. Their bodies slump on the sidelines, exuding a self-defeating attitude. On the field of play their bodies tighten and they play tentatively. In close games, they believe they are going to lose. All of this is part of the crayfish effect. Professional coaches know that confidence is the key ingredient for any team, one that is just as important as sheer talent. And once that confidence is lost, it is usually only a series of wins that can get it back, no matter how many sports psychologists and motivators are brought into the locker rooms.

In chapter 4, we talked about the outcome expectancies of the five core instinctual-emotional drives and how if we meet those expectancies, we are rewarded with feelings of happiness and elation by our pleasure system. If we fail to meet those expectancies, such as in a social defeat, our "unpleasure system," which apparently includes the amygdala, will punish us with feelings of despondency, sadness, and frustration. And if we are an imbiber, it might push us toward the bottle.

For many of us, it is that automatic. We cannot rationally will ourselves to feel otherwise, although some of us are more capable than others in masking those feelings.

I play singles tennis from time to time with Herb Weintraub. If he is winning, he struts about the court like a crayfish, chest out, happy, enthusiastic, and slinging taunts, like "you're on the way out, buddy." If he is losing, he slumps, looks depressed, and says little.

"You know what you're doing?" I said to him one day, "You're displaying the crayfish effect. You win, you strut; you lose, you slump."

"The crayfish effect, you say. Well, that's okay. I'm the same way when I play poker, which is why I lose a lot."

In other words, he is unable to display a "poker face," a mask that some of us can contrive that hides the churning of the instinctual-emotional mind and makes it exceedingly difficult to understand what some of us are really thinking. The psychopath, hiding behind a mask of sanity, is obviously expert at this.

In his book *The Ape and the Sushi Master*, zoologist and ethologist Frans de Waal, a leading expert on primate behavior, compared human behavior to how chimpanzees react when they lose status. He quoted from the Bob Woodward and Carl Bernstein book *The Final Days* on how President Nixon reacted to his loss of power: "Between sobs, Nixon was plaintive. . . . How had a simple burglary . . . done all this? . . . Nixon got down on his knees. . . . [He] leaned over and struck his fist on the carpet crying, "What have I done? What has happened?" The book then described how Yeroen, a dominant chimpanzee in the world's largest chimpanzee colony at the Arnhem Zoo in the Netherlands, who was being challenged by a younger male in a series of scrapes and began to realize that he would lose, began to have tantrums similar to Nixon's.

[He] would in the middle of a confrontation suddenly drop out of a tree like a rotten apple and writhe and squirm on the ground, screaming pitifully, waiting to be comforted by the rest of the group.

The expression "being weaned from power" is particularly apt because Yeroen's relapse into childlike behavior was the same as that of a juvenile being weaned from its mother's milk.[7]

On the other side of the crayfish effect, we all understand that social victories can change how we feel. If we know someone upon whom greater status was bestowed because of hard work or extremely good luck like winning a big lottery, we'll frequently ask, "Did it go to their head?" We know innately that we all have a propensity to become arrogant, to begin to look down on others, to become, in other words, a power freak.

One of my favorite movies, *What a Way to Go*, produced in 1964, starred Shirley MacLaine and in one of a series of segments, Gene Kelly played the role of Pinky Benson. Pinky was a down and out dancer in a loud and busy nightclub who danced each night in a clown costume with heavy face makeup. He was self-deprecating, modest, and humble. He didn't care if the crowd continued to talk as he started his routine, barely paying attention to him. Then one night he was late and his friend, Louisa, played by MacLaine, encouraged him to dance without a costume or makeup. He was frightened to death to do it, but went on. At first the crowd paid no attention, some even booed. But as they saw Pinky's dance routine progress, they quieted down and at the end they gave him a standing ovation.

Pinky subsequently married Louisa and began to quickly garner a series of ever more important engagements. As his stature as an entertainer grew, he became more self-important, growing quickly out of the old, self-deprecating Pinky. He changed the way he dressed, how he acted with others. Then he became a movie star and now he had all the trimmings, the fawning entourage, the home in Beverly Hills, the swimming pool, the Rolls Royce, the limousines, the publicity agent, the showy wardrobe, and the arrogance to demand that he be named the producer and director of any movies in which he appeared. At the zenith of his career, he became haughty, arrogant, disdainful, overbearing, and domineering. In short, he was a status-obsessed power freak, mimicking in some respects the characteristics of the psychopathic power freak described in the previous chapter.

How many times have we seen professional athletes, some of them fresh out of high school, who with their status suddenly elevated, become unapproachable? They become patronizing, imperious, overbearing, and self-important. They refuse to sign autographs, ignore the media, become no-shows at charitable engagements at which they promised to appear, and insist on traveling only on their private jets. The stardom and the wealth their job brings had been their dreams since youth, but their new status "goes to their head," and they become status-obsessed power freaks, the kind of people most of us would go out of our way to avoid.

In the business world, I had dinner with an acquaintance whom I had known for several years as a down-home type of person. He had recently become CEO of a Fortune 500 corporate division, one of this corporation's smaller divisions with fewer than 200 employees. The first thing he did at dinner was take out his car keys, with a large Mercedes insignia on it, and a cell phone and placed them both in the center of the table. Then he snapped his fingers at the nearest waiter and ordered a bottle of wine in French. He began talking of how difficult it was to find good restaurants these days because the help was so inefficient. The cell phone rang and it was his stock broker, with whom he spent fifteen minutes, naming some of the important stocks he had and what the stock broker should do with them. Then his son called and he brusquely cut him off, reminding him that he was having a business dinner. I kept thinking of one of those custard pies they use in the movies that someone throws in your face . . . that maybe one of the waiters he insulted would treat him to one. But then he would probably complain about the flavor.

Fortunately, the instinctual crayfish effect doesn't affect all of us. Fred Rogers, who produced, wrote, and starred in the PBS series *Mister Rogers' Neighborhood*, and now retired, apparently didn't change very much in temperament, if at all, during the thirty-three–year history of the series. The show began as a black and white public television production in Pittsburgh and grew into a national powerhouse with 3.5 million viewers weekly. In an article in the *New York Times*, his wife said that nothing ever changed him. Even his office remained the same, consisting of a "vintage 60's couch of gold paisley, its pillows supported by a wooden plank and a roomy leather chair."[8]

Singer Perry Como, who died in May 2001, was another person who didn't let celebrity go to his head. He began his career as a barber, later singing part time with a band, and eventually he had one of the longest running television shows in the history of the medium. Asked to describe his success, he said; "I've done nothing that I can call exciting. I was a barber. Since then I've been a singer. That's it."[9]

In chapter 4, we described how our pleasure or reward system may be flawed because it can addict us to substances it perceives as rewarding, but which may eventually kill us, like cocaine and heroin. It would appear that the part of the crayfish effect that manifests itself after a social victory—our feelings of arrogance and dominance—is not so much a flaw as an anachronism of this system. It is out of date.

Presumably the genetic design of this part of the system after a social victory was to drive us to feel arrogant, dominant, overbearing, and imperious so that we'd have more confidence when we challenged the next person up the ladder. It made perfect sense when we lived in caves. The attitude would help carry us as far up dominance hierarchy as we were able to go. If we were defeated in a challenge before we reached the top, our attitude would totally change. We would become submissive and slink away.

But in the modern world it would appear that we no longer need the extremes of the crayfish effect. In the field of sports as in the business world today, we have much greater respect for the heroes who have taken their teams to championships or the organizations they manage to new heights of success, but who remain modest and humble. They did their jobs. They met the challenge, the competition, transforming into the power freak mode while doing so. They were rewarded with feelings of elation and happiness, but when the challenge was over, it was over. They did not become arrogant, haughty, and domineering because of their successes. We like people who exhibit this attitude, who keep the innate drive to become arrogant and domineering under control. They are part of the true adaptive humans of the twenty-first century, who feel the urges of their primitive, instinctual drives but are disciplined and keep them in intellectual check.

Unfortunately, there aren't enough Perry Comos, people who ostensibly understand innately that these feelings are biological, that if we win at something big, we should enjoy the body chemistry that is giving us a temporary high while realizing that it hasn't made us the king of the world. If we lose, we need to withstand the chemistry that is creating our "unpleasure," knowing that this too will pass and in the greater scheme of things, including the fact that we have absolutely no rational idea of what we are doing on this planet or what the ultimate purpose of life is in general, that the event, under this type of perspective, was relatively insignificant.

STATUS-OBSESSED POWER FREAKS WHO ARE BORN INTO IT

What about status-obsessed power freaks who are born into it?

At some point, their families acquired wealth and status and began acting imperiously. The offspring, if they began to display arrogance, learned it by imitating their families and the other people around them. In effect, they *learned* how to act like the strutting crayfish.

England's duke and duchess of Windsor, during the early stages of World War II, refused to board a ship taking them from a port in Spain to the duke's new post as governor of Bermuda until they had their "proper bed linen." Unfortunately, the bed linen was still at their home in France, in Nazi-occupied territory. An attempt was actually made to retrieve the bed linen through diplomatic sources, but it was unsuccessful and they departed.[10]

In a more recent display of status obsession, Sophie, the wife of Prince Edward of England, made news in April 2001, when she was secretly taped making imperious remarks about others. Sophie was said to have referred to "Prime Minister Tony Blair as 'too presidential,' [and] his wife Cherie as 'horrid, absolutely horrid, horrid, horrid.'"[11]

The customs of higher society in nations throughout the world have been chronicled in books, movies, and in the news. The theme throughout all of it is that "we are who we are and you are who you are and we don't want to mix."

In their book *Social Dominance*, psychologists Jim Sidanius and Felicia Pratto chronicle several class divisions throughout the world. They describe in detail the caste system in India as being relatively intact after 3,000 years, even though it is

> no longer part of the legal order of Indian society and "untouchability" was outlawed after Indian independence in 1947 . . . [it] remains an extremely important aspect of Indian social and political life.
>
> For example, most marriages are still made within castes, politicians rely on the "caste vote," castes continue to act as economic and political pressure groups, castes are still ranked in terms of purity and pollution, and intercaste violence continues to the present day.
>
> While the United States is a more socially dynamic nation than

India and is, of course, not nearly as old, the U.S. version of the caste system shows every sign of being highly stable as well. Despite intense efforts to eliminate racism from U.S. life, the relative dominance of Euro-Americans over African-Americans has remained unchanged since the European occupation of the New World more than 400 years ago.[12]

The authors used the term "arbitrary-set systems of social hierarchy" to define class hierarchies based on "such characteristics as clan, ethnicity, estate, nation, race, caste, social class, religious sect, regional grouping, or any other socially relevant group distinction that the human imagination is capable of constructing."[13] They pointed out that these systems of "group-based hierarchies abound and can be found in both the ancient and modern worlds and on every continent."

They offer a "partial list of modern nations to include: Mexico, Japan, Sumeria, Nigeria, Germany, Israel, France, Canada, the United States, Taiwan, Zaire, Korea and South Africa. . . . [O]ne is truly hard pressed to find a society anywhere in the world that does not have an arbitrary-set stratification system."[14]

In his book *Japanese Etiquette and Ethics in Business*, author Boye De Mente describes how Japanese society in general is based on a ranking system:

> Everything and everybody is ranked, within whatever school they attend or organization they work for, first on the basis of their educational background, then on their seniority, and finally on their ability to get along with others, their personality and their talent. . . . The higher ranking the employer is, the higher the status will be of any individual in the organization. This status is visually exhibited by the company or organization lapel button worn by employees of most major corporations and government bureaus.[15]

Even in the old Soviet Union, an entity originally based on the ideas of Karl Marx's classless society, the more privileged had access to such things as the best apartments, houses in the country, and well stocked grocery stores, while the remainder of the "classless people" had to live several to a room, stand in long grocery store lines, and suffer other inconveniences spared those of higher status.

Children who are born into families of higher rank who support caste conditions may be more readily imbued with their prejudices and domineering attitudes because it is part of the culture and because their own instinctual drive for power and status may be helping them absorb these attitudes. Those whose drive is less intense may escape with their attitudes undistorted. They're the lucky ones.

Then there are the parents who are status-obsessed in our present-day hierarchal societies. While they may attempt to mask their caste propensities with a "we're just plain folks," veneer, they insist that their children go only to the "right" schools and befriend only the "right" children, and they continue to dominate their children with demands to do the right thing even after the children become adults . . . marry the "right person," have the "right" job, and so on. Any sublimation of the status of the children would result, in their minds, in a diminishment of their own status or a curtailment of their efforts to gain a higher status.

Further, some of these status-obsessed parents are unable to give their children credit for anything they do at any age, even if the children do all the "right" things, because the admission would diminish the parents' own status. In their minds, only they are capable of achievement. And so the children, if they are in need of parental nurturance, become ripe for a personality disorder of their own.

In some of the reference materials exploring the subject of social dominance, scientists conjecture that the hormones testosterone and serotonin in some combination are the culprits that create the drive for status. Catherine Marler, Associate Professor of Psychology at the University of Wisconsin, alerted me to several studies involving the hormone testosterone. She stated, for example, that "There is a study demonstrating that testosterone increases in fans supporting the winning team and decreased in fans supporting the losing team."[16]

Remember that how we think, feel, and act are controlled by approximately fifty different chemicals in our brains. At the Health/Emotions Research Institute symposium previously mentioned, I asked several of the leading psychiatric neuroscientists in the world which brain structures carried this drive that creates the dominance hierarchy and our need for status. The answer I received is that it is "broadly distributed," which means that they haven't tracked the system as yet.

Then in a conversation at the symposium with Dr. Mary Ellen Oliveri, chief of the Behavioral Science Research Branch of the National Institute of Mental Health, I asked why this subject of social dominance, status, and the ranking system was relatively understudied by neuroscience, since it appears to be primarily responsible for warfare, terrorism, hatreds, and racism, among other bad things. She replied that most of the research money is being spent on discovering the causes of mental illness, which could lead to medication and other solutions to alleviate suffering.

This made sense to me; but it might be a wonderful thing for mankind in general if we could find some way to adjust permanently the circuitry and chemicals in our brains. Then we could moderate *extreme* instinctual drives for power and status that continue to create such havoc in our lives. It is a near certainty that 300 years from now, if the human race survives its own primitive instinctual-emotional system, a method will be found and employed that does so.

OTHER CHARACTERISTICS OF STATUS-OBSESSED POWER FREAKS

One additional characteristic of status-obsessed power freaks is an unquenchable hunger for higher status. No matter how many possessions they have, or what their current status is, it will never be enough. They must, at all costs, keep up appearances and at the very least, remain on a par with their peers, or find richer and more powerful peers. We wonder at professional athletes who want to squash their current contracts paying them millions a year, if a teammate or a player on another team with the same or lesser ability, in their perception, gets a contract for more money.

In the spring of 2001, Frank Thomas of the Chicago White Sox baseball team threatened to walk out of spring training camp if his contract, which paid him $9 million annually, wasn't voided and a new one drawn up. At the time a player on another team, Alex Rodriguez, was given a ten-year, $25 million per year contract and Thomas was upset because he felt he was equally as good as Rodriguez. Thomas actually had some sportswriters sympathizing with him, even though he later backed down.

Thus, the salaries paid to sports stars and CEOs, among others, are not necessarily based on talent, but on "market value," which can be interpreted as the salary level when an intense drive for status meets an outcome expectancy. And because this expectancy is buried behind the walls of the instinctual-emotional mind system, it is resistant to rationality. We cannot walk up to these people and tell them that they are acting stupidly because they are being held captive by their instinctual status expectancies. They would think that we are the ones who are crazy. Their actions appear perfectly natural and normal to them.

Still another characteristic of status-obsessed power freaks is their need for an entourage. We see them following sports stars and movie stars particularly, because these people are so visible to us. But entourages also exist in the business world, where they are called "inner circles."

The subordinates in these circles need to earn their way into the entourages by displaying trustworthiness, submissiveness, and loyalty under extreme circumstances. It is only when these traits have been displayed that the extreme power freak can feel comfortable with them, whether they are a foreman on a production line or in the CEO's suite. Members of the inner circle will never directly challenge their boss. If they want to get an idea across, as described in chapter 11, they will do everything they can to make it ultimately appear as if it is their boss's idea, not their own. This inner circle serves, among other things, to give extreme power freaks the perception that they are normal.

In the business world, status-obsessed power freaks do not mix with subordinates. They will not eat at the same table with them. If forced to do so they will look uncomfortable and may make demeaning remarks. Like status-obsessed parents, the people with whom these CEOs associate must have just the right credentials, the right family, the right upbringing, and the right education, including the right private schools and universities.

Oddly enough, psychopaths and the status-obsessed may exhibit many of the same traits in their intimidating and demeaning behavior toward others, including their lack of empathy, guilt, remorse, or shame and their personal sense of entitlement. While the status-obsessed most often take on these behavioral patterns after a series of social victories as manifested by the Pinky Bensons and successful athletes and businessmen, among others, the psychopathic appear to do so early in their lives, before the age of fifteen.[17]

It is possible that we could end up, under the worst scenario, of having to deal with a status-obsessed power freak who also exhibits traits of psychopathy, sadism, narcissism, and paranoia; is in the power freak mode with everyone in their lives except perhaps those who have authority over them or can offer favors; has twisted, distorted outlooks on life; and is impervious to rationality, but could also come off as being glib and charming at times to make our lives not only miserable, but confused.

As Dr. Gilbert M. Hefter, a clinical psychiatrist and associate professor of psychiatry at Northwestern University and my collaborator on *Battling the Inner Dummy*, would frequently say, "these people are no bargain."

CHAPTER 7

Situational Power Freaks

On more than one occasion my boss ate my lunch, knowingly, without telling me ahead of time, leaving me without enough time to get another one.[1]

Situational power freaks are apparently transformed into the power freak mode only under specific situations and circumstances. Once in the mode, they can display characteristics that are identical to the extreme power freak and they become just as resistant to reality. The difference is that after the situation normalizes, so do they. In most cases, they act as if nothing ever changed within them.

It would appear that these transitions into the power freak mode have more to do with status-seeking than gratifying psychopathic urges. In almost all cases, the situational power freak is responding to a challenge to his or her status, that is, to either maintain or enhance it.

While in the situation, both the challenger *and* the challenged may take on several of the characteristics of an extreme power freak.

In many instances the scenario would be akin to one chimpanzee in a chimp group challenging another. Among chimps there will be "charging displays," hair rising making their bodies look deceptively large, foot stomping, loud hooting, climbing into trees, and sharply swinging branches. Eventually, the challenge will usually culminate in eye stares and sometimes a struggle before one contender turns his behind to the other and submits. Once it's over, it's over. In other words, each chimp transforms out of the power freak mode and returns to normalcy. Jane Goodall described the aftermath of one such encounter in her book *In the Shadow of Man:*

From then on it seemed that Goliath accepted Mike's superiority, and a strangely intense relationship grew up between the two. They often greeted one another with much display of emotion, embracing or patting one another, kissing each other in the neck. . . . Afterward they sometimes fed or rested quite close to each other, looking peaceful and relaxed *as though the bitter rivalry had never been* [emphasis added].[2]

However, Goodall also points to examples in her books where the dominant male, once fallen, not only becomes sulky and grim, but remains an outcast. Nevertheless, the point is that once it's over and the chimps are out of their power freak mode, they return to relative normalcy.

It is possible that this behavior is also part of the general design of the crayfish effect. Just prior to a challenge by another, we become as ruthless and determined as our brain chemistry will allow, to give us the greatest possible odds for a victory. Goodall talked about one chimp named Hugo who transformed as follows in a charging display: "[H]e would sit, with hair on end, his sides heaving from exertion, a froth of saliva glistening at his half-open mouth, and a glint in his eye that to us looked not far from madness."[3]

Perhaps the characteristics that situational power freaks take on in a challenge is the human version of a "charging display." Certainly we have observed glimpses of madness when the linemen of two professional football teams face off together. After the game, the devout Christians from both sides will frequently gather in a huddle with arms about each other and pray together, assuming their normal temperament.

Under this theory, we would envision the crayfish effect as a continuum. Our "charging display" characteristics would manifest themselves in the preparation and battle segment of the continuum. When the challenge is over, the effect presents itself by driving us to become elated, happy, and puffed up if we win or dejected if we lose. In any event, when the competitive match or challenge is over and we have made the transition out of the mode, we are capable, assuming the challenge was non-traumatic, of resuming our normal temperament.

In the following categories I employ my own descriptions of situational power freaks in modes of behavior. Further, I have used actual examples of power freak mode behavior from my own experience, primarily in the business world, or from books or articles as noted, in an attempt to make the differences between the classifications as clear cut as possible, acknowledging that there are crossovers and similarities.

CHALLENGED POWER FREAKS

In the business world, the challenged power freak is the most common of the situational power freaks. This person might be a perfectly normal manager at any level in the management hierarchy, until he or she is threatened with some form of challenge. Frequently it involves managers who have a new co-worker thrust upon them, one whom they perceive as a potential threat to their job position and status, whether real or not. Within days, these basically normal managers are transformed into the power freak mode. Their realities become distorted and they are driven to irrational fantasies and actions, when, only the week before, they were totally competent managers with a strong sense of reality. For example, they may become extremely angered and suspicious if they spot one of their subordinates talking to the challenger. The people in their departments soon become aware of the fact that they had better take one side or the other, which destroys the teamwork and comity that must be part of any company that is to remain successful over the long term. In meetings, constant clashes emerge between the two sides, with each side actually sitting across from each other in groupings. Subordinates have to be careful not only of what they say, but where they sit in meetings. The turf is carefully staked out.

In other circumstances, the challenged power freak might also be the challenger. She might have been a perfectly normal manager in a previous position, but when taking a new position and confronted with an incumbent peer who is perceived by the challenger as threatening, the same metamorphosis can take place. Within days, these challengers find that they are acting just as foolishly as some of the challenged. It is akin to the madness that chimpanzees exhibit during charging displays, when one is challenging the other for rank, part of the crayfish effect.

Here is an example of a challenger who turned power freak. The names and circumstances are changed, but I watched this episode take place:

John Kroll was vice president of sales and marketing of a large company engaged in the manufacture of outdoor barbeque grills. He was reaching retirement age and was asked by the management of the conglomerate that owned the company to begin seeking out a replacement, who he could train for two years to take his place, after which he would retire.

After a long search, Kroll settled on a man he had known in his industry, Ron Abbott, who was national sales manager of a company that made charcoal briquettes and thus knew many of Kroll's company's most important customers, a distinct advantage in this industry, which sold its products to a myriad of retail customers.

To give Abbott space, Kroll took on the new title of executive vice president of sales and marketing and gave Abbott his old title of vice president of sales and marketing.

In what should have been the most amiable of transitions, the power freak factor apparently reared its ugly head. Abbott, who had an excellent track record as a manager with his last company, became impatient with the internal loyalty that continued to be shown by his department's employees to Kroll. Instead of seeing this as a normal reaction to a transition of power, something to be valued and nurtured in a company that had a long reputation as a people-oriented organization, he began to perceive the reaction as a threat to his authority. Within three months of his hire, Abbott began to distance himself from Kroll and replaced many of the district sales managers in the country with sales representatives from his previous company, who owed their allegiance to him.

Kroll had little choice but to sit and watch while district sales managers who had been loyal to him for twenty years or more were replaced. Kroll would question Abbott about these actions, but Abbott would quote sales statistics that were shaped to prove his point. Then Abbott began replacing people in the internal administrative departments who also reported to him, whom he perceived as more loyal to Kroll than to himself. This was all too much for Kroll to bear, as he was a man whose aggressiveness and toughness combined with an amiable disposition had helped propel him to the top of his career field, although these traits began to dissipate as he approached his retirement. In a step that was a disappointment to the conglomerate that owned the company, Kroll simply retired early.

Kroll later told one of his friends, "In a nutshell, I simply made a poor choice when I hired the guy. When all the shit started to fly, I could have fought him and won. But it would have hurt the company and what would be the point? To show that I was as good as I ever was when it came to a challenge? It's just better to know when to get the hell out."

With Kroll out of the picture, Abbott became what he was at his previous company, a perfectly normal manager who tried to foster harmony. But the seeds of what he had sown to hurt Kroll ran too deep and within a year after Kroll had left, he was terminated.

There are endless variations of situations in which the challenged power freak emerges and then recedes, usually with one or the other of the challengers leaving the picture, oftentimes, the less competent of the two. There isn't "kissing and making up," as between certain chimpanzees who reemerge from a challenge, at this level of the corporate hierarchy. But when one or the other is transferred or leaves the company, the two participants usually revert to being the normal managers they were before the incident began.

Here is another example of a situation involving challenged power freaks which I witnessed. Again, the names and circumstances have been changed:

Alex Ferris, owner of Ferris Industries, worked for more than forty years to build his business of electrical specialities. Conduit, cable boxes, switches, the company produced more than fifteen hundred such items, which it distributed to electrical wholesalers nationwide. Upon his death, his two sons took over the business, as co-presidents, with the stock divided evenly between them.

The succession began ideally, as the elder Ferris had envisioned it. The two sons always got along; their love for each other was obvious. One son, Tim, oversaw the manufacturing operation, the other son, Jeff, handled marketing and sales. Then one day, Tim's desk drawer became warped and difficult to open. So he ordered a new desk. Jeff's wife, visiting the company one day, noticed Tim's new desk and complained about it to Jeff.

"Did you see Tim's new desk? You should order a new desk, too. And maybe a small conference table and chairs." Jeff was amused, but went ahead and did it to keep his wife happy.

Then Tim's wife visiting the company one day, saw the new conference table and chairs, and said to Tim, "If he has a new conference table and chairs, you should have them, too." And Tim went along with her suggestion and ordered them.

Next it was a company car. Tim ordered a BMW and Jeff did the same, this time without much encouragement from his wife. Then it was the size of their offices in a new addition. The relationship between the two brothers became strained for the first time in their lives. They tried to act pleasant enough at family events, but it was plain that a competition had developed. The power freak factor in both of them apparently intensified significantly. Eventually, whatever Jeff wanted to do to further the company's distribution system, Tim disagreed with. Whatever Tim wanted to do to improve the factory, Jeff disagreed with. Then lawsuits ensued and they were forced to hire an outside executive as CEO. However, the distrust grew so strong that both sides insisted the CEO have a lawyer in his presence at all times to assure that he wasn't favoring one side or the other. This included when he went to the bathroom, believe it or not.

"My intestinal system was never the same after that experience," this CEO told me years later when we bumped into each other.

In the meantime, the company was struggling with the conflict and disorganization as each brother coerced employees that worked under him to make a choice between the two brothers. Sales and shipments went into a downward spiral and the company was eventually sold for a third of the value that had existed at the time that Tim ordered a new desk.

The annals of business are filled with stories like this: families torn apart when just a little communication, organization, and the injection of pure reason could solve the problem. Instead, the instinctual-emotional system's power/status drive of the participants is allowed to take over and the law of the jungle presides. In other words, their amygdalas go into overdrive and chaos ensues.

This type of situation also takes place in families and may be reflective of family life in general. There might be a minor disagreement over who should cut the turkey, a status issue for many families on Thanksgiving. This was exemplified in the movie *Avalon*, where an older brother arrived late at the home of his younger brother who was wealthier and more successful. Because the younger brother didn't wait for his older brother, who traditionally carved the turkey, the older brother on seeing the turkey carved, turned around with his wife and walked out: In his mind, his status was diminished and a deep family split was created.

I have seen many families disrupted because of temporary issues of status when biting words, harsher than usual, were exchanged. Maybe a daughter ended up not talking to her father. Or a father ended up not talking to his son. Or a brother wouldn't talk to a brother. And it would grow from there, splitting the family for months or years, all of which probably began over an insignificant challenge, such as who should cut the turkey. The instinctual power/status drive that continues, for generation after generation, to be passed on through our genes, can, as we've observed, be the scourge of the earth.

I personally witnessed a CEO of a successful company turn down an acquisition that was priced right and made perfect sense because it was suggested by an executive vice president he had inherited when he was named to the CEO position and whom he saw as a potential challenger. Yet this skilled manager always stated his positions honestly and without a separate agenda in staff and board meetings, though they frequently were in disagreement with the positions of the CEO.

"I won't take action on anything that s.o.b. suggests," the CEO told me in private. "He'll only use it to try to get my job."

In all other respects in his relationships with peers and subordinates, this CEO was apparently normal. He became a challenged power freak only in situations involving this one subordinate.

The variations that drive a challenged power freak into a power freak mode can be endless. And it all has to do with not losing status, which will make us feel bad, or gaining status, which will make us feel good.

COMPETITIVE POWER FREAKS

A competitive power freak might be described as someone who transforms into power freak mode when he or she is in a contest, a competitive challenge. We previously described John McEnroe, who on the tennis court can display the signs of "madness" described by Jane Goodall in challenges between two chimps.

I know a corporate executive who likes to play in amateur basketball leagues. Off the court, he is a warm and concerned person who is consensus-oriented in his managerial approach. On the court, though, he turns into a maniac. He elbows opponents, screams at teammates, tries to cheat on the score, picks fights after the games, shows no empathy toward his teammates; in short, he becomes temporarily psychopathic. I saw him one night on a local health club basketball court out of control as he attempted to attack a member of the opposing team. His own teammates were holding him back. I thought to myself that if he had had a gun, he might actually try to shoot the guy he was mad at. Shortly thereafter, he was banned from every private basketball court in the city.

I had lunch with him about two months later and alluded to this problem. He told me that when he steps on the basketball court, something inside of him snaps and he is driven to do anything it takes to win. He must win at all costs. Later he finds it difficult to remember the incidents.

Michael Jordan might also be described as a competitive power freak, because as we detailed in chapter 1, he is driven to win at anything that offers a challenge, whether it is a card game or a pick-up basketball game at a local gymnasium. I saw him one night eating dinner at a restaurant he owns in Chicago, talking happily to his wife, and you would never think he had a competitive bone in his body. However, if somebody brought a deck of cards over to his table, the competitive craziness would undoubtedly have kicked in.

There are any number of professional football players playing on defensive lines who gladly tell sports reporters that they would like nothing better than to severely injure the opposing quarterbacks to the extent that they would be out for the season or for good.

On the tennis court, I have played with people who are so intent on winning that in a close match when they are behind, they begin to call balls out that are obviously in. Many of these people are the owners and managers of large companies where their management style is apparently normal.

Then there was figure skater Tonya Harding, a prototypical competitive power freak, who encouraged members of her "inner circle" to attack her main competitor, Nancy Kerrigan, prior to the 1994 Olympic games. Kerrigan was coming off the ice after a practice when she was clubbed in the knee. Her removal from the competition would have greatly increased Harding's own chances to win an Olympic medal, but Kerrigan recovered from her injury and was able to compete.

Competitive power freaks, similar to challenged power freaks in general, may have a relatively normal power freak factor. But when their instinctual-emotional minds perceive they are in a competitive challenge, their power freak factor is apparently notched up to a level eight, nine, or even ten and manifestations of a "charging display" emerge.

Lawyer David Boies, who represented Al Gore in the Florida recount battle of the 2000 presidential race and was later retained by the prosecution team that pursued Microsoft in an antitrust lawsuit, was featured on the program 60 *Minutes*. Boies was casual, charming, and mild as he was interviewed by Mike Wallace, but attributed his success to his intense need to win. And like Michael Jordan, he pointed out that this need to win involved any situation in which he was competing, including gambling and athletics. The crayfish effect, again.

Boies stated that he was handicapped by a disorder that made it difficult to follow notes. And so he needed to study each case so thoroughly that he could make his case or question the opposition with incisiveness through only casual reference to notes. During one sequence, we could hear him off-camera, sharply and successfully questioning Microsoft chairman Bill Gates, who had the defeated look and demeanor of that chimpanzee who knew he was going to lose his dominant role to a challenger that was getting the best of him.

In the business world, I have seen competitive power freaks at every level. Many years ago, one of my clients was bidding on the lighting system for a new manufacturing plant being built by a leading aircraft maker. He lost the bid and couldn't figure out why. Only later did he learn that the winning bidder was represented by an agent who had made an insider deal with the head of the purchasing team that determined the winner. The winning company was allowed to bid low with a rigged bid arranged by the agent, with the promise that they could make up their losses with add-on systems to be added to the specifications after the job was let, and with high, set prices for replacement lamps.

The agent who put this crooked deal together and was later indicted was president of his local Junior Chamber of Commerce and entertained children in local hospitals with magic tricks, like murderer John Wayne Gacy. But on the field of battle, when he was in competition with agents from other companies, he obviously turned into a competitive power freak and became irrational.

As pointed out on page 243, there are many companies that work to recruit competitive power freaks. In the book *Palace Coup*, about Harry and Leona Helmsley, author Michael Moss described the competitive attitudes of real estate brokers working for one of the many corporations that Harry Helmsley owned:

> [T]he high standards of decency toward other dealers that Helmsley held himself have not been enforced, or even encouraged, down the ranks of Helmsley-Spear. Brokers are free to fight for sales as best they know how. Except for Helmsley buildings, every property in the city, the country, the whole world is fair game.
>
> "He bred killers," said one former Helmsley broker. . . . And they tend to set the pace inside the Helmsley empire, turning it into a microcosm of New York City business at its most vicious.
>
> Harry Helmsley's reaction when he has been asked to mediate fights among his brokers has been to turn to the loser and shrug, as if to say, "Why did you let that happen to you?"[4]

Unfortunately, in this world of greed, avarice, and gluttony, there is a market for the competitive power freak. Many of us would prefer a David Boies to a mild-mannered lawyer with equal intellect if we were involved in a lawsuit that we desperately needed to win. Most of us would also want Michael Jordan on our basketball team. However, there are many companies where this type of temperament isn't encouraged.

What's the message here? I'll get back to you on it.

VINDICTIVE POWER FREAKS

Vindictive power freaks develop from the disputes between the challenged and the challenger. If the dispute was particularly painful, one or the other may begin to harbor feelings of long-term vengeance. According to the theories of evolutionary psychology, as described in an extraordinary paper, "Evolutionary Explanations of Emotion," the potential of creating the feeling of anger and vengeance in a challenged opponent may be just enough to keep the challenger at bay and to prevent him from trying again.[5]

In other words, the mechanism during primitive times was one more useful, evolutionary, peace-keeping device for our lives. But we continue to carry it in the mental software of our instinctual-emotional system today and it frequently leads to irrational outlooks and attitudes. If the vengeance is less traumatic, somebody has taken our parking space and we want to harm the culprit in some way, scratching their car or letting the air out of their tires, the feeling, if we walk away and let it alone, will soon dissipate. But if the incident was severely traumatic—a manager unjustly fires us while our wife is pregnant with our fourth child—our vengeance may last for quite a while and may never dissipate until we've had a chance to get back at the person. Until revenge is achieved, a vindictive power freak can become temporarily psychopathic, displaying these symptoms as adapted from chapter 5:

- More impulsive in their actions than they were before
- Lack of empathy for the person(s) they feel vengeance against
- Lack of remorse or guilt toward these persons
- Becoming cunning, callous, and manipulative in attempting retaliation
- Is more predisposed to do whatever they please against the person(s) they feel vengeance toward
- Is amused by, or takes pleasure in, the psychological or physical suffering he or she causes

At the extreme level of the vengeance syndrome we have the effect of postal and other workers who have led basically normal lives and have shown no obvious signs of being imbalanced. However, a deep vengeance is triggered when such people are traumatically intimidated at work or laid off, in their minds for no apparent reason. They have been drastically challenged and their power freak factor has been ramped up, perhaps to a level ten. Perhaps this transition was exacerbated by problems at home, their marriages might have been dissolving, or they had some mental problems to begin with. To take their vengeance, they come back to their places of work with a gun and attempt to shoot those who caused their pain, without the slightest sense of remorse or guilt and knowing they will go to prison, if they don't shoot themselves at the end of the rampage.

This is only different in degree from a client, "Art," I had many years ago, who was a small manufacturer of a specialized computer network software. He had previously been active in another company with a partner, "Gary," who used a clause in their original agreement to force Art out of the business. Art soon formed a new company in the same industry, but with a far superior software system. His primary objective with this new business, however, was to force Gary and his old company into bankruptcy, which he eventually did. His vengeance, obviously, ran long and deep and actually impaired the growth of his new company.

"Art," I said to him, "your obsession with Gary is crazy. You have a chance to really grow this business, but all you want to do is go for his strongest customers. There are other customers and markets you can go after."

"I don't care, I want to destroy that sonofabitch."

"But it's holding you back."

"I know it is and I don't care."

Gary had come back to him several times, asking for forgiveness, but it fell on deaf ears. After Gary was forced to close his doors and was out on the street, Art said to me, "You know, this is the first time since that guy screwed me that I feel any real happiness." In other words, he was able to recapture much of his former temperament only when the situation that drove him into becoming a vindictive power freak was resolved, irrational as the whole situation was.

In most milder incidents, once the vengeance has been taken, both the challenged and the challenger are capable of resuming their normal temperament. An excellent example of this is described in the book *Adult Bullying, Perpetrators and Victims*, by sociologist Peter Randal. He relates the story of "Greta," an office manager, and her problem with "Danielle," who returned to the workforce as an accounts technician at the age of thirty-seven. Danielle worked under Greta, was twelve years older than Greta, and had been hired without Greta's approval, who obviously became vindictive about it:

> Greta told her on the first day that she hadn't wanted someone as old as Danielle, she didn't like older people and she would make sure that Danielle left or be transferred. From that time onward she:

❀ Made a point of criticizing the quality of Danielle's work.

❀ Put her down in front of other women.

❀ Clock watched to make sure that Danielle, a punctual woman, by habit, did not lose a minute of work.

❀ Harassed her verbally whenever the opportunity arose.

Danielle lasted seven months and then asked for a transfer. On the day she left Greta told her that it wasn't anything personal. She simply didn't like older people and she had to make a point about Danielle being appointed without her approval.[6]

Greta, we might assume, simply went back to her job, the feelings of vengeance over, but would probably repeat her vengeful behavior if another subordinate was appointed over her head.

Perhaps feelings of vengeance are another facet of the crayfish effect. A challenge takes place and the instinctual mind of the loser, instead of submitting gracefully and slinking off to the periphery, believes that the challenge *isn't* over. The ruthless determination to win in the end, the manifestations of the "charging display" are kept alive until there is a resolution—the postal worker comes back and attempts to kill his former superiors, the ultimate victory for that worker—or enough time passes that the memory of the challenge is dimmed.

The more normal of us may feel the need to take vengeance from time to time, but we have hopefully learned how to handle it without retaliation.

EMPOWERED POWER FREAKS

"Empowered power freaks" is an arbitrary descriptor I've given to those persons who assume a dominant, Napoleonic role in specific situations. The best example I can think of is a man I knew several years ago, "Norman," who was an administrative assistant working for a client of mine. You would see him in the office as usually pleasant and friendly. But Norman had a sailboat. And once he boarded his sailboat, which needed a crew of at least four to sail on the open waters of Lake Michigan, he would turn into a tyrant, a Captain Bligh. A "madness" would overtake him. He would scream out orders to his shipmates. If anyone made a mistake, Norman would berate them loudly in front of the rest of the crew. For the annual race to Mackinac Island in northern Michigan, a 333-mile marathon from Chicago involving about 300 boats, he increased the crew to six, and one year took his supervisor along, who had asked Norman if he could participate.

The supervisor, "Lou," told me later that it didn't matter that he was Norman's boss. Within miles of the starting line, Norman began screaming at him at the top of his lungs, for forgetting to tie some line to some hook. This behavior lasted the three days it took to reach Mackinac. Once they got there, Norman turned to Lou and said in the pleasant tones he used in the office, "I hope you enjoyed the trip. It was a lot of fun, wasn't it?"

Lou said he was intent on firing Norman the minute they both got back to the office. But Norman became his usual, mild-mannered self and Lou felt his anger, or vengeance, leave him. "I couldn't do it," he told me. "But hell will freeze over before I go back on that boat again."

We might presume that people like Norman have the instinctual propensity to be alphas, but have been held back because they simply weren't up to it. In the primitive caves, we can envision them off in a corner, plotting ways to topple the alpha leader, whom they were unable to beat physically. When the leader, busy with another chore, put a person like this in charge of a hunt, we can imagine this frustrated man taking charge and acting Napoleonic. Back in the cave, he would resume his submissiveness, but inwardly not liking it.

We might assume that when empowered power freaks are given an opportunity to lead, they shed their veneer of civility and take on some of the pathological traits described in chapter 5:

- ❧ Grandiose sense of self-worth
- ❧ Lack of empathy for other human beings
- ❧ Unreasonable or exaggerated sense of entitlement
- ❧ Exploitive attitude toward others
- ❧ Frequent fantasies of greatness

My son, Andy, who is a part-time ski instructor, tells me that the same phenomenon happens to many ski instructors, who in their normal lives, have little or no authority. Once they take on a group of students, however, they become empowered and turn Napoleonic in wielding authority, taking on much of the Captain Bligh behavior that Norman embodied on the sailboat.

On the business side, I know a woman, "Kim," who went to work for another woman providing in-home pet-care services on the near north side of Chicago. The woman who owned the business used to be a secretary, but decided she wanted to be off on her own. Kim, who is her only employee, told me one day that the owner definitely treats her like an employee. "In every little way," Kim told me, "she makes sure that I know that she is the boss and I am an employee, belittling me in the most subtle of ways where she can. But there are only the two of us in the business. I don't understand it."

We've probably all known people who have taken on Napoleonic complexes when they were elected to head a PTA chapter, or a committee at church, or whatever. Or, as described in chapter 2, they become empowered in their positions as a bank teller and make people wait needlessly, or as a maitre d' they begin to think they are the king or queen of Spain. They become situational power freaks in the sense that they take on this complex only when they are given authority. When this authority is removed, they become submissive.

Life is wonderful, isn't it?

Directional Power Freaks

"I was working as a tool and die maker and had a boss who was convinced that he knew more than anyone else about mechanics. Even though my work was praised by customers, he took evident delight in joking with other supervisors about my work and the work of others. After I built a machine for a department in the plant, he stood in the middle of the department and questioned the selection of the types of steel I had used. He did so disparagingly and in a cynical tone. When I tried to defend my work, he simply smirked and, in front of everyone, turned away. In fact, turning away from me was the single most humiliating thing I can remember him doing."[1]

A directional power freak appears to be another form of the situational power freak. They have specific views that when challenged or intruded upon will transform them into the power freak mode.

A prejudicial power freak may become intimidating and snobbish only when she is thrust into the company of members of a minority ethnic group she detests. At the country club over lunch with her friends, she may appear apparently normal.

A messianic power freak may become intimidating only when dealing with a challenge to whatever mission with which he is obsessed. A fundamentalist cleric in a Middle Eastern country may beat women with sticks on the street who in his perception aren't properly covering themselves, but act apparently normal with colleagues in a local coffee house.

When directional power freaks are in the mode, however, they can be just as impervious to reality and as intimidating as the extreme power freak and must be dealt with as per the techniques suggested, beginning in chapter 11.

As described earlier, it would appear that some of us have a propensity for absorbing beliefs, attitudes, and specialized knowledge that make us feel superior when we are "in our elements." I recall knowing many years ago a professor of mathematics who had the reputation of being tyrannical and arrogant in the classroom with his students. Yet on the tennis court, where he wasn't very good and knew it, he was submissive and kindly.

As with situational power freaks, the following categories use actual examples of behavior from my own experience or from books or articles as noted to make the differences between the classifications as clear-cut as possible, with the understanding that there can be crossover.

MESSIANIC POWER FREAKS

As pointed out, the brain/mind seems to have a propensity to form an extreme attachment, an addiction, to all sorts of things beyond substances, from lovers and children to religious, political, cultural, and philosophical beliefs. It then follows *that our thinking can become more or less distorted within the subject range of the addiction.*

Sigmund Freud used the term "obsessional neurosis," rather than addiction, in describing people who are irrationally passionate or fanatic about a mission or system of beliefs, including religion, which is as good a definition as any of what drives a messianic power freak. Messianic power freaks are completely captured by their "emotional beliefs" (described on pages 57–59) and are unable to see any other form of opposing thought, no matter how apparently rational.

We might safely conclude that Marshall Applewhite, the leader of the Heaven's Gate cultists who committed mass suicide in 1997, had an obsessional neurosis. As a messianic power freak, he wielded absolute authority over his adherents to the point that they all willingly committed suicide with him, a step not taken lightly, obviously. Then there were Adolf Hitler, Pol Pot, Mao Tse-tung, and Joseph Stalin, as formerly noted, who caused the deaths of tens of millions because of their obsessions with beliefs that had no basis in reality. As the lyric goes in a song from the musical *The King and I*, "He'll [the human male will] fight to prove that what he does not know is so."[2]

However, not every issue that a messianic power freak is involved with is treated as a life or death issue. In fact, only the most publicized are. It is possible that our instinctual mind releases rewarding feelings when it senses that specific outlooks, attitudes, and specialized knowledge are capable of raising our status. We soon become addicted to or obsessed with these attitudes or knowledge and consider any challenge to them a threat to our status. We then transform into the power freak mode at levels much higher than we normally exhibit. In a sense, we take on the manifestations of the "charging display," resuming our normal temperament only when our thought processes turn to other subjects.

Many years ago when I was married, my wife and I lived in a suburb of Chicago that had nice schools and community facilities. But one of my neighbors became fixated on the idea that we needed a community center with a gymnasium and other recreational facilities. We kept reminding him that schools were kept open for use of the grade school children after school and there were two community centers already in existence, run by religious groups, but open to all. However, over a period of two years, he became totally fixated, messianic about his vision. If his wife or children disagreed with him, he would quickly become angry and begin shouting at them.

No matter where we ran into this fellow, in the grocery store or on the street, the subject would turn to the community center. He would start preaching like a television evangelist, angrily putting down people who didn't agree with him.

It was apparent that he felt he was wielding power because of his stance on this issue, which had now become an obsessional neurosis, an emotional belief, ensconced behind the walls of his instinctual-emotional mind and impervious to reality. Any challenge to this belief, no matter how well reasoned, was taken as a challenge to the man's status and so the crayfish effect emerged and he took on some of the manifestations of a "charging display."

In another example, how many times at social gatherings have we mistakenly walked into a discussion of politics between people of one party or another and with eyes glazed, listened to the messianic views of each, none willing to give an inch to an opposing view?

In the business world, I met a young man who was launching a dot.com company. He was barely out of college and was absolutely convinced that the public would prefer to buy shoes over the Internet, rather than going down to a local shoe store. He already had a venture capital loan of about $3 million and had talked his widowed mother into adding her life savings. A number of us cautioned him about the risk, but he looked at us like we were dinosaurs.

"Bricks and mortar stores are dead," he said. "Why go into crowded malls and stores to shop when you can get the same things in the quiet of your own home?"

"But some people like the experience of shopping, and like to try on shoes before buying them," we replied.

"You don't get it," he replied. "That thinking is dead, dead, dead."

The last I heard of him, his company, whose stock was at one time worth about $20 million, had collapsed and he was living with his distraught mother, trying to make ends meet.

To echo Dr. Hefter's words again, "these people are no bargain."

CONTROL POWER FREAKS

Control power freaks are driven to be in charge of everything in which they are involved. They are never completely happy in any situation in which they are engaged if they are not in total control.

I know a man who is driven to be in charge of anything he participates in. He is chairman of the local little league, he heads the major committees in his church, he is president of his local PTA, president of his own company, and president of the trade association to which it belongs.

Control power freaks appear to believe implicitly that they can do things better than anyone else in their fields of endeavor or in activities they know something about, or think they know something about. They tend to be opinionated and know-it-alls. If you challenge them about this knowledge, you will usually get a frosty stare in return, or worse, some taunting remark that hurts. They usually loathe to delegate responsibility to others beyond their low level of trust. They need to be in charge, to hover above the entire field of play. If they had their druthers, they would want to know what you're doing at all times of the day and why you're doing it. Their presence is more stifling than intimidating. They are like the parents of a man forty years old who insist he call them twice a day to report what he is doing.

In his book *The Control Freak*, author and professor of psychology at Seattle Pacific University, Les Parrott III, gives the following example:

> Henry, a manager of a successful consulting company leaves nothing to chance. He hovers over his staff, providing exhaustive instructions on how to handle jobs they have done countless times before. On any given day, you might find Henry down in the mail room making certain that the mail is properly sorted. You might find him in the washroom making certain that central supply has bought the right soap. But you are most likely to find him going from desk to desk, monitoring everybody's phone calls, shaking his head or writing a say-this note, or maybe drawing a finger across his throat if he decides the phone call is going badly. . . . Only with clones [of himself] could Henry overcome his reluctance to delegate.[3]

We might presume that the idea of being the sole authority or needing to be needed raises the status of the control power freak. When the opportunity presents itself to be the authority, his power freak factor is raised. If he is challenged, he manifests characteristics of the "charging display," becoming puffed up, aggressive, nasty, mean, and ready to do battle.

There are some similarities between the control power freak and the perfectionist power freak described next, particularly in their similar distrust of the ability of others to perform as well as they can.

PERFECTIONIST POWER FREAKS

Perfectionist power freaks are obsessed with the concept of perfection. In the field of psychology, there appears to be a division between the "healthy perfectionist," someone who believes in the pursuit of excellence, and a "neurotic (or compulsive) perfectionist." Healthy perfectionists have been described as persons who watch the details, who strive for excellence in their endeavors, who set high standards, and work diligently to meet them. Neurotic perfectionists are described as "people who strain compulsively and unremittingly toward impossible goals and measure their own worth entirely in terms of productivity and accomplishment."[4]

As with most personality characteristics covered by psychology and psychiatry, if the perfectionist tendencies are present in small doses as quirks or a personality style, they are considered within the range of normality. However, it is when these traits begin to dominate our lives that they become personality disorders, as previously described in chapter 5.

Some years ago a creative director of an ad agency I knew about was perfectionist to the point that the designs and copy he was working on by himself or with others were never good enough. They could always be better.

"Ray," his colleagues would say, "let go of the damned thing already. We have a deadline."

"Not yet, I'm not sure of the headline."

"But that's the tenth headline you've come up with."

"I know, it's still not good enough."

This would go on with everything he did. Was this normal or neurotic? Probably somewhere in between.

Psychologist Sidney J. Blatt of Yale University notes that investigators have identified at least three types of perfectionists:

- **Self-oriented:** This involves "exceedingly high, self-imposed, unrealistic standards and an intensive self-scrutiny and criticism in which there is an inability to accept flaw, fault or failure within oneself."
- **Socially prescribed:** Such people believe "that others maintain unrealistic and exaggerated expectations that are difficult, if not impossible to meet, but one must meet these standards to win approval and acceptance."
- **Other-oriented:** This perfectionist "demand(s) that others meet exaggerated and unrealistic standards."[5]

The perfectionist power freak in the context of this book would comprise the latter two.

It is one thing to have to deal with extreme perfectionists in our lives who are "self-oriented" and don't necessarily demand the same levels of performance from us. It is quite another thing to do deal with the perfectionist who becomes intimidating and threatening when we don't live up to their unrealistic standards. Perhaps they have developed these unreal standards as a reason for intimidating others.

There can also apparently be elements of one of the ten personality disorders in the perfectionist power freak, who may have character traits that meet some of the criteria for obsessive compulsive personality disorder (OCPD). This disorder, by the way, differs from obsessive compulsive disorder (OCD), which is characterized by repetitive acts or thoughts. The criteria for OCPD includes the following, the last of which complements Blatt's description of "socially prescribed" or "other oriented":

- ❋ Inability to complete a project because own overly strict standards are not met
- ❋ Preoccupation with details, rules, lists, order, organization, or schedules to the extent that the major point of the activity is lost
- ❋ Unreasonable insistence that others submit to exactly his or her way of doing things, or unreasonable reluctance to allow others to do things because of the conviction that they will not do them correctly.[6]

I knew one perfectionist power freak, "Marvin Axel," who was a mid-level manager running a department of about twenty persons. I was in his area one day when he had his entire group gathered about him as he put on a demonstration of where to affix a paper clip to documents of more than one page. He wouldn't allow stapling.

"Stapling is not good," I heard him say. "If I want to edit your document, I must use a staple remover and that leaves tears in the pages. Do not use a stapler. Is that clear?"

The gathering nodded their heads.

"Fine, next, when you use a paper clip make sure it is precisely one-half inch in from the left hand border in a perfectly vertical configuration. I know this must sound like nit-picking, but if we don't watch the little details we will all become sloppy."

This manager never allowed anyone to have any paper on their desks other than the ones they were working on. At night, all desktops had to be absolutely clear.

Perfectionist power freaks presumably find status in their fanatic obsession for perfection. When challenged about it, the crayfish effect manifests itself and tempers flare. Perfection to these people is no laughing matter.

PREJUDICIAL POWER FREAKS

Prejudicial power freaks transform into this mode when they are thinking about or dealing with members of groups they detest. If you are African American and working for a company whose culture fosters discrimination against African Americans, you are going to feel intimidated no matter if your law degree is from Harvard and you hold a doctorate in nuclear physics from Yale. The academic term that encompasses this behavior is "group-based social hierarchy." The basic premise is that we not only have a status-seeking predisposition to rank ourselves individually like a group of chickens, but we are predisposed to rank ourselves against other groups as well, as per the caste systems described in chapter 6.

In the book *Social Dominance*, the authors point out that we can be biased against other groups on the basis of race, sex, nationality, religion, and social class.[7] Group bias is a handy mechanism for those of any culture to use when seeking out someone to discriminate against. There were many members of the Ku Klux Klan who were poor and uneducated and looked down upon by other whites. The African Americans who had emerged from slavery were handy folks to be looked down upon by these down-and-out whites, no matter what an individual African American's credentials were. Not many years ago, some African Americans in Chicago were accused of discriminating against immigrants from Vietnam who had set up businesses in African American areas. Humans, as we've already observed, appear to have this innate predisposition to look down upon someone else, unfortunately an integral part of the ranking or pecking system. It ostensibly also reinforces our status to perceive others as beneath us.

David M. Buss, in his book *Evolutionary Psychology*, describes the theory that the thought process that creates these prejudices will "emerge prior to, and separate from, other types of reasoning strategies."[8] The reasoning, it would appear, is most likely imprinted on the instinctual-emotional structures that make up this side of our minds, becoming another emotional belief impervious to reason. You can't walk up to someone who is innately prejudiced against Albanians and state that his or her views are primitive, irrational, unrealistic, and need to be changed. He will look at you as if you are the one who is irrational. His fixation is as deep as the emotional memory that generates a phobia against flying and any change requires intense effort.

A second theory of evolutionary psychology about the causes of group prejudice has to do with our survival/fear instinctual program. As described previously, this theory suggests that an innate dislike of and aggressiveness against strangers is built into our instinctual drive for survival. The theory, as noted, is that when we lived in the caves or on the savannas, we never knew if the tribe approaching us was friendly or not. Consequently, we were automatically predisposed to be suspicious, distrustful, hateful, and aggressive against them, basically taking on the characteristics of the "charging display" to give us the greatest odds for winning a battle.

The recent mapping of the human genome, announced in early 2001, revealed that the difference in DNA between races of humans, as previously pointed out, is practically *indistinguishable*. Among humans, we are 99.9 percent identical.[9] The 0.1 percent difference contains the variances in our shapes and sizes, our susceptibility to such things as heart disease or cancer, as well as our melatonin production, which is thought to lead to variations in the color of human skin and hair.[10] "Race Gene Does Not Exist," is the title of the article just referenced and there were probably hundreds of others just like it, following the announcement of the mapping of the genome. Yet, ministers, priests, rabbis, and other religious leaders were not likely at their pulpits during services the following days, waving copies of the articles and saying, "Look, there is no genetic difference between us and any other race of humans on this planet. Nobody as a group is smarter or more intelligent then any other group. We are basically all equal. So let us stop these stupid, prejudicial beliefs that remain locked in our inner minds." Nor were politicians or any other leaders covered by the media bringing up the subject in any meaningful way.

Prejudicial power freaks are among the most heinous of all power freaks because they bully, intimidate, taunt, and even kill their victims, not for anything their victims did—against which some defense might be mounted—but because of what their heritage is. Their victims are dead meat right from the get-go. The only defense, as described in chapter 13, is calculated avoidance.

I recall having lunch with someone who was trying to sell us an extension to our computer system. Midway through the lunch he told me he lived in an area of Chicago that had become "overrun with people from India," and he couldn't stand it. "These people are practically subhuman," he said. "Their apartments are dirty, they are snobbish, and they still practice arranged marriages." He went on and on like this and so I thought I'd take a crack at him.

"Of course, you know that the cerebral cortex of your brain, your reasoning power, is composed of sixteen ounces of neurons, about 300 hundred million of them, which are connected by trillions of connectors called axons and you had nothing to do with how all this was put together."

"I don't understand you," he replied.

"I mean the brain you are thinking with and telling me about Indians with was constructed by a few thousand genes from the genetic structure of your mom and dad. It grew by itself in the womb and you had nothing to do with it."

"Well, of course I know that."

"But what you don't appear to know is that if you removed your brain and mine, and compared them with those of Indians, there would be no difference, other than the usual differences between people."

"Look, I don't care about that, these people are different, I live among them."

"But that is thinking from the mental software of your brain that you had no part in constructing. The point is, we don't know how we think. How we think remains a mystery to science. And so it is irrational to have such strong opinions, particularly when we know that we don't know how we think, what the actual physical process is, so how about just trying to be kind and curious and accepting of others?"

"Yeah, well I know how I think."

At this point he knew he was losing the sale with his drivel, but he persisted in his tirade, which proved to me Buss's point that these prejudices are separate from other types of reasoning strategies.

He left me with the check.

SYMBOL-LADEN POWER FREAKS

All of us tend to use symbols to display our status to others, including those of us low on the power/status scale, whose symbols are a display of having no symbols. "We aren't into that," they broadcast, which has a status of its own. If we discount natural ornaments such as peacock feathers, the use of symbols is primarily a human characteristic, since peacocks, chimpanzees, and crayfish don't have vacation homes, cell phones, or SUVs. On the other hand, the dominant chimpanzee male will usually travel in the middle of a troop on the march, putting subordinate chimps out to the flanks to absorb any surprise attack by predators. Thus, where we locate ourselves can be a status symbol.

Jean Godden of the *Seattle Times* described some of Seattle's top status symbols, during the 1998 heyday of the dot.coms:

* An unwashed blue Volvo station wagon
* An Internet connection at your cabin in Mazama (a resort area in Washington state)
* An extra-large blue camping tarp
* Microsoft stock options
* Reservations for Table 24 at Stars restaurant in Pacific Place
* Relatives buried in Lake View Cemetery

Godden also pointed to lavish events as being a status symbol, reporting on a party after the wedding of forty-seven-year-old John Elroy McCaw Jr., "one of the billionaire McCaw brothers who sold Seattle-based Cellular One to AT&T," to twenty-eight-year-old international model Gwendolyn Hoyt:

> McCaw spent an estimated $1 million on the party, flying in kegs of Guinness from Ireland and hiring song-and-dance man Tommy Tune for an opening act. Taking the stage after dinner was Stevie Wonder, who belted out three hours of hits. McCaw and Hoyt popped a bottle of champagne while Wonder sang "Ribbon in the Sky," the couple's favorite song.[11]

One might imagine that McCaw viewed Hoyt herself as a status symbol.

Then there are the top status symbols of baby-boomers as reported by Boomers International Newsletter Online:

* Vacation home
* International vacations
* Working as top executive in large company

✖ Living in an exclusive neighborhood
✖ Owning expensive jewelry
✖ Owning an expensive car[12]

Tattoos, uniforms, guns, and clothing have also been mentioned as prominent status symbols. So too are cell phones. Natalie Angier in an article in the *New York Times*, describing a research study in Liverpool, England, entitled "Mobile Phones as Lekking [mating] Devices among Human Males," reported the following:

> Not only did significantly more men than women appear to own cell phones, but they clearly wanted everybody else to know they owned them, too. . . . [T]he men would take their phones out of their jacket pockets or briefcases upon sitting down and place them on the bar counter or table for all to see.
> . . . The researchers theorized that "the men are using their mobile phones as peacocks use their immobilizing feathers and male bullfrogs use their immoderate croaks: to advertise to females their worth, status and desirability."[13]

Still other status symbols include memberships in exclusive groups or clubs; income and education; and at-work titles (doctor, judge, CPA, director, manager, esquire, president, captain, general); and the size, decor, and location of one's office.

Even religions have status symbols. In the Catholic Church, status is demonstrated in the hierarchy of the Church's ministers, from priest to cardinal, and the dress or vestments they wear that display their status. It is akin to the titles and dress that symbolize the hierarchies of the military.

We are basically beset with symbols of status wherever we look. There appears to be a fine line, however, as there is with all psychological predispositions, where the use of symbols begins to dominate one's life to the point that one can be afflicted with what we might unofficially label status symbol disorder. This would partially manifest itself in what George Simmel, a venerated professor of sociology, wrote around the turn of the century, and was reported by the National Research Council, Institute of Psychology: "When social groups are ordered by rank, agents imitate symbols designating the higher hierarchal levels and abandon those designating the lower level ones."[14] This means that as soon as existing status symbols favored by those higher in a hierarchy are copied by others, they quickly find new and better status symbols to take their place. This was soon labeled the "Simmel effect," and is a phenomenon that we all recognize, even as we wonder about it.

We have watched the tattoo craze and wonder why some people start with one or two tattoos and eventually end up with them covering almost every visible area of their bodies. The Simmel effect would apparently dictate it to those who are symbol-laden power freaks. As soon as everyone else in their social groups have one or two tattoos, they will thirst for more . . . or more body rings or a bigger and blacker motorcycle, or more chest muscle, or whatever.

Presumably Simmel understood that some of us may actually define our status by the symbols we display. If we're one of them and our neighbor down the street buys a newer and better-grade car than we have, the Simmel effect will kick in. At first, we may feel angered and dejected. But then we decide the challenge isn't over. Some of the manifestations of the "charging display" might emerge: now we feel aggressive, puffed up, our thinking becomes distorted, and we may buy an equivalent or *even better car*, though we can't afford it. In this sense, the Simmel effect would be a derivative of the crayfish effect, applying primarily to our interaction with symbols.

If our body is laden with tattoos, if every conceivable fold of our skins sags from the weight of jewelry and we believe that because of this, our status is enhanced among our peers, we would feel crestfallen, defeated, when we see someone who is even more impressively covered and more admired by our peers. Not until we find an even more outlandish skin treatment will we again be rewarded by the Simmel variation of the crayfish effect.

I have known corporate executives who have upgraded their corporate jets because too many other executives began flying the same model that they did. I have also known high-ranking executives with the authority to do so outfit their offices with outlandish decor, at costs of tens of thousand of dollars, with custom-made furniture and cabinetry, steam rooms, and exercise areas. The Simmel effect has made the private executive bathroom too common. The most successful executives I have known, however, have done little of this, some having offices you couldn't distinguish from anyone else's.

In a paper titled "The Fight for the Alpha Position: Channeling Status Competition," the authors describe the problem of Govert, an analyst working for a Dutch pharmaceutical firm:

> A change of building led to Govert having a desk that was 10 cm shorter [about 4 inches] than the one he had before. This was clearly beyond the pale; Govert was furious. "It was as if Govert's prestige could be measured in terms of his desk's surface area." And whenever Govert felt his status threatened he browbeat those below him and became increasingly non-compliant with his peers and superiors. His focus on status brought down morale in the whole office, distracted management, and perhaps worst of all, threatened to contaminate others to begin their own focus on status. This example will sound familiar to many managers—status striving is commonplace in organizations.[15]

Govert's aggressive behavior was obviously the result of the Simmel version of the crayfish effect. His desk was shortened, his status was challenged, his "charging display" emerged so he browbeat people beneath him. What a life.

Being in attendance at important meetings is also a status symbol. I have read that in the White House, the most important symbol of your ranking is in the level of the meetings you are invited to attend. In the business world, I recall being in a corporate meeting of about six managers when we were all advised to keep our voices down.

"Why?" I asked, "the door is closed."

"Well," one of them replied, "every time 'Craig' is not invited to a meeting that has nothing to do with his area, but he thinks it has, he will make it a point to walk by the door almost continuously, drop a pencil, or stir a cup of coffee while pausing at the door, to see if he can hear any conversation."

And so it would appear that the power freak who is addicted to status symbols may not only use them to show rank over and dominate others, but can be easily crushed when the symbols he or she needs are imitated or denied.

Stealth Power Freaks
Manipulating While Undercover

An anthropologist named Ralph Galin asked the director of a mental hospital to allow him to spend some time on a ward for a research project. He wished to be admitted as if he were a mental patient, and remain in this role undiscovered until the end of his study; he asked the psychiatrist's recommendation. The psychiatrist's advice was simple. "Be yourself and act naturally."[1]

Stealth power freaks might be defined as those who are not overtly intimidating and demeaning, they don't bully and taunt; in fact, on the surface they may appear to be gentle, kind, warm, and caring. But they will do anything they can, including sacrificing friendships and destroying the careers of peers and subordinates, if it will help them achieve greater status and power.

In his book *Mask of Sanity*, professor of psychiatry Harvey Cleckley asserts:

> Certain people, as everyone knows, may for many years show to a certain degree the reactions of schizophrenia, or manic-depressive psychosis, or a paranoia without being sufficiently disabled or so generally irrational as to be recognized as psychotic. . . . It would, however, sometimes be not only difficult but unfair to pronounce a person totally disabled while most of his conduct remains acceptable.[2]

In other words, despite twisted urges that may be pathological, some of us appear to have the intellectual capacity to wear a mask of innocence and kindness, when it better serves our interests.

This capacity is a complicating factor in human relationships because we can never be sure of someone's true personality. As Gertrude Stein might say, "I know it is you, but who is the real you in you?"

In the business world, our capacities for stealth, cunning, and undercover manipulation can wreak havoc on an organization at any level that harbors an extreme power freak with these capacities. Those working on production lines or in office administrative positions can sabotage the efforts of a co-worker or a supervisor they consider a threat to their status, by subtly creating defective work at appropriate times, in a way that shifts blame to their targets.

A memo might be innocently passed for review via e-mail to a peer who is a stealth power freak, for example. The peer subtly injects a couple of lines of data that he knows is incorrect and if it's undetected when returned to the sender, it can make the sender look bad when the document is distributed.

At the upper levels of management, executives can create similar havoc, undercutting the work and efforts of others, as they hide behind their masks of kindness. Among other devious capacities they harbor, they can, with great aplomb, say one thing and do another.

Cleckley, whose book focuses on psychopathy, makes the point that it is frequently difficult to unmask even the more severe psychopaths who are capable of covering their malicious intents with a "mask of sanity." If psychiatrists such as Cleckley have had a problem in discerning some psychopaths, what chance do the rest of us have, particularly if the psychopath was just hired as our new boss and appears to be as charming as Cary Grant?

In the business world as well as in family and community life, what we might call "the stealth factor" at a given level of intensity usually surfaces when the extreme power freak:

- Believes that the use of stealth, cunning, and undercover manipulation will better suit his needs than an outward show of authoritarianism. He or she would simply prefer to work behind a mask of kindness and sympathy, while doing such things as playing one person off of another.
- Is phobic about intimidating or in other ways hurting peers and

subordinates on a face-to-face basis. And so she simply stabs them in the back.

The use of cunning and manipulation, as noted in the characteristics of psychopaths listed in chapter 5, is apparently a standard weapon for extreme power freaks with psychopathic traits. For them, it is presumably quite natural and justifiable to use whatever means it takes to defend or raise their status. Remember that they have no sense of guilt, remorse, or empathy.

In the executive suites of some of the largest corporations, for example, it is not unusual for the CEO to leave senior managers whose services are no longer wanted to "twist in the wind," as their superiors and peers begin to ignore them, hoping that they'll get the hint and resign. It is a cruel form of manipulation. I witnessed two such events.

Many years ago I was having breakfast with the president of a large, publicly held company, whose CEO was a power-driven man with a long record of success. The CEO had promoted this man, who had been one of his divisional presidents, to president of the corporation. They had a falling out of some kind, but the CEO refused to fire him, probably because this man was his appointee and the termination would have reflected poorly on him.

The president and I were having breakfast at one of the corporation's facilities being used that day for a planning session. As we were eating, we heard the loud roar of the CEO's helicopter as it came in for a landing. Minutes later, the CEO and the vice chairman of the company strode in, passing through the breakfast area. They ignored the president and they ignored me, probably because I was sitting *with him* that day. The look of pain on the president's face was pitiful. If we could have done a brain scan of his amygdala, the social defeat would undoubtedly have had it looking like a supernova. The president later resigned his position and fortunately was rewarded for his long years of service with a lucrative consulting contract by the firm.

The second example involved another large company. The executive involved, "Dennis," was in charge of sales for a specific category of customers. When he took the position, the executive vice president for whom he worked was extremely cooperative, because the company had not had much success in this category and was under pressure from the board of directors to do better.

Within two years, Dennis's efforts were successful, particularly with one major customer, and the company was racking up tens of millions of dollars in volume. But Dennis watched in wonderment as his superior, the executive vice president, began to undercut him in meetings. It became clear to Dennis that this man was tired of hearing about Dennis's success and wanted him out so that he could take total credit for the amazing growth that was taking place. Soon Dennis was unjustifiably left out of meetings and isolated in the company. When he would see his superior in the hall and say something like, "Look, I really need your help in serving this customer better," the superior would reply, "There is nothing I can help you with." E-mails and voice-mails would go unanswered. After a few months of this, Dennis had no choice but to resign to maintain his sanity. "I wish I could have sued that guy for mental cruelty," he told me.

Extreme power freaks can be jealous and envious of subordinates who have had great success, even though that success reflects on them in a positive way. Because an overt confrontation might be bad form, in view of the subordinate's success, the extreme power freak may find the use of cunning and manipulation as the best weapons for undercutting successful subordinates.

Crazy? You bet.

In the fifteenth century, Niccolo Machiavelli wrote a book called *The Prince*, which became the basis for what are now known as Machiavellian strategies. In his book, *What Would Machiavelli Do?*, Stanley Bing, a columnist for *Fortune* magazine, pointed out a number of characteristics that Machiavelli would suggest as appropriate to emulate today, if you want to be successful. The following two characteristics reminded me of executive managers who use the manipulative "twisting in the wind" technique with subordinates they don't want to fire, but whom they want to leave:

※ Make people fear for their lives
※ Torture people until they are only too happy to destroy themselves

Some of the other Machiavellian characteristics noted by Bing include these:

* Scream at people a lot
* Have no conscience
* Be proud of cruelty and see it as a strength
* Lie, when necessary
* Carry a grudge forever
* Embrace your own madness
* Treat yourself right[3]

Not exactly church choir material.

Stealth, cunning, and manipulation are also weapons of choice among extreme power freaks who are somewhat phobic about direct confrontation and intimidation or who simply prefer to wear a mask of warmth and innocence as a personality device.

The following story is a bit long, but it was related to me by an industrial psychologist who prefers to remain anonymous. It is an excellent example of an extreme power freak who is good at wearing a mask of innocence while using stealth, cunning, and manipulation to claw her way upward. The names of the persons and their companies have been changed.

Ed Young had just joined the well regarded Osborne Consulting Company as a marketing specialist, at the age of thirty, after receiving an MBA from an accredited university, attending nights and weekends over a five-year period. Osborne Consulting was attracted to Young because he had been a district sales manager for a high-tech company and so had sales and marketing experience in the field to go along with his MBA.

After two months at Osborne, Young was riding high. His first client was a mid-sized Internet access company which we'll call PriorityAccess, operating in a number of key markets in the midwest, and whose proprietary software gave them a definite edge over other access providers. His assignment was to develop an expansion plan into eastern markets. He had completed his market surveys and was ready to present his findings and initial recommendations to his client's senior management committee. His immediate supervisor was Hilda Chamberlain, who, although three years younger than Young, had made her way quickly up the cor-

porate ladder to a mid-level managerial position. She was outwardly
warm, pleasant, and cooperative and had reviewed Ed's findings and
approved his presentation. However, at the last minute, he added several
points on his own with which he was sure Ms. Chamberlain would agree.

The presentation was scheduled for the following afternoon.
Young had been fine-tuning his Power Point presentation for a week.
The next morning he turned on his laptop computer for one more
review using a computer projector, and found that the file was missing.
Distraught, he searched through his entire file directory, but there was
nothing.

He grabbed his laptop and rushed down the hall to Chamberlain's
office.

"Hilda, you won't believe this, but the client presentation file is
missing," he held up his laptop helplessly.

"That's impossible, Ed," she answered. "Maybe you misfiled the last
entry. Did you check thoroughly?"

"Yes, yes I did, for God's sake. And I didn't make a back-up. We're
going to have to postpone the presentation, that's all there is to it."

"I'm afraid that's impossible, Ed. Three of the six committee members are in from out of town, specifically for this presentation. Look,
I've been keeping track of your findings and working them into a presentation of my own that includes other materials. Why don't I give this
presentation on your behalf, skimpy as it might be, but including the
salient points to show the good progress we've been making?"

"I don't know, Hilda, I have a personal sense of the material that I
can add as background information."

"No problem, Ed. You can chip in with your comments any time
you like. We'll keep the presentation loose and informal."

That afternoon at the meeting, Hilda told the committee about
the problem and stated that in the interests of time, she would present
her findings, which would at least cover the most important points. Ed
made his apologies for the inconvenience, pointing to the useless
laptop he brought to the meeting. He noted that the PriorityAccess
people didn't look sympathetic.

Then Hilda began her Power Point presentation. Young's mouth
went agape. The presentation was not only identical to his own, but it
contained the additions he had never covered with Hilda prior to the
meeting. Worse, Chamberlain presented the materials as if they were
her own, talking about how she had verified information with tele-

phone surveys and database checks. She never once glanced at Ed, never asked him to comment. The committee members were overwhelmed by her presentation, asking questions only of her, ignoring Ed.

The CEO of the company said, "Hilda, we couldn't have asked for more. I am going to call Gene Osborne tomorrow, as you know I know him very well, and tell him what an outstanding job you did."

Hilda accepted the accolades, barely acknowledging Ed.

When the meeting was over, the CEO asked Hilda to stay on to meet with him privately. Ed was expecting a similar invitation, but again was ignored.

The next morning, Ed was furious. He strode into Chamberlain's office and began rebuking her for stealing his presentation and showing him up at the meeting.

Chamberlain denied his accusations and went on the attack herself, berating him for not making back-ups. "If I hadn't been working on this along with you, the entire situation would have become a disaster," she said. She dismissed him out of hand. The next day he received a copy of a negative report about himself that she had submitted to her supervisors and which was placed in his personnel file. His new career had its first strike against it, and after only three months on the job.

A year later Hilda Chamberlain was asked to resign from Osborne Consulting. It finally became apparent to her superiors that what she did to Ed Young she was doing all along to other subordinates and peers alike.

The industrial psychologist who related this incident to me said that in an exit interview with Hilda, she readily admitted to her misdeeds. With regard to the needless squashing of Ed Young, she said she had seen this kind of power play behavior when she first entered the business world and thought that for her to become successful she would need to emulate it. "You know, everyone in the organization was relatively pleasant on the surface, but that never fooled me. I knew that everyone was out to get one another and I just joined in as best as I could. I also thought Young was out to get my job."

The industrial psychologist also told me that he was surprised that Hilda got by with this behavior for so long because the Osborne corporate culture was relatively benign. Harmony and teamwork were emphasized there. He related how he had gone back to the files and interviewed all those like Ed Young who had previously complained about her and realized that her supervisors were simply misled by her outward personality and her talents.

"I think that in their hearts they would have liked to keep her on because she was so good at what she did," he told me. "But word had gotten around the organization about her unacceptable behavior, although I'll tell you that it is acceptable in other companies I've worked with. I believe she is working for one of them now."

One of the companies where Hilda's behavior might have been acceptable was real estate broker Helmsley-Spears, at a time a number of years ago when Leona Helmsley worked there as an employee, before she married Harry Helmsley, as discussed previously. "He bred killers," one former Helmsley broker said about the culture of the organization. "The whole world was fair game."[4]

Most of the brokers were overtly pleasant to one another, inquiring about family and such when they bumped into each other in the corridors, but they all seemed to understand that it wouldn't be considered inappropriate if one broker stole a deal from another broker, if the circumstances arose. Apparently in their minds, as so many Mafia characters in motion pictures have put it, "It's just business."

One of the key elements that creates this type of consistent backbiting may reside in the atmosphere of a particular corporation. I knew one executive, "Michael," who left a corporation in a consumer products business notorious for its dog-eat-dog environment. This corporate culture is not usually immediately recognizable upon meeting people from this company and others like it. Employees all appear pleasant, joke with each other, ask about each other's families, but behind the scenes, they appear to constantly scheme for ways they can back-bite their peers and supervisors, intent on moving up the corporate ladder.

Michael soon left this company and joined another at a higher managerial level, a promotion for him. His new company had a normal corporate culture that stressed comity and teamwork. Nonetheless, it took Michael at least two years before he stopped looking behind his back, suspecting that subordinates and peers were waiting for an opportunity to sabotage him. His outlook, we might assume, had become distorted because of the many traumas he suffered in a dog-eat-dog environment, where his only defense was to toughen himself to assume that the worst was going to happen, and so that he could play the game as well . . . which, by the way, he unfortunately did.

Cunning and manipulation are also favored weapons of the relatively normal executive whose position is suddenly threatened and so transforms into a challenged power freak. Because these persons are apparently not as innately aggressive as an extreme power freak, they may find it difficult to confront others whom they perceive as a threat. And so they will use stealth and cunning, hoping that they won't get caught.

The following story was related to me by a public relations consultant:

> The public relations agency, "Anderson & Associates" employed a young account executive named "Ralph," only a year or two out of journalism school with a major in public relations. He was doing quite well with the agency, which considered him a rising star. Ralph had about him an aura of humility and modesty. Then the agency hired an experienced reporter named "Wally," who had worked for several years on a daily newspaper, and put him in the same office with Ralph, asking Ralph to watch over him and break him in.
>
> Despite the fact that Wally was a warm and caring human being, who had taken this job only because it provided a greater income for his growing family, Ralph was completely intimidated by him. He saw Wally as a threat to his status because Wally not only had a degree in journalism, but had served on the front lines for many years as a reporter with a major daily newspaper. The owner of the agency explained to Ralph the differences between pure newspaper journalism and the practice of public relations, which can involve many things beyond the writing of news stories on behalf of a client. He told Ralph how both he and Wally could benefit from each other's experiences. Ralph was unable to accept the explanation. He became addicted to the belief that Wally was a threat to his career.
>
> During the following weeks and months, with both in the same office, Ralph gradually transformed into a challenged power freak. He truly liked Wally, had met his family, but at the same time did his best to make Wally look bad, without seeming to do so. Wally would ask Ralph to look at an article or a speech he had written before sending it to a client. Ralph, on appropriate occasions, would notice errors, but fail to alert Wally. Wally would then be criticized not only by the client, but by the supervisor of the department. In an extreme form of manipulation, Ralph would loudly defend Wally, telling the supervisor

that he had missed the error as well. He knew that in the mind of the supervisor, the error would nevertheless be attributed to Wally.

Over a period of four to six months, there were about eight of these errors, scattered through various projects, and Wally was becoming uneasy and losing confidence in his ability to do the job. This attitude began affecting his writing and his dealing with his clients, so within the year, Wally resigned to go back as a reporter on another major daily.

Ralph later became a key executive at the agency and no longer felt challenged enough by anyone new to repeat the same tactics. But he did admit to the person who told me this story that he would do it again in a heartbeat, if a challenge did emerge. "I owe that to my family," he said.

The only positive about the use of cunning, stealth, and manipulation, whether in the business world, among siblings, or in charitable organizations or wherever humans gather is that sooner or later, the persons who employ such tactics are almost always found out. Once they are, they should be dealt with in the same manner as any extreme power freak. We'll get into that shortly.

CHAPTER 10

The Power Freak Factor

Can We Measure Ourselves?

"I'm employed at a company where the CEO definitely needs to sit in a locked office all day! The company had to construct a new head office entranceway so the people sitting in the lounge could not hear her screaming and yelling obscenities! She treats her employees like crap, bullying them so much so that three quit in one week. Experience means nothing to her, everyone is replaceable, except her of course. . . . This is the worst!!"[1]

To know how to deal with the extreme power freaks in our lives, we need to have some idea where we stand on the power/status scale ourselves. The higher we are, the more probable it is that we bristle at authority and the more difficult it would be for us to be compliant to a superior in the workplace who is intimidating. Further, the higher we are on this scale, the more deluded we may be about our own personalities and temperaments.

Following is a brief description of a case study included by Paul Babiak, an industrial/organizational psychologist, in his article, "When Psychopaths Go to Work: A Case Study of an Industrial Psychopath." It is an example of an industrial or business (the terms are interchangeable) psychopath, or in the jargon of our book, an extreme power freak with psychopathic traits:

Dave's boss discovered that the first major report he produced included large amounts of plagiarized material. When confronted, Dave brushed aside the concerns, commenting that he considered it a poor use of his time and talents to "reinvent the wheel." He frequently "forgot to work" on certain uninteresting projects. . . .

Dave was frequently unprepared and late for staff meetings. When he did show up he could be counted on to deliver a verbal tirade. When his boss asked him to control his outbursts, Dave responded that in his opinion fighting and aggression were necessary forces and that people needed them to advance in life. His boss commented that he never seemed to learn from the feedback he received, never acknowledged that he had done anything wrong and always acted surprised when given feedback, insisting that he had never been told that he had done anything wrong before. Dave's co-workers were consistent in their descriptions—they found him rude, selfish, immature, self-centered, unreliable and irresponsible.[2]

Dave was unable to see his own failings. He was deluded about himself and worse, he believed his behavior was beyond reproach.

This points back to parts of this book, where we observed that the primary cause of delusional thinking is the fact that we ostensibly can become addicted to or fanaticized in a particular belief and that our *thinking can become more or less distorted within the subject range of the addiction.* As noted earlier, Marshall Applewhite actually *believed* there was a new life for his Heaven's Gate group on a spaceship hidden behind the Hale-Bopp comet. Adolf Hitler actually *believed* that the Aryan race, as he called it, was superior to all others and worth purifying by killing millions of those he thought would pollute it.

As Freud noted, human behavior is largely driven by unconscious and nonrational drives, which we rationalize and justify in terms of logic and reason and that some of these beliefs may become an obsessional neurosis. Thus, we can sit in front of someone who thinks we should drop atomic bombs on China or some other nation and hear very convincing arguments structured in a logical and reasonable sequence. As previously mentioned, this vulnerability of the rational mind to the infection of twisted realities, created by the instinctual mind, is among the human race's greatest weaknesses.

Add to this Freud's observations that these twisted realities have no sense of time, awareness, or logic and we can see that the problem is compounded.

And so it is impossible to get positive results from simply walking up to extreme power freaks like Dave and saying, "Behave yourself, you're acting unreasonably, you are intimidating and hurting other people, you are leaving misery in your wake. You don't need to manage by intimidation, you don't need to be arrogant. The best managers today hold their subordinates accountable, but do so in climates of motivation, nurturance, and teamwork."

People like Dave, who are delusional, would not have the slightest idea of what you are talking about. During periods when you are trying to give them feedback, advising how they might straighten up, they would probably be looking at you with a sly grin, trying to figure out how you are trying to get the best of them. They are in their own worlds and that is why they are so difficult to deal with, as described in the next chapters.

Extreme power freaks can also read some of the most effective books on management and many of them obviously do, but they don't get the message. For example, in the book *Get Better or Get Even: 29 Leadership Secrets from GE's Jack Welch*, the author, Robert Slater, reports that the values that Welch looked for in those who would succeed when he was CEO at GE are exemplified in four types of managers:

1. The first type delivers on commitments—financial or otherwise—and shares GE's values. "His or her future is an easy call," says Welch. "Onward and upward."
2. The second type does not meet commitments (read "bring in a healthy balance sheet") and does not share GE's values. "Not a pleasant call, but equally easy."
3. The third type misses commitments but shares the values. "He or she usually gets a second chance, preferably in a different environment."
4. The fourth type delivers on commitments but does not subscribe to GE's values. This is the most difficult type to deal with. This is the individual who typically forces performance out of people rather than inspires it: the autocrat, the big shot, the tyrant.

Too often all of us have looked the other way—tolerated these "Type 4" managers because "they always deliver"—at least in the short term. And perhaps this type is acceptable in easier times, but in an environment where we must have every good idea from every man and woman in the organization, we can't afford management styles that suppress and intimidate.[3]

In other words, people with psychopathic traits and/or status obsession need not apply.

Extreme power freaks would also find unbelievable the following suggestion made in the best-selling business book *The Boss's Survival Guide: Everything You Need to Know about Getting through (and Getting the Most Out of) Every Day*:

> Your role as a manager means that you, too, may be in a position of facing a moment of truth: Is it in the best interests of the business to terminate an employee? Deciding "yes" is one of the hardest things you will ever do as a manager. Most terminations will feel like a loss to you, to the employee and probably to others in your company. Even if the employee "deserves it" because of poor performance or insubordination, it is still one of the most stressful events in a manager's life. Expect to face anger, hurt and fear and no matter how many times you terminate someone it doesn't get easier.[4]

It doesn't get easier? To an extreme power freak, firing someone can make their day, particularly if the person being fired is about to be made miserable and has a family with kids. The tougher the hardship on the terminated employee, the more intense the "high" the extreme power freak may feel. Warped? Absolutely.

Some of us may pride ourselves on being open-minded, but yet are attached to emotional beliefs that may not be rational at all. As a result, we may be unable to see the full picture and can miss opportunities.

Several years ago, the communications manager of a client would persistently complain to me about his superior, the company's marketing manager.

"He's close-minded," he would say. "Everything always has to be done his way."

I would nod as he continued.

"He barely acknowledges that I live, for god's sake. It's like he tries to avoid me, because he definitely knows that I have better ideas than he does and so I'm some kind of threat. That must be it."

When I talked to his superior, whom I knew, and the conversation drifted to the communications manager, I could see him grit his teeth.

"This person has no relationship skills," he said. "It's always his way. He doesn't know the first thing about persuasion. He has some good ideas, but to tell you the truth, I just can't stand dealing with him. The guy always has to be in control."

From my perspective, it was the communications manager who had the problem. He complained about his boss being power hungry, but it was he, in fact, who was the power freak in the situation. After several sessions with an industrial psychologist, he seemed to settle in and remained on the job. I asked him one day what had changed.

"Look, I have kids," he muttered quietly to me. "I need this job. I've just learned to shut my mouth and get along."

So his "positions" didn't change, merely the mask he put over his personality. All it would have taken was a few fine adjustments for this manager to move up the ranks. He just couldn't do it.

Others have, however. I've seen people with personalities similar to the communications manager one day wake up and transform. "What happened to you?" I remember asking one of them. "You're acting like a Dale Carnegie instead of the asshole you used to be."

He laughed and said, "Hey, I saw the light." He talked about how he had dinner one night with an executive higher up in the company who was like a father figure to him. This executive was tough with him, told him how he was acting and the reaction it was having on others. He wouldn't let up.

"Somewhere within that conversation it hit me that he was right and I was wrong. It was like a religious epiphany. I never felt such a feeling of relief. I saw what an asshole, to use your term, that I had been. I had the best night's sleep I ever had. The next day I came to work relaxed and in tune and it has been great ever since."

So it can happen, particularly with those who become blinded by the arrogant, haughty, and domineering behavior that derives from status obsession. These behaviors don't appear to lie as heavily on us as they do when they are spawned from psychopathic origins.

RATIONAL ASPIRATIONS VERSUS OUR PRIMAL DRIVE FOR DOMINANCE

It is difficult to separate the measurement of rational aspiration or the intellectual desire to succeed, to do a good job, from the measurement of sheer primal pressure for dominance. Philologists appear to use the word "ambition" to cover both the more ennobled term "aspiration" and the primal drive for dominance. *Webster's International Dictionary* defines ambition as "having a desire to succeed or achieve a particular goal . . . aspiring," and an "ardent desire for rank, fame and power."

In his book *Ambition*, essayist and writer Joseph Epstein, who teaches at Northwestern University, alludes to the confusion that clouds the term:

> [T]here can be no blinking the fact that ambition is increasingly associated in the public mind chiefly with human characteristics held to be despicable. Ambition is most often confused with aggression; and aggression, make no mistake, is scarcely thought to be an admirable quality. The ambitious person is generally thought to be single-minded, narrowly concentrated in purpose, bereft of such distracting qualities as charm, imagination or introspection of the kind that leads to self-doubt. Success is said to beget success, but ambition begets distrust.[5]

Gilbert Brim, director of the MacArthur Foundation Research Network on Successful Midlife Development, in his book *Ambition: How We Manage Success and Failure throughout Our Lives*, reinforces Epstein's views: "[I]n earlier times and to some extent today, a drive for ambition is associated with selfish purposes. In early Roman days, ambition had the connotation of greediness and selfishness and of being individualistic and competitive."[6]

It appears far easier to isolate the power/status drive in its purest form among animals, where the existence of high intelligence doesn't confuse the issue. In the animal world, if a chimpanzee named Herman has the instinctual drive to become an alpha, and has low levels of fear and nurturance and the physical wherewithal, he can become an alpha, and we can witness the result. After the final challenge, a primatologist would not likely report that it was Herman's "blind ambition" that drove him to defeat one challenger after another, but his natural drive for power and dominance. And so it would appear that the word "ambition" has more of an intellectual cast than a primal one.

Nonetheless, because of the ambiguity of the term's definition, it appears to make more sense to use the term "aspiration" to describe our rational desire to advance in life, to be industrious, to compete hard and to succeed, without necessarily wanting to step all over others in a drive to dominate them—what Brim in his book calls a "cooperative ambition" versus a "competitive one." This concept of rational aspiration would help us better understand a leader like George Washington, who gritted out the hardships of the Revolutionary War, won a victory, and was asked to become the first king of the United States. He refused the offer, wanting only to return home to the life of a planter. It is hard to imagine a Bobby Knight or Al Dunlap doing the same.

"You want me to be the king, is that correct?" one or the other might have said if they were in George Washington's position at the time.

"Yes, we do."

"Well, I suppose someone has to do that nasty job and it might as well be me."

Think of the extreme power freaks you have known in your life and how they would have reacted to such an offer. And so we have a conundrum. Why are a George Washington or an Abraham Lincoln or a Robert E. Lee perceived as decent humans by their followers, though they did tough and hardened things, including sending soldiers into battle and to their deaths, while extreme power freaks with psychopathic traits such as an Adolf Hitler or a Joseph Stalin are not?

We might presume that part of the answer lies in the intensity of their primal drives for status and dominance and that the intensity was less for Washington and Lincoln than it was for Hitler and Stalin. Because Washington and Lincoln were noticeably aggrieved by the deaths they caused, we can also suppose they had higher levels of nurturance than Stalin or Hitler. One of Stalin's famous quotes was "One death is a tragedy. A million deaths is a statistic."

It is also apparent that the higher we rate on the scale of the drive for power and status, the more our outlooks become distorted and delusive. Stalin and Hitler both were deluded, among other things, into thinking that their autocratic social and governmental concepts were worth killing millions for and were not open to feedback. It was their way or the firing squad. Washington and Lincoln had a better handle on reality. They understood the difficulties of defining the right thing to do. You could disagree with them without fearing for your life.

Based on these premises, we might assume that those of us at the lower to mid-range of the power/status scale can feel the primal pressure within us, but we have it under intellectual control; we have disciplined it. Because we know it is there, however, we can call upon it to be tough and hard when we are challenged, and revert to our normal state when the challenge is over. Thus the true heroes of the world are apparently not the power-motivated alphas who thrust themselves into situations of conflict with the sole purpose of achieving and maintaining dominance and acquiring the rewards these positions bring. The heroes appear to be those lower on the power/status scale, the fours and fives, maybe even some threes, who are called upon under troublesome circumstances to take charge, rise to the occasion, and allow their primal drives to be released. Win or lose, they relinquish authority, allow their displays of aggression to subside, and retire to the normalcy of their former lives.

These are presumably the heroes that were so popular in the classical Western movies, the Gary Coopers and Jimmy Stewarts, whom we admired in their character roles as aspiring to do the right thing at the right time; they eschewed conflict, but became so irate at watching the bad guys pick on the weak that they finally picked up their guns to fight. After they defeated the bad guys in a final battle, they gave up their power, dropping their guns or their badges on the street, and rode away into the sunset. In this sense, we might assume it was more their rational aspirations to maintain an equanimity among humans than a primal drive for status and dominance that motivated them initially.

This appears also to be the key to the likability of our leaders. We like people whom we perceive as not driven to dominate, who are balanced, who are more like one of us, but have leadership qualities and handle the role of leader with grace and equanimity. We tend to dislike, on the other hand, the alphas and alpha pretenders whom we perceive as relishing a dominating position, who show off, tell us how great they are, and who can be abusive and intimidating. Because of their plethora of distorted outlooks, including paranoia, they come across as uptight and artificial in their humor. When they succeed, they look for adoration, but don't get it.

"Why don't people love me?" we frequently hear them ask.

"Because you are an uptight, power-driven jerk," most of us would like to respond.

It would appear that the extreme power freak wants power for power's sake, whereas the level fives to be described shortly, those in the middle of the scale, the Washingtons, Lincolns, and Lees, want power in defense of a cause.

In the last book of his trilogy about Franklin D. Roosevelt, *FDR: The War President*, Kenneth S. Davis, historian and student of psychology, comments about General George C. Marshall, who basically headed the war effort in World War II and later served as secretary of state:

> Marshall did not make idle threats or use them merely to gain tactical points; he was remarkably free of personal arrogance [read status-obsession] and lust for power; and he had at this conference [the first joint conference of World War II between the United States and Great Britain] firmly established himself as the dominant military figure of the Allied war command.[7]

The upshot appears to be that in the modern world of humans we most applaud those with leadership qualities who are reasonable, who have not been captured by their instinctual power/status drive, who in their own graceful way, using their intelligence and creativity, manage to get the job done. We loved Jack Kennedy for those qualities and for the fact that he appeared to aspire to a higher and more ennobling life for the rest of us. We disliked Richard Nixon, in general, because we perceived him as being driven to dominate, too attached to the trappings of power and too uptight due to his paranoia and other distorted outlooks. In the end Nixon was driven out of office because he mistakenly assumed, as most power-driven people do, that the rules that govern the rest of us didn't apply to him.

MEASURING THE INTENSITY OF OUR POWER/STATUS DRIVE

In the field of psychology a variety of scales are used to measure the intensity of personality characteristics, including disorders. Some are heavily structured mathematical models, others are simple, a one-to-four or one-to-five scale or endpoints, as they are called. Others have a much wider measurement, such as the well known Taylor Manifest Anxiety Scale, which after a short test, measures your anxiety level from one to fifty.[8]

David G. Winter, as noted earlier, is one of the leaders in the study of what he and other psychologists call the "power motive," which is the title of his book. He authored the n Power Scoring System, which has been in use since 1973, with n standing for "Need," or need for power. It is, however, a highly technical system, covering approximately 105 pages in his book and is intended to be administered by trained practitioners. At the heart of the system is the use of photos and stories, which the practitioner employs to determine power imagery and other feelings that are elicited when the respondent views the photos and hears the stories. The scale of intensity ranges from 0 to +11 for each photo or story.[9]

I am certain I have not done his system justice, due to the mathematics needed to interpret his Power Scoring Sheet. Because trained practitioners must administer the system, it doesn't include lay descriptions of the varying intensity levels of the power drive (or motive) beyond "fear of power," and "need for power." These need to be interpreted in more detail by the psychologist conducting the tests.[10]

My first book, *Brain Tricks: Coping with Your Defective Brain*, included a hypothetical scale of the power drive, with descriptions for each level.[11] The scale was augmented in my recent book, *Battling the Inner Dummy: The Craziness of Apparently Normal People*.[12] The augmentation was developed in conjunction with two graduate students working for their Ph.D.s, at the University of Wisconsin department of psychology, Nanmathi Manion, who has since earned her doctorate, and David Amodio.

The scale was also placed on a Web site in 1994, with a simple quiz (available at the end of this chapter) that allowed anyone to determine, roughly, where his or her own power temperaments placed them on the scale. For the first two years that the quiz appeared on the Web (www.powerfreaks.com), we asked for detailed feedback from participants so that we could adjust the questions in an effort to make the results as accurate as possible. As of early 2002, primarily because of a link to a psychological section of America Online, the quiz has been taken by more than 500,000 people. Separate software monitors the tally.

Now, the scale described below has been refined once again. Among other enhancements, it delineates the levels. Levels one through three are described as a power drive that is difficult to detect and passive. At these levels, as Winter, McClelland, and other authorities concur, there may be a "fear of power." The power drive at levels four and five is described as mild; six and seven as moderate; and levels eight through ten as extreme.

The scale suggests a measurement of the power/status drive as a whole. The deluded outlooks of the situational and directional power freaks in particular are not directly addressed. As we've seen, these people are transformed into extreme power freaks only in specific situations—a competitive event or when challenged by a peer, for example. Thus, tennis player John McEnroe might be a level five during most of his waking hours, but when he steps on a tennis court, he takes on many of the characteristics of a level eight or nine. In December 2001 a Chicago Bulls basketball player who is normally mild mannered kicked a chair into the stands during a game, injuring a spectator. He then made the comment, "I know it's a little ridiculous. It's like I turn on a switch before [each game's player] introductions. I can't help it."[13] A racist member of the Ku Klux Klan might also be a level five during most of his waking hours, but when he comes in contact with a minority group, something "switches" in his mind and he takes on the charging display characteristics of an extreme power freak for the duration of the contact. He is unable to rise above it and we don't excuse him. A control power freak may be relatively normal until someone cuts her off in her car or in other ways challenges her authority, her territory. Then she is temporarily transformed or switched into an extreme power freak as well.

It would thus appear that the descriptions of the extreme power freak levels that follow can also be used to describe in part the intensity levels of situational and directional power freaks, when they are in this mode.

HYPOTHETICAL SCALE OF POWER /STATUS INTENSITY LEVELS

Difficult to Detect

Level One

These are apparently people who have many Jesus-like characteristics, in particular with no recognizable concern for power or status. You insult them and they turn the other cheek. "We are all God's children after all," they might say. "We all have flaws." They are unconcerned with wealth or possessions and are generally kind and considerate. They can be hard workers and have aspirations, but appear unconcerned with promotion or achieving a higher rank. If it comes, they are embarrassed to acknowledge it and may fear it. They would gladly give away everything they owned, it seems, if they thought the cause was a noble one. They are humble, modest, and polite in their dealings with others. There is something in their brain chemistry that obviates or significantly dampens such normal emotions and drives as jealousy, envy, hatred, and vengeance. It would appear, unfortunately, that the design of the power/status system allows only for a relative handful of people like these on the planet. Were there only more of them.

Passive

Level Two

These are people who appear almost as saintly as those on level one, but do, apparently, feel some stirring of power and status. They will feel mildly upset if insulted, although probably not significantly vengeful. They may have strong aspirations, but are not mentally punished after defeats. They are not overly sensitive to the expectancies of power and rank. If they win, fine. If they lose, fine. They are usually submissive to authority at work or in the home and even when this authority is stifling, they won't complain, or if they do, it is not strident. They are not contrarian. Whether happy or not, they are probably accepting of their station in life.

Level Three

These people can be hard workers and diligent in other ways; they want to succeed in the tasks they do, they may have high aspirations for a more ennobling or rewarding life, but are not seemingly anxious to rise to any position where they need to supervise others, particularly in the workplace. The thought of being in authority appears to make them uncomfortable. They are content to defer to leaders at work and stronger family members and stay out of the limelight. Nonetheless, they can feel mild jealousy and envy if someone on their block has a better car or a neighbor or co-worker was promoted. They can be accepting of other ethnic groups. They are the worker bees of society and content with that role.

Mild

Level Four

These people are apparently not preoccupied with gaining power, but accept it if comes their way. At home or in the office they are content with being in a subordinate role, if that's the way it is. As supervisors they would tend to promote harmony and readily accept input from colleagues and subordinates. If challenged in the workplace or home, they will feel anger, resentment, and vengeance, but the feelings won't be as long-lasting as they might be at the higher levels. They will feel jealousy and envy when those in their social circle gain in status, but again the feelings aren't lasting as they more quickly adapt to reality.

Level Five

Level five people may be ambitious and have strong aspirations to be successful in their endeavors in order to satisfy their expectancies as well as better provide for their families, but they are not abusive in the process. They won't walk over family, friends, and co-workers to get ahead or achieve their goals. They might be disappointed in achieving less than a high leadership rank, but they accept it and get on with their lives. As supervisors they would tend to promote harmony. They are prone to normal levels of jealousy and envy when others they know gain status over them in terms of career promotions or having a better car or backyard deck. Some at this level may look down on others, measuring their status against them, but it is usually not overt. Among the fives (perhaps also the fours and even the threes) would be those humans we consider the salt of the earth. These are the Washingtons and Lincolns and the characters frequently played in the classical western motion pictures, as previously described, who take the mantle of leadership and handle it gracefully when it comes their way, but then reject enduring dominance and authority when offered to them, preferring to ride off in the sunset.

Moderate

Level Six

These people presumably like the feeling of power and will work hard to gain it, even though the quest doesn't entirely consume them. They would like to be at the top, want to lead, and are extremely disappointed when they don't succeed. They may accept failure, but only grudgingly. It rankles as punishing feelings such as anger, hostility, and resentment linger. As supervisors they may have their moments when they intimidate and abuse, but it isn't something they crave to do. Their aggressive and intimidating moments emerge in the heat of battle, as they pursue perfection or authority or attempt to win a competition or a challenge. They wonder in calmer moments why they lost it and may feel guilt and remorse.

Level Seven

These people strive even harder to gain power and status. As supervisors they can be intimidating, abusive, and bullying if they think the behavior will serve their purposes. They will feel only small levels of guilt or remorse in the midst or aftermath of such behavior, but not enough to keep them from repeating it. They enjoy the feeling of being in a dominant position, it gives them a high. They would be extremely jealous and envious of peers who gain status over them. They will do practically anything to match or better them. When faced with a challenge or in a competition, they can be excessively aggressive. They may be prime candidates for some form of bigotry. They may need others to look down upon. In situations where they find themselves being perceived as lower in rank, they will feel annoyed, resentful, and humiliated.

Extreme

Level Eight

These people are apparently consumed absolutely with moving upward in their families, careers, and avocations. They need to dominate. They feel a pathological high from the fight and challenge of moving upward as much as being there. They are arrogant, rude, selfish, and egoistic. As supervisors, they can be naturally intimidating and abusive, feeling no guilt or remorse from the experiences, but on the contrary, savoring a mild high. They can be cunning and manipulative against their own peers and supervisors as they try to maneuver themselves upward. They can become insanely jealous, envious, and vengeful if others in their circle gain status over them. If someone on the block gets a better car, they will be out shopping for an even better one that same week if they can afford it, and even when they can't afford it. On the social side, they probably believe they are better than others, even though they may be found on a Sunday morning feeding the poor at a shelter. The experience makes them look humble, but in fact gives them a rewarding feeling of status. They can be messianic in their beliefs and attitudes. They know it all, you don't. As a sailboat captain on a small lake, they would be Napoleonic. In competition, winning is not everything, it is the only thing. Do they have rational aspirations? Perhaps so, but they are apparently overwhelmed by their need to dominate. Nothing that goes wrong is their fault.

Level Nine

These people are everything the eights are, but are also willing to do anything they deem necessary to claw their way to the top in whatever their endeavors. They are willing to sacrifice family, friends, peers, subordinates, whatever it takes to succeed at whatever enterprise or competition in which they are momentarily engaged. They will plagiarize and cheat, if they think they can get away with it, without compunction. As supervisors at work, they are absolutely dominant. They are beyond arrogant and egoistic. Being intimidating, rude, and abusive makes their day, it gives them highs that emanate from their flawed reward or pleasure systems. Their authority or knowledge can't be questioned. At work, they are trusting of only an inner circle that has proved loyal over the years. If they are thwarted in their rise to power at work, they will become bullies to those they are successful in subjugating, even spouses and children. On the social side, they know they are better than anyone else, and in particular members of any other social group. Outside of work they are comfortable only with friends who have reached their station in life and belong to or patronize their elitist clubs or watering holes. They can feel intense bigotry. They are paranoid about potential threats to their position and will take unreasoned actions against others they perceive as being out to get them. They may relish formality and disdain informality. They are frequently unable to tolerate being addressed by their first names by people they perceive as beneath them. They will meet challenges and competition with the equivalent of panzer tanks, if that's what it takes. These people, in other words, are not a lot of fun.

Level Ten

These people have all the characteristics of a level nine, but they are more intense. In psychiatric measurement, they may be described as "severe" extreme power freaks, and in their case it's not redundant. They include the Adolf Hitlers, Pol Pots, Joseph Stalins, and Slobodan Milosevics of the world. Dominating and subjugating others makes their day. They are definitely psychopathic and would kill without compunction if they thought they could get away with it. In the case of the Hitlers, Pol Pots, and such, they were in a position to authorize murder and did so. The level ten in the workplace is restrained from killing by the threat of punishment, the most common form of controlling psychopaths throughout history. Their brain structures are incapable of creating the chemicals that develop feelings of guilt and remorse. Thus, they can be merciless in eliminating whoever or whatever gets in their way. As psychopathic alphas, there is probably a messianic aura that surrounds them, frightening many others while at the same time attracting them and molding them to their wills. They think they know everything, there is nothing you can teach them. They will defend their turf to the death, if necessary, and believe that they are better than anyone in the world. They look down on everyone. Stay out of their way.

At the end of this chapter are the questions for the quiz that might help you determine where you stand on this scale, or you can take the quiz interactively at www.powerfreaks.com. As previously mentioned, the

Web site containing the quiz has been ongoing since 1994. From the beginning, we had software that monitored the number of people who daily visited the site and their country of origin. In 1998, we added additional monitoring software to tabulate the scoring results of the quiz. There was no capture of names, addresses, or any other private data. Thus, of the more than 500,000 people who have taken the quiz since its inception, the scoring results of more than 274,952 of them were monitored as of January 28, 2002.

It should be noted that the results are based on a self-selected group and are not scientifically rigorous. Nonetheless, they provide an indication of trends, one of which is that the power/status scale appears to be structured on a bell curve, as demonstrated below.

Level	Percent	No. of Responses
ONE	2.7	7,529
TWO	2.9	7,905
THREE	9.2	25,160
FOUR	19.5	53,701
FIVE	26.7	73,288
SIX	21.3	58,656
SEVEN	10.6	29,067
EIGHT	3.8	10,523
NINE	1.5	4,057
TEN	1.8	5,076

Interestingly enough, the percentages have changed very little from the initial sampling of approximately 50,000 that was published in *Battling the Inner Dummy*, with results through June 1999.[14] The extreme power freaks of levels nine and ten combined comprise 3.3 percent, which would be approximately equivalent to the number of people in our midst who are psychopathically and narcissistically disordered. If we add the level eights, we are at 7.1 percent. Does that number make sense? I would imagine it would depending on where we work and live.

But why the bell curve? Why are most of us in the apparently normal range? Who can say, but we should probably be happy it isn't worse. Viewing this from the positive side, 93 percent of the people we come across are probably not going to browbeat us, humiliate us, or try to stab us in the back.

As we've observed, high intelligence can help us discipline our instinctual drives, but when the strength of those drives is such that they overtake us, a high level of intelligence then, in an ironic twist, makes us more capable of better rationalizing the more irrational of those drives.

One of the best examples of how high intelligence can go hand-in-hand with psychopathy was exemplified in the 1920s by law student Nathan Leopold, who along with a friend, Richard Loeb, kidnapped and murdered a fourteen-year-old boy in 1923. Leopold's intellectual credentials included being a graduate of the University of Chicago, attending law school, and planning to attend Harvard Law School later that year. He was very accomplished in the study of languages, being fluent in five and familiar with fifteen. Richard Loeb was a star undergraduate student at the University of Chicago.

Both men came from families that were not only traditional and normal, but wealthy. Albert Loeb, Richard's father, was a millionaire executive in charge of Sears, Roebuck's prosperous mail-order business. Nathan Leopold Sr. was a wealthy shipping and manufacturing executive. Both men were highly respected members of the community.

The subsequent investigation and trial of Leopold and Loeb brought out the fact that both men "understood the consequences" of their act, but believed they were intelligent enough to do it and not get caught.[15] They considered it to be a challenge to their intellect.

Like most extreme power freaks with psychopathic traits, they didn't believe that the common-sense rules of life applied to them. If they were alive today, they would presumably deny the extreme power freak categorization and offer reasons for their distorted thinking and actions in perfectly rational and logical terms, such as, "The killing was an intellectual exercise. We wanted to see how smart and clever we could be. It was nothing personal."

Thus, the extreme power freak at work, on the factory floor, or down the hall in an office, because he displays intelligence, or a specific talent or expertise, or loves and cherishes his children, or because of the glibness and charm that he is capable of externalizing, may not feel that he is an extreme power freak at all. He would look at the descriptions of levels eight or nine and say, "This is absolutely not me, I have my moments, but I'm really a nice guy," and he believes it. Nothing that you can tell him rationally can change his mind. One can be an extreme power freak, in other words, and not know it because the real nature of our own personalities and temperaments can be apparently buried behind a wall of delusive and distorted outlooks.

THE DELUSIVE OUTLOOKS OF AN EXTREME POWER FREAK

The following distorted and delusive outlooks are my own interpolations of the characteristics that define psychopathy or antisocial personality disorder; sadistic, narcissistic, and paranoid personality disorders; as well as status obsession. We might all agree with three or four of the statements, but if you find yourself agreeing with more than five, then please . . . stay away from me.

- Nobody can do the job better than me. Without me, this place would fall apart.
- I know I am better than anyone else. That's a fact.
- I could do anything in the world as well as anyone if I just had the time and put my mind to it. Golf, mathematics, the arts? Just give me time and practice and I'll be among the best.
- If you don't do the job exactly as I say you should, you will get it wrong, I can guarantee you.
- I may intimidate and abuse and yes, even bully others, but it is usually for their own good, particularly if they've made a mistake or are acting in ways that are contrary to what I consider proper behavior. Not only that, being intimidating and abusive to people can give them the discipline that they lack.

❈ Under my authority, the ends justify the means, whatever they are. If that requires back-biting and hurting people in the process, so be it. I'll do whatever it takes under whatever circumstances.

❈ You need to be tough and hardened in today's world. Guilt and remorse are for softies.

❈ I can truly say that the mistakes made under my watch have been because of the incompetency of others. They either didn't measure up to the job or they didn't do as I asked. My record where I am involved in a situation is close to perfect, if not absolutely perfect.

❈ Why should I feel sorry for anybody? If I made it in this world, anybody can. If they are down and out and need some help, I say tough luck.

❈ And by the way, that includes firing people. People are fired because they deserve it. When I fire people it doesn't bother me at all. As a matter of fact I feel good about it because through the dismissal I am improving the company.

❈ I don't need to be loved by anybody. I'm my own person. And it doesn't bother me that I find it difficult to feel love for others. That romantic stuff belongs in the movies, not in the real world, where believe me, it's dog-eat-dog.

❈ I expect others to admire everything I do. If they don't admire me, I question their intelligence and judgment.

❈ I expect others to be compliant to me. I know better, after all. If I offer a direction, if I give orders, I expect them to be followed and not questioned. If you question me, that means you have no respect for my position, my knowledge.

❈ I may be haughty, cocky, and arrogant, but in my position I deserve to be. That's part of the reward of being successful, isn't it? I get a kick out of looking down on and ignoring people I perceive as beneath me. Give them the time of day, or an autograph? Forget it. They'll only go peddle it and make money off of it that should be mine.

❈ I know what I believe is true. I feel it in my head, in my gut, in my very soul. If others don't believe as I do, they are simply wrong.

❈ Most classes of people are beneath me. I can just feel that. I may not hate them, but I don't want to be around them.

❀ I am quite willing to help the poor and the homeless, but I want credit for it. Why else should I be helping these lazy people?

❀ Naturally I flirt with people of the opposite sex whom I find attractive. When they're married it's even better.

❀ I dislike authority figures. Who knows better than me what is best for me?

❀ Nothing anybody else does is of real interest to me. As a matter of fact, when they start telling me about their exploits, I find I get bored in a real hurry.

❀ "Why, everywhere we go, do you always like to be the center of attention"? I was asked. That's not it at all, I just like to be around interesting people. Most people bore me. It's true I may tend to monopolize conversations, but that's how I keep from being bored.

❀ Winning is definitely not everything, it is the only thing. And sometimes it's necessary to cut a few edges in the process. "You mean like lying, hurting and cheating?" I was asked. People don't understand that stupid rules don't apply to me. All the great leaders in the world felt they were exempt and I am no exception.

❀ I don't need to be grateful to anyone. Whatever they did for me I deserve. They are lucky I gave them the chance to help me.

❀ I like a lot of tattoos, I like a lot of rings on my body, I like to be seen out with only the right people. I like to dress exactly like my peers, even though their pants are torn. These things make me feel good. What is it your business?

❀ I like the right brand of car, the right brand of clothing, the right sunglasses, the right architects and interior designers, I like the best of everything and I shun anything else. And I shun people who don't think the way I do. What's wrong with that?

❀ All that really matters is getting what I want or what I think is right. Who might get hurt in the process is just another part of life.

❀ Whatever I have or possess, I deserve better, I want more. Nothing is ever enough. You may not like that attitude, but unless you think that way you'll never get ahead.

❀ Some nights when I can't get to sleep I wonder why I am not better recognized for the greatness I bring to everything I do.

🕸 Hey, this is my sailboat. And when you're crewing on my boat or doing anything else, whenever I'm in charge of things, you follow orders or else you're history.

🕸 Am I ever jealous or envious of others? Of course I am. If you don't feel jealousy and envy, you are not properly motivated to get ahead. The worst news I can get is that somebody I know did something noteworthy. Even worse news is when I learn they did something better than I did. It ruins my day.

🕸 You really can't trust anybody. Everybody is after something they can get out of you, including your job. My secret is to let everyone know, even my closest subordinates, that I am suspicious of them, and to keep as much important information as I can to myself.

🕸 Confide in people? Whatever I confide is merely to set them up for the result I am trying to achieve. Confiding your personal feelings in anyone is setting yourself up for an eventual fall.

🕸 Am I vengeful, do I bear grudges? Of course I do. Do they go on forever? Maybe not forever, but for a long time. People have to know there is a price to pay for incompetence or disloyalty, I don't care how minor the circumstance.

This list of distorted and delusive outlooks can go on and on. The more you recognize some of your own outlooks among the listings, the more difficult it will be, as a general rule, for you to be compliant or submissive to bosses or other authority figures in your life whom you perceive as extreme power freaks. If you must deal with these extreme power freaks and you don't have "recognized competence," as described in the next chapter, compliance may need to be one of a number of strategies you'll have to practice.

🕸 🕸 🕸

If you haven't recognized your power ranking level and are curious, the quiz questions are below.

THE POWER RANKING QUIZ

Instructions: Answer each question by selecting a number. Select a 10 if the question asks you about an urge you feel is tremendously strong; a 1 if you don't feel it exists at all; a 5 if you feel you're about in the middle, or the appropriate numbers in between. Then add up all the numbers and divide by 12, and that's the approximate intensity of your power level. See pages 159–65 in this chapter for a description of your level. The results will usually give you a rough indication of where you stand on this scale. If you think your results are inaccurate, try again in two to three weeks. If you believe your score is too high, visualize how it might portray your behavior in the power freak mode . . . in a challenged or competitive situation, for example. Remember that no one will see your answers, particularly if you write them on a separate sheet of paper. So you can be totally honest, checking your instinctual thoughts and urges as you ponder. If you would like to take this quiz interactively, log onto www.powerfreaks.com and click on limbic quizzes, then the power quiz. When you are finished with the interactive quiz, click the "Submit" button at the bottom of the screen and a description of your ranking will automatically pop up.

1. How envious do you feel when a neighbor or friend gets a big promotion and begins to earn more money than you? _____

2. How angry do you get when someone at work gives you a direct order to do a menial chore? _____

3. How willing would you be to destroy a friendship if it meant getting a promotion? _____

4. How strong is your dislike of at least one other ethnic group? _____

5. How much do you like to be in the limelight? _____

6. How angry do you get when driving a car and another car cuts in front of you? _____

7. How strong is your urge to win when you are
   in a competitive activity? _____

8. How resentful would you get if one of your equals
   at work was promoted over you? _____

9. How difficult is it for you to trust others? _____

10. How resentful do you feel when you are ignored when a
    decision is being made that you think requires your input? _____

11. How easy is it for you to stare strangers in the eye? _____

12. How willing would you be to physically harm people if it
    meant you could reach a higher station in life and get away
    with it? _____

Total your numbered responses: _____

Divide by 12
Your Power Ranking _____

Now that we have a good idea of the thinking and behavior of an extreme power freak, we'll be covering, in the next three chapters, the basic strategies for dealing with them.

CHAPTER 11

Dealing with the
Extreme Power Freak Boss

Monkeys living in social groups form dominance hierarchies; that is an animal can outrank others by displacing, threatening, or attacking them without reciprocal action and claim priority in competition for access to food, sexual objects, and affinitive relationships.[1]

While the strategies suggested in this chapter are focused on the extreme power freak boss, many of them can be adapted to use against any authority figure in your life. It is the extreme power freak boss, however, who is probably the most difficult person we need to deal with. You may have a power freak mother, father, or sibling, but as described in chapter 13, as an adult, you are free to avoid them entirely or limit contact with them to reduce the pain and degradation. You may have a power freak peer—a colleague or co-worker on an equal level with you—but while she may cause you great discomfort, she may not be any immediate threat to your livelihood.

An extreme power freak boss is in a unique position because he has say over your job, your livelihood; a boss can hire and fire. Unless you can move to another position, you may be the target of daily degradation. When you are an adult, a boss can have the same degrading, stressful impact on you that an abusive and/or alcoholic parent might have had when you were a child. If you have a family to support, the stress is greater, because you know you can never just walk away. And so until this extreme power freak boss is terminated or transferred, or you find another job, you need to find ways to deal with him or her that create the least amount of discomfort. Some of us can be much better at this than others.

Those of us who have been in the military or have lived in authoritarian environments have a pretty good idea of how well we can stand up to an extreme power freak authority. If we were in the military, during basic training we had a drill sergeant stand directly in front of us on a daily basis, screaming epithets, telling us how dumb and low we were. Many of us were able to take it, understanding that we were being trained for blind obedience and that we were acting a role. Others high on the power scale themselves, who had great difficulty and struck back, bore the brunt of the unfortunate results.

It would appear that one of the major personality attributes we may need in our ability to deal with an extreme power freak boss—which we'll now simply call "power freak boss"—is our capacity for role playing in our everyday lives. Some of us appear to have a greater capacity for role playing, depending on whom we're with, as noted earlier. We can act one way with our mothers, another way with our closest group of friends, another with our spouse, and still another with our superior at work. Some of the best salespersons utilize role playing as an integral part of their job. If one customer is stiff and arrogant, the salesperson is all business from the first moment. If another customer is warm and friendly, the first moments are spent talking about family and friends. If another customer is a jokester, the first moments are spent sharing the latest jokes.

Franklin Delano Roosevelt, thirty-second president of the United States, was known as a consummate role player who used this aspect of his personality to help sell his ideas and points of view. Historian Kenneth S. Davis describes how FDR would use "walls of words" to elicit the information he needed and the personal responses he desired:

> Consistent with this was the endlessly repeated observation . . . that Roosevelt was the "consummate actor." What could this mean save that he was a master of make-believe, a role-player, capable of becoming convincingly whatever "character" it suited his purpose or need to become in the perception of those who saw him and heard him?[2]

Abraham Lincoln was also known for his role playing, a technique he honed from years as a lawyer spent in trial courts. If two of the greatest presidents of the United States could use role playing to good measure without being called "phonies," then how wrong might it be for the rest of us, if we need to survive a power freak boss, who is either pathologically disordered or status-obsessed, or both?

On the other hand some of us don't need to role play at all. One of the best salespersons I ever knew, "Ronald," years ago worked for a company we represented that sold both residential and commercial groundwater pumps. Ronald, unlike Presidents Lincoln and Roosevelt, never varied his personality, no matter whom he conversed with, whether it was the president of his company, his fellow salesmen, his closest group of friends, his largest customer, a municipal water utility, or his smallest customer, a rural pump dealer who served mostly farmers. Ronald had a quiet, sincere, patient demeanor. No matter whom he was dealing with, he would deliver the facts, answer questions, and leave. The president of the company would call him in from time to time to get a feel of what was happening in the field and the agenda would be the same. Ronald would tell his story, answer questions, and get out. His immediate boss, the vice president of sales, was high on the power scale, trusted no one, and was known to lash out at members of his sales force. Ronald's meetings with this man were no different than they were with anyone else. He would enter the office, give his report, and answer questions. If the vice president exploded, Ronald would just sit there patiently and wait for it to end, looking and acting unflustered the whole time. He would then leave gracefully.

It turned out that Ronald was recognized as the most competent member of this company's large sales force in that he knew the product line and its applications inside and out. He worked hard covering his territory and was immediately responsive to phone calls from his varied roster of customers when they had problems or needed information. From the most complicated and technical pump for a water utility to the smallest farmhouse pump, Ronald knew which product was appropriate for each application, and what to do if a problem arose. He was so good at what he did that people didn't care what his personality was like and so he didn't have to vary it, even for his immediate superior who was at least a level seven on the power scale.

Ronald had a key element for dealing with a power freak, which is "recognized competence."

RECOGNIZED COMPETENCE

Recognized competence appears to trump most personality conflicts in the workplace, or most anyplace, for that matter. Al Dunlap of Scott Paper and Sunbeam might have been the epitome of an extreme power freak when he fired thousands of employees and gloated about it in public interviews; he might have been hostile and brutal with managers on his staff; but when his actions raised the stock price of first Scott and later Sunbeam, he was lauded as a genius. It was only later when allegations were raised that he manipulated sales figures to enhance earnings and was forced out as CEO that he was generally derided.

On the other hand, Dunlap, like other executives I've known, was probably not intimidating at all with someone on his staff whose competence he recognized was absolutely vital. One president of a corporate division I worked with, "Leonard Hull," was devastating to most members of his support staff, except for one person, who was employed in his information technologies department, and always made himself available to help Hull with his computer problems, both at the office and at home. "I can't get along without Albert," Hull would laughingly brag as he tried to show his human side. "When something happens with my computer that I can't figure out . . . and I don't take but a minute to even try, Albert saves the day."

Hull "recognized" Albert's competence and so Albert became invaluable to him. On the other hand, Hull had a vice president of sales, "Ed Gregory," who was one of the most competent sales executives I've known. However, Hull had been recruited as president from another company and had inherited Gregory when he came in. Because Gregory was not submissive in the least to Hull, and simply wanted to be left alone to do his job, Hull viewed Gregory as a member of the old regime and a threat. He became intent on getting rid of Gregory, even though he was recognized as the best there was in that industry.

The first thing that Hull did was insist that Gregory take him on the road to meetings of the firm's largest customers so that he could establish his own relationship with them. As soon as he felt satisfied that he had established these relationships, he began to make Gregory's life miserable, making cutting remarks about him in staff meetings, realigning the organization so that managers who previously reported to Gregory would now report directly to him, making irrational deals with customers without Gregory's knowledge, and then exploding at him when Gregory objected.

Hull did not "recognize" Gregory's competence, which went far beyond the personal relationships that Gregory had built up with the firm's customers over a period of many years. Gregory was expert at fore-casting sales and at digging out new product opportunities, then guiding them to fruition in conjunction with his engineering and manufacturing peers. He was expert in launching these new products into the market, understood how to spend the company's marketing and sales budget effi-ciently, and was superb in motivating his field sales personnel. Hull, how-ever, in a delusion common to power freak bosses, believed he could do everything that Gregory could do and better, and so he made Gregory's life miserable enough so that he would leave the company, which he did. Hull then brought in a vice president of sales who had worked for him at a previous company in another industry and with whom he felt comfort-able. The company, however, suffered for more than a year as the new man tried to learn the industry and made a number of errors in judgment.

The point is that just because you may be extremely competent and rec-ognized as such by others, it is not always enough to protect you from the wrath of a status-possessed and delusional superior who *doesn't* recognize that competence. Nonetheless, the higher the level of your core competency, the better your chances are of dealing and surviving with a power freak boss, whose own agenda supercedes that of the company that pays him. There is the chance that at some point your competency will be recognized. Compe-tency is a strong factor, but *recognition* of that competency is the key.

A university fundraiser I know told me of an experience she had with a power freak boss in the earliest days of her career.

"This woman was the ultimate power freak. She didn't know how to guide anyone. She would scream her way through the day, yet with potential donors, she could be as sweet as Little Orphan Annie.

"I was one of her victims until she learned that I was really good at raising money, after which she did make an effort to tolerate me."

And so competency may be recognized along the way. But even when recognized, that competency must be perceived by the power freak boss as one that is growing.

In this sense, it is axiomatic in the business world that to survive and advance, one's core competency must be consistently widened and improved. You may be the only one in your office who knows how to work an outdated copier, or knows where everything is in the storage room, or understands the total bidding system of the purchasing department or the nuances of the accounting system. But if you hold that information close to your vest in an effort to protect your position in the company, it will never be enough for a new power freak boss who is brought in as your superior and is looking to become a hero by whatever means, including eliminating or consolidating your job assuming that your competency can be quickly learned by others.

The best managers I've known are people who continue to be unsure about their own knowledge, whatever station they have reached, and who reach out for new information and challenges related to their competencies in a myriad of ways that will allow them to do their jobs better. In other words, they are never satisfied with their existing competency, but constantly strive to improve it.

However, that still might not be enough to survive under a power freak boss.

COMPLIANCE

A number of excellent books have been written about getting along with difficult people, including bosses, peers, subordinates, even members of one's own family. In most of these books, there are interesting techniques described for coping with power-driven superiors. In the *Complete Idiot's Guide for Getting Along with Difficult People*, one of the best books I read on the subject, written by Brandon Toropov, an expert on business and communication techniques, the following is observed: "People who take things personally tend not to do well with very difficult bosses. Suffice to say that stress management is an extremely important part of working with bosses in this category."[3]

Toropov then goes on to describe methods for reducing stress levels instantly, including watching your breathing, drinking water, doing word tricks in your mind, recounting a scene from an old movie, and balancing a quarter on your finger to help divert and still your mind. I tried the quarter trick when someone really angered me recently and I ended up throwing the quarter against a wall. That seemed to help. It would appear that among all the books that have been written describing stress management techniques, one has to work hard to find techniques that can successfully calm our individual temperaments.

The point, however, is that some of us are better at being compliant or submissive than others.

Ronald, the pump salesman, could take his boss's ranting and raving with complete equanimity. He knew his boss was in charge and if he wanted to explode, Ronald's outlook was "be my guest." Others might become extremely stressed under the same pressure. Still others might become angry, bitter, resentful, and vindictive to the point that they would want to confront the boss and yell back. Once that happens with a prototypical power freak boss, it is usually all over. It will only be a matter of time until the boss somehow nudges them out of their position.

In a recent article in _Fortune_ magazine, Joe Torre, manager of the New York Yankees baseball team, describes how he gets the most out of his players while getting along with the owner of the team, George Steinbrenner, who is well up there on the power scale. Steinbrenner has fired twenty-one managers in the twenty-four years he has owned the ball club, and was quoted as follows: "Joe doesn't have to keep being reminded that there is a boss. And I don't have to keep reminding him that I am the boss, see?" The article also reported:

> Torre isn't a stranger to tough bosses . . . which has helped him appreciate Steinbrenner's less offensive qualities, notably his total commitment to winning. "You can't pick and choose the part of him you want to keep and the part you don't want to keep," says Torre. "He's a package and you gotta accept the whole package."[4]

Torre accepted Steinbrenner, but how effective would the rest of us be at doing this? Obviously, there were many managers prior to Torre who knew their business, but didn't know how to handle Steinbrenner, with perhaps their own power freakishness being their greatest barriers.

In the world of higher animals, as noted earlier, rank is achieved through physicality, ranging from eye stares to pitched battles. In the end, the loser via the crayfish effect automatically becomes submissive to the winner. Among chimpanzees whose limbic brain structure we share, and whose striving for domination is totally exposed, submissiveness is manifested through what primatologists have labeled as "status rituals." A "pant-grunt" is one such ritual, the lower ranked chimpanzee using soft, soothing sounds that recognize the status of the chimp of the higher rank. Another ritual involves the lower ranked chimp grooming the higher ranked and stopping occasionally to clap hands or feet as if in applause of the higher status.[5]

In the world of humans, as mentioned before, physical prowess doesn't count for very much. Nerds who look like they can get blown over in a strong wind can become CEOs simply through their intellectual capacities. Those nerds, however, can still become arrogant, display psychopathic and other pathological traits, and demand submissiveness just as readily as the physically empowered alpha male did when we lived as primitives on the savannas. In today's world that alpha male with natural traits of arrogance and empowerment may have to be submissive to the nerd, and he probably has frequent fantasies of punching the nerd in the nose. In other words, alpha males—as well as alpha females—find the act of being submissive extremely difficult. On the other hand, those lower on the power scale, who work to avoid power and responsibility, obviously have less of a problem in being submissive to a power freak boss.

Almost all of the experts who deal with the problems of dealing with "difficult people" (there are at least fifteen books in print with that phrase in the title), refer to the fact that being submissive involves developing "coping behaviors," tricks of the mind, in effect, that allow the more power-driven of us to be submissive with some degree of comfort.

In the book *The Control Freak: Coping with Those Around You, Taming the One Within*, Les Parrott, author and professor of psychology at Seattle Pacific University, suggests "Try on Your Manager's Shoes": "The first step in getting along with any Control Freak, even your boss, is to see the world from his or her perspective. The more empathy you have for the person who irritates you the most, the less likely that person is to disturb you."[6]

Is it possible to be empathetic with a power freak boss? Perhaps so.

In *Coping with Difficult People*, Robert Bramson, an authority on the prevention and management of difficult and nonproductive behavior, gets more to the core of the challenge with a coping behavior he says may have a sizeable psychological cost:

> The cost is that you have to swallow your pride and purposefully act deferentially to these "superior" beings, even when they are your organizational equals or subordinates. You will listen attentively, blink your eyes, and, with careful diligence, dance to their tunes. In effect, you will be saying to them, "All right, you great big wonderful, all-knowing fountains of wisdom, give me advice, lay out the plans, tell me what you're going to do and I'll help you do it." By taking this subordinate stance, your interactions should become reasonably free from static and generally more comfortable. . . . More to the point, if you can carry it off, you should feel less tension and anger.[7]

Of course, some people find this coping behavior very difficult to adopt. A good friend of mine, Larry Dore, who made a career in sales and marketing, was excellent with customers, doing whatever was necessary, within reason, to win their business. But he could never be submissive to his bosses, including stints as the head of sales and marketing for divisions of two large, publicly held companies, although he was always respectful. I asked him why he could be so flexible and submissive, when necessary, with the customers of the companies for whom he worked, but couldn't be submissive when he had superiors with whom he clashed, and it would have been to his advantage.

"I think it was because I grew up in a tough, Irish Catholic neighborhood and it was a mark of weakness to suck up to whoever your boss was. . . . Most of us had part-time jobs after school . . . and that behavior has just stuck with me."

"But yet I've seen you submissive with customers."

"That's different," he said. "It was okay in the neighborhood to be submissive with customers because that was understood as something that was necessary."

Is it possible for those of us like Larry who have trouble exhibiting submissive behavior to think of ourselves in the role of "selling ourselves" to our power freak bosses? Could we even imagine ourselves going as far as using the "mirror and matching" technique used in the world of salesmanship, considering it a test of our ability to role play, remembering that two of our greatest presidents, Abraham Lincoln and Franklin Roosevelt, did it, and were not exactly known as suck-ups? In his book *Advanced Selling Strategies*, sales expert Brian Tracy described the technique as follows:

> In mirror and matching, you assume the same bodily posture as your customer, with a five-second *delay* after your customer moves. For example, if you were sitting at a conference table and your customer relaxed and leaned back to ponder what you had just said, you would wait about five seconds and then you would gradually lean back and match the same posture, as though the customer were looking in a mirror. If the customer straightened up and leaned forward, you would wait about five seconds and then gradually straighten up and lean forward as well. . . . After you have followed your customer several times, you can test whether or not you are fully attuned to your customer by leaning forward in the conversation. After a few seconds, if you have established a high-enough level of rapport, your customer will lean forward to synchronize his body language with yours. At that point, you can gently lead your customer, as you would lead a partner in a dance, into the postures of careful listening, paying close attention and readiness to take action.[8]

I'm not sure I could go this far. Maybe if the kids were starving. And yet a power freak would love to have his or her subordinates exhibit this form of compliant behavior, they would love for you to be constantly trying to sell yourself to them in a human versus chimp pattern of panting-grunting and grooming.

If your competence is recognized and you are compliant to a power freak boss, that may be all it takes. If not, there is still another element you can use.

TRUST

Recall from chapter 5 that extreme power freaks with psychopathic traits almost always have high levels of paranoia. These paranoid traits include the following:

- ❀ Expectation of being exploited or harmed by others
- ❀ Questioning the loyalty or trustworthiness of friends or associates
- ❀ Reading hidden demeaning or threatening meanings into benign remarks
- ❀ Reluctance to confide in others, fearing the information will be used against them

In the section of his book titled *Why Trust Is Everything*, Brandon Toropov says, "When they [tough bosses] encounter a subordinate who can be counted on to act with discretion, tact and loyalty, they may change their fundamental behavior patterns *with the person whom they trust* [his italics] and no one else."[9]

Tough bosses, he says, look for people who will work with them and not against them. This is quite true. It is extremely difficult to gain the trust of anyone with a high level of paranoia and particularly a power freak boss who feels that those whom he perceives as against him are secretly plotting his demise. This is why most power freak bosses have an inner circle usually composed of less than a handful of people that he can trust implicitly. It takes time to gain this kind of trust and you may never achieve it, but like recognized competence, it can trump most other perceived shortcomings.

The following are some of Toporov's excellent suggestions for gaining trust over time. I have added my own comments following some of his points:

1. Never tell tales out of school.

This is an extremely important suggestion. If the power freak boss learns even once that you have broken a confidence, that you have told others what the boss confided in you, it is all over in terms of ever gaining his or her trust. One misstep can blow the entire program. Learn to keep your mouth shut, if you don't already know how to do it.

2. Know what the boss's guiding objective is and talk about it as often as you can.

If your boss is under pressure from the head office to get sales up by 15% this quarter, you should be interested in and willing to get sales up by 15% this quarter.

3. Do what you say you'll do no matter what.

If you promise the boss the report will be on his or her desk by Monday morning at 8:00, find a way to get it onto that desk by Monday morning at 8:00. Another extremely important suggestion. Keep your word, keep your commitments, no matter what.

4. Never make excuses . . . don't make a long-winded song of woe.

Be prepared to take the heat when you make a mistake. Stand up and take the heat as if a drill sergeant was screaming epithets at you and then move on. Don't take it personally, it is part of the show. Moreover, few effective superiors, power freaks or not, like to be around whiners and complainers. When you get an assignment, ask questions if necessary, but your response at the end should reflect "yes, sir," "can do," "no problem," "consider it done."

5. Assume personal responsibility when you do, in fact, screw up.

They absolutely *love* this. If you can avoid blaming others do so. It is always best to take the responsibility, but never make it appear as if you are covering up for others. Don't come off as a martyr in other words. Just take the heat, apologize, and move on.

6. When in doubt, quote them appreciatively.

As we've mentioned, an extreme power freak may have great intelligence, which bears little on the distorted views of his instinctual-emotional mind. Along the way, therefore, your boss might have said some insightful things. When you can do so prudently, quote them back when he is present. You can always use mouthwash later.[10]

In their book *Neanderthals at Work*, Albert J. Bernstein, a clinical psychologist, and writer Sydney Craft Rozen, also have excellent suggestions for gaining the trust of a difficult boss, some of which reinforce Toporov's. I have collated them as follows from different pages of the book and added my own comments.

1. Follow the rules. Know what you're supposed to be doing and see that it's done.

In short, don't be an embarrassment to your boss. Watch your personal days and vacation days. Don't take vacations during periods when it is important that you are in the office. Don't stretch your expense accounts; you don't want to be questioned.

2. Recognize your boss's limitations.

Do everything you can to recognize and then compensate for your boss's limitations. Do it quietly and unobtrusively. Never call your boss's attention to what you did to cover up one of his or her oversights. He or she will eventually learn what you are doing and the information coming to him in this way will be much more valuable in earning his or her trust.

3. Allow your boss to criticize you without going off the deep end. Accept criticism quietly and with dignity.

Tough to do for most of us. We don't like to be criticized by anyone. It violates our status program, engages our crayfish effect, and spurs us to fight. If you've made a costly mistake, most power freak bosses will lose their temper. While they are doing so, acknowledge the mistake ("I know, I know I did that") and look remorseful. If you are being criticized over a difference of opinion and you think you are right and your boss is wrong, present your point of view succinctly and without emotion. If your boss insists that you do it his way, then simply say something like, "Well, I thought you'd like to hear my point of view, but don't worry, I'm going to knock myself out to do it the way you want it to be done." And then do it that way, throttling any feelings of anger or vindictiveness. He or she may be right. If it doesn't work, don't remind the boss that it was his or her idea. Simply say something like, "Maybe we did something wrong in the execution. Maybe we ought to try it again with this adjustment," and then make a suggestion. Let your boss take it from there. Work hard to divert the blame from him or her. Did you think life was easy? Remember, you're working for someone who is probably psychopathic. Accept the responsibility for any misconceived assignment that came from your boss if it went through your hands. Act the role of whipping boy or girl. If you're a masochist at heart, you might come to enjoy this.

4. Don't expect your boss to follow your standards of fairness. If you do, you're apt to be disappointed.

This really falls under understanding your boss's limitations. Very little is really fair in the business world, where the ultimate objective is to make a profit on investment capital and where nurturance isn't a priority. One of the strategies frequently used to meet that objective, however, is to keep employees happy and secure under the theory that they will work harder. But not every employer uses this strategy; many utilize fear and intimidation instead. The boss is apt to get away with this more easily during tight economic times when employee replacements come cheap. The point is that what your boss thinks is fair and just within the corporate culture may be miles removed from your own beliefs. And if you stand in judgment of your boss's concepts he will eventually come to know it and his trust level in you will be diminished. He is looking for total acceptance and you need to be willing to give it. Remember that many people have it a whole lot worse than you. You're not homeless, for example. Does that work?

5. Develop your own sources of information.

Peruse the trade magazines, read appropriate books, watch business television shows, and make notes of things that would be of interest to your boss. Pass them along to him with a handwritten cover note . . . "For your info," for example. But in addition to outside industry information, you need to keep your eyes and ears open about what's going on within the company. This doesn't mean that you need to become a gossip and spellbind the boss with intriguing tales of who is having an affair with whom, or who is having trouble at home, or who is having trouble doing his or her job. It is, instead, to develop important nuggets of information on an *infrequent* basis that you know will be important to the boss. For example, if an important project is running behind schedule and you learn the cause, you might tell your boss about it in a way that doesn't castigate anyone. Something like, "I heard through the grapevine that engineering is struggling with the wiring on the new product design. I don't know if it's true or not, or if it's important to the project at this point, but you might want to look into it."

6. Don't ever go over your boss's head. . . . This is as risky as trying to corner a wounded wolverine.

This is a big one. You may be in a situation where you see your boss is in trouble and it is due to his or her own incompetence. Or he or she may be blaming you incessantly for things that are not your fault and you are on the brink. You feel you can't take it anymore. You know your boss's boss. You are tempted to walk in there and tell him or her the story. *Don't do it.* If you do it one time, and your boss finds out, the element of trust between you will be lost forever. Beginning on page 203 there is a description of what you might do when confronting your boss when you are absolutely at your wit's end. If you do that and the problem continues to the point that the stress is affecting your health, then, you might as a last resort speak to your boss's boss. But before that, start drafting your resume.

7. Find techniques that allow you to transcend your temper. Your best strategy is to listen to what the boss has to say, ask what he or she wants you to do, and get out.

Losing your temper with your boss and coming out a winner has terrible odds. The chances are about one in fifty that your boss will come out with newfound respect for you. "Look at Peters, there, he is finally standing up for himself. Now I can really work with him." Dream on. How far you can go with a power freak boss in standing up to him is a judgment call that is crucial. In the *Fortune* article about Joe Torre, Jerry Useem writes, "during one of their occasional shouting matches—this one over Torre's contract extension in 1998—Torre stopped midway to ask, 'We're not mad at each other, right?' Steinbrenner responded, 'No, we're not.'" Torre, described by Useem as a "master business manager psychologist," knew exactly how far he could go . . . and when he was unsure, he stopped, broke in with a droll question, and moved on to assure that the discussion was not personal. He could get away with this, but maybe you can't, depending on the nature of your personality. The best policy in any hot confrontation with your boss is to stifle your anger, leave at the end of the meeting with as much grace and dignity as you can muster, then go home and destroy your dining room table with a bat. The cost to you in the long run will be far less.

8. Always know what's going on in your department. Be ready at all times to cite facts and figures.

You don't need to work for a power freak to understand this advice. I have known department managers, for example, who feel they are simply "orchestra leaders." They delegate almost all of their responsibilities and keep their desks absolutely clean, coming in every day to get involved only in those problems that may require their attention. The problem with this type of behavior is that when a serious mistake is made by one of their subordinates they are taken completely by surprise and it may be too late to correct the situation. Then, if they have a power freak boss and need to tell her about the problem, they will be torn apart not only because of the mistake itself, but for their ineptitude in running their departments. Whatever trust level you have established with your boss will then be diminished. From a single incident, the paranoia of this boss will drive her to continually question, in her mind, whether you know how to handle your job. Whether through staff meetings or one-on-one meetings, it is essential to be kept abreast of what the workload is in your department, its nature, and potential problems.

9. Warn your family that your boss may demand extra work, long hours. . . . Make sure your family recognizes that you'd rather be with them than toiling for the ogre.

Great advice, if it works. My two divorces were caused primarily by being away from home, either because of out-of-town travel or nights at work. I read somewhere that it is possible to have more fear of an irate wife than a dominating boss. I'll attest to that. There are many managers today who are under stress at work because of the demands of a power freak boss who wants the assignments done right now, no questions asked. Then they come under even greater stress when they go home at night because their spouses, who feel *their* status is being violated and become embattled—the crayfish effect . . . it follows us everywhere—think that they are being abandoned for love of the work. The point is, if you need to work for a living, if you haven't significant job choices, and it is your lot to work for a power freak, then you need to choose the work, however demanding it may be at the moment. Power freak bosses do not like to hear excuses like the kids' recitals, doctor appointments, and such. They want you to sacrifice all for them and you'd better do it or start working on your resume. For better answers to the problem of how to handle spouses who are unsympathetic to the demands of your work, read some good books on relationships. With my divorce record, I am obviously not in a position to give this kind of advice.

10. Keep records of what your boss is asking you to do.
Log conversations and directives and send the latter for initialing.

You may do this, but it's really not the way to build trust. Further, when your power freak boss calls you on the carpet, pulling out papers with his initials is not going to help the situation. He will say something like, "Yes, I might have initialed that, but you didn't explain it to me properly." Remember, a power freak will practically never accept responsibility for mistakes. Count on the fact that he will always blame others and if you are involved with the mistake, it will be you he blames. As previously described, you need to take the heat, perhaps as Brandon Toporov suggests trying to recall a scene from an old movie, as the tirade continues. The better idea when you have a memo that you sent to your boss summarizing the nature of his directive and with which he didn't disagree at the time, is to bring it in and say something like, "I must have misunderstood your instructions right from the beginning. Here's the memo I wrote and obviously I was wrong with understanding these two points. So here's what I'd like to do to set things right." To maintain your level of trust with a power freak boss, this is the kind of response he wants, regardless of the facts. Remember that he is delusive to begin with and you are simply playing the game, acting out a role. When he is terminated or leaves and you are given a normal boss, you can resume your normal personality, if you can remember what it was.[11]

There is one other key element for dealing with a power freak boss that has to do with trust, but is important enough to require focused attention, and that is communication and advice seeking.

COMMUNICATION AND ADVICE SEEKING

In the *Fortune* article about Joe Torre, the statement was made that "Where most saw a bully [George Steinbrenner] Torre simply saw a man in need of reassurance, which he deftly set about providing."

Most power freak bosses are willing to delegate responsibilities to others as necessary, but the very fact of doing so may violate their status program. As the power freak boss is watching his or her subordinates in action, he or she is probably thinking, "I am the best, I am in charge, if I had the time, I should really be doing those jobs, if they are to be done right." As one result, when a subordinate succeeds in doing an excellent job on a project, he or she will probably not get any credit from the power freak boss, who is being emotionally punished by an instinctual-emotional mind that is now thinking, "I could have done better, I should have gotten the recognition, I don't like anybody else getting recognition, I am going to fix that sonofabitch."

The subordinate who did the great job ends up being puzzled. "Why does the boss appear mad at me? He thanked me through gritted teeth, for God's sake. I knocked myself out to make sure that job was done right. What went wrong?"

Remember, as we've observed, a power freak's thinking can be distorted and delusive. You are not dealing with rationality.

How many times have we seen a movie or play when a son or daughter of an extreme power freak after a great success appears uncertain on how to approach the parent with the good news? Like the power freak boss, this parent is actually jealous of his offspring, he wants the recognition, he wants the power and status that accompanies a success, he wants to feel the high their pleasure system gives them after such a success. Deep down, these parents may feel an attachment to their offspring. They may actually weep for a brief time if an offspring meets with an untimely death, but in the day-to-day world the attachment program, apparently the weakest of the instinctual-emotional drives, is swept away within the minds of these extreme power freak parents by the force of their need for uncontested status and power.

So how do we deal with this characteristic of a power freak boss?

The objective needs to be that when you come in and tell the boss that you have had a great success, you should say, "*we* have had the suc-cess," and really mean it. One of the rules of thumb in dealing with a power freak, described in a little more detail later in this chapter, is that you can never take the sole credit for any success . . . and if possible, attribute any idea that worked to the influence of the boss. "By God, Mr. Matson, that idea you gave me about reconfiguring the proposal to the Apex account really worked." When it's we, instead of I, the resulting reaction of the power freak boss can be totally different.

"So it worked, James," he might say happily, no artificial pleasure forced through gritted teeth. "That is wonderful. You know this problem reminded me right from the beginning about something we did for the Biggs & Crowley account back in the 1980s, and it worked then. Did I tell you that story?"

"No, Mr. Matson," you reply with great aplomb, practicing the con-cept of role playing and crossing your fingers behind your back.

"Have you got a moment?"

"Oh, yes, sir." And then you sit back as Matson recounts the story you have heard dozens of times in detail, awash in the rewarding emo-tions he is feeling from this joint success, as you try to remember some scenes from an old movie so you won't appear bored. Method acting in the office, we might call this . . . akin to the young actor purportedly asking the great Broadway director George Abbott, "what is my motiva-tion?" and he answers, "your paycheck." You have to find your own moti-vation, in other words, as Matson drones on.

Underlying this approach is an overall strategy of communication that you need to establish with a power freak boss that allows you to seek advice and thus attribute any success to a joint effort. Any failure, of course, needs to fall directly on your shoulders. This is never a fair and just two-way street. You can never walk into a power freak boss and say, "Well, we lost the Apex account, I guess our idea didn't work." You need to say something like, "I want to apologize for letting the Apex account slip through our hands. If we had done absolutely everything you suggested when we talked about it, I'm sure this wouldn't have happened." Mouthwash time.

You may think that attributing failures to yourself while attributing successes to the power freak boss may make you vulnerable, that he'll begin to think he doesn't need you. However, he is going to think that any success you've had was attributable to him anyway . . . and that any failure was attributable to you. It will be better, in most cases, for you to be out front with these attributions.

Many of us, of course, are incapable of this kind of method acting. My friend Larry Dore, who learned as a youngster in his Irish Catholic neighborhood never to "suck up" to an authority figure, could never have attempted this. "This jerk is not going to turn me into a phoney," he might say. Others of us might be able to come closer to this kind of role playing, knowing that having to work for a power freak boss is the result of happenstance, working for the wrong company at the wrong time. And so role playing, you might say to yourself, is a coping strategy and not a mark of phoniness. Only you know whether this can sit right with you.

How close you can come to genuinely seeking advice and how successful you are in keeping a power freak boss from intimidating you depends to a great extent on the communications strategy that you use with him or her. And the key to this strategy comes from knowing how open your communication with the power freak boss can be, since all of them differ from one another to some degree. Some of these bosses want to know a lot about what you're doing. They want to be informed of all the meetings you're having, problems you're dealing with and how you're dealing with them, decisions that are pending, whom you're having lunch with, how things are going at home, and maybe even when you go to the bathroom. Other bosses want to be kept informed of only the more important matters. They want you to use your judgment on which matters you bring to their attention. They don't want to hear about your personal life. They don't want to be bombarded with constant questions and information they don't deem to be important. "Please, I can't do my job and yours as well," these types of power freak bosses might say.

The most difficult types of power freak bosses, in terms of a communications strategy, are those who don't want any communication at all. They don't want to communicate in the interim with you so that they can explode fully and with justification when you fail. If you succeed without giving them credit, they won't be happy with you, telling you that, "In our business, what you did may be good, but it is basically insignificant to the major successes that this company needs and deserves. So please, for your own sake, try harder." When you fail, expect an explosive tirade. There is absolutely no way to win with this type of power freak boss, except by sheer luck. The best you can hope for is co-existence with some level of discomfort.

If you are fortunate enough to have a boss who wants to know everything, then tell them everything. How hard can this be? Yet, I've known people who resent it. They feel that the boss who wants to know everything about their jobs doesn't trust them to do the job or is somehow invading their privacy. Trust in doing the job? Without communicating what you are doing, they will never have trust in you. Invading privacy? You are not being paid to hide your activities, but to do the best job you can under the most trying of circumstances. Take advantage of the power freak boss who wants to know everything. The reason they do is probably based on their paranoia. If they don't hear from you for a week or two, if they hear from others about an activity you are undertaking they are unaware of, they will become suspicious of you. No matter how well you have done in the past for these bosses, they will think you have "something up your sleeve." Maintaining the trust of a power freak boss is a full time job unto itself, because it is never fully earned. It has to be earned every week and sometimes every day. Even the chosen few that make up the inner circle of an extreme power freak have to be careful every day on how they phrase their wording when they are in his or her presence. One mistake, one lapse in phrasing can trigger the status or paranoia programs and the trust may be lost forever. "I knew that down deep, James was never truly a team player," this boss could be thinking to himself or herself.

So another rule of thumb: If you have a boss who seeks a lot of information about your activities and you begin filling him in, continue doing so and pay attention to the process. Lapses could cause serious repercussions. Avoid triggering his paranoia. Focus the communication on the following:

- Does the boss want a daily meeting with you to be updated? Then do it. If weekly, then do that.
- If he doesn't want a meeting, but would like you to phone him to update him, then do that. Or if he wants you to e-mail him, then do that.
- Provide the ongoing communication his way, not yours. Maybe it's a combination of the above or something else all together. Go along with it.

❧ As we've noted, pass along interesting documents frequently. Put a note on it: "Mr. Matson, Thought you would be interested in reading this. James." Or, "Mr. Matson, Here is some progress on the Apex account. James." Or whatever. If he wants to know and see everything, then make sure he does. If you're unsure of how much he wants to know at the beginning of the relationship, then err on the side of overdoing it. If he is getting too much information from you, he will let you know so that you can adjust downward.

❧ Seek advice on how to handle important projects. More detail on this follows.

What about the power freak boss who wants to be kept informed of only important matters? There may not be a daily or weekly meeting with this type of boss, but he wants to hear from you. He wants to know for certain that you are still on the team, that you are compliant and trustworthy, that you are not hiding anything. And so you may have to go out of your way to find documents that you can forward to this person, that he will perceive is important enough for his attention. If you send something that is obviously not important, this will also violate his status program. "Does James think I'm some kind of dummy that I need information like this? I guess I'll have to keep my eye on him."

The job of communicating with this type of power freak boss is thus much more difficult than the boss who wants to know everything. It requires a little more thought because once again, what you may think is unimportant he or she may think is important and vice versa. Over time, if you work to become perceptive enough, you'll learn to know which matters are truly important in the minds of bosses like these. You have to think through the process everyday, in addition to performing the job you are being paid to do. Remember, in this sense, that you are also being paid to contribute to the success of the company as a whole, regardless of the fact that you have a jerk you are reporting to. So this *is* part of your responsibility.

When it comes to seeking advice on important projects, one rule of thumb is never to go in empty handed. Never go in and say, "Well, sir, here is a letter from the Apex account threatening to start using another vendor. What do you think we should do?" Some power freak bosses will think, when you use this approach, that you are setting them up to take responsibility for a failure. Rather, go in with a list of your own ideas, preferably bullet-pointed on a single sheet of paper. Two pages, in a meeting like this, might make the power freak boss anxious. There is too much to review. Many of these people are not mental giants. Then go over your strategy one point at a time. "Here is what I was thinking to begin with." Then get her reactions to each point and make a note of them as she talks. _Make sure you take notes._ If you don't take notes, she will think that you think that what she is suggesting is unimportant. At the end of the meeting thank her for helping you out with the advice and state that you're going to get right on the project. As stated previously, if you keep the Apex account, let her know that it was her advice that did the trick. If you lose the Apex account, find some way to absolve her in your explanation of any responsibility. Take it all on yourself, if absolutely necessary. In the end, this will prove less painful to you.

With the power freak boss who doesn't want to hear from you because he always wants you to be set up as the fall guy or girl, the process of seeking advice can be critical. Select those matters of only crucial importance. One selection criterion might be thinking in your own mind how mad and jealous this type of power freak boss will be when he finds out that you were successful in resolving the problem. Irrational? Of course. In these cases, work hard to set up a meeting. "Mr. Matson, I hate to bother you on this, but this matter is extremely important to the company and I just need a few minutes of your time to review some of the ideas I have," you might say to him via phone or e-mail. If he allows you to meet with him, then come in with your single page of bullet points and take copious notes as he talks. If he doesn't allow you to meet, then via phone or e-mail ask him for advice on a single, innocuous question. Or find some way to get even the smallest amount of input. Then when you have a success, you can focus on that one bit of input as being a "tipping point" in getting Apex to see the light.

This is definitely all craziness, but don't forget, it's a crazy world to begin with.

PROACTIVE

In the world of sports, the axiom is a good offense can sometimes be your best defense. If we view dealing with a power freak boss as a sport, it certainly is a contest, then this axiom may apply.

In their book *Working with Difficult People*, business psychologists William Lundin and Kathleen Lundin cite the experience of Margaret, who in "trying to cope with one of the more distressing, difficult behaviors in the workplace, an angry boss, decided to be proactive in her relationship with him." Following is a segment of the interview Ms. Lundin had with Margaret:

Margaret: He came up to me in the morning like he always does. This time I didn't remain seated. I jumped up and said, "I'm glad you're here. I was about to call you. I have an idea for simplifying this form. It might save us time and make our reports easier to follow." And I gave him a big smile.

Kathy: Sounds good to me. What did he do and say?

Margaret: He stood there. He didn't actually wilt, but he was overwhelmed. He had to smile. What else could he do? He wanted to study it. He never had a chance to get that mean look.[12]

In *Neanderthals at Work*, the authors reinforce the proactive strategy with the following advice: "Take risks, take the initiative, and take the heat if you're wrong." However, this may not work for everyone. As with communication, you have to find the correct balance of proactivity in dealing with the power freak boss.

There are some power freak bosses who don't want to hear any of your ideas. Whatever you suggest they will squelch. If the idea is presented verbally, they will cut you off. If the idea is presented on paper, they may scrunch it up and toss it across the room. I've seen this happen. They may be narcissistic to the point that they actually believe that any new idea, regardless of what it is, must come from them to have validity.

Your job is to carry out their ideas in a strictly reactive mode, which is covered in more detail shortly.

Other bosses may be open to your ideas, but only reluctantly. "Mr. Matson," you might say, "I have some thoughts on how we can save time in screening new vendors without lowering our vendor standards."

"Have you thought this completely through?" Mr. Matson might reply skeptically.

"Oh, yes sir, I have."

"Well then write it up and let me review it."

This type of power freak boss knows that he or she doesn't have all the ideas in the world, but is guarded in accepting ideas from others for fear he or she may ultimately take credit for them if they work. And so you write up the idea and submit it. In some instances, the boss will call you in and say that "you do have some interesting thoughts here, but here's the way I'd like to handle it." He then gives you his ideas with which he has ownership. Basically, you have succeeded. You have been proactive in submitting an idea, which the boss eventually took to be his own. He will never thank you for the idea, he will never even recognize the fact that you started the process, but you should be happy because somewhere deep in the recesses of your boss's instinctual-emotional mind, the chances are good that there has been a recognition of your competence.

Other bosses may never respond to your written idea. And you shouldn't remind them about it, except perhaps once: "Mr. Matson, have you reviewed that idea about screening vendors yet?"

"Not yet, James, but I'll get to it."

Then one day, you're sitting in a staff meeting and the boss says, "I have developed a new process for screening vendors I would like to test immediately." He then hands out a proposal that practically mimics all your ideas. He gives you no credit for developing it, and you must not take any credit for proposing it, even to your colleagues. It is the boss's idea and again you have succeeded. "*Yessss,*" you can say to yourself like a basketball player who has just made a three-point shot to win the game. Deep down it is probable that your boss will remember where the idea came from and if so, again you have reinforced your recognized competence.

In either situation with this reluctant boss, just because you had one victory, you mustn't rush in with other good ideas, even though their immediate implementation may help the company. If you rush in with them, the boss will begin to suspect you are after his job and will find ways to squash them completely. So you are not doing him, you, or the company a favor by being perceived as an "eager beaver." Your ultimate objective must be to help your company regardless of the power freak boss obstacle put in your way and so you must string your proactivity out. Perhaps you wait six weeks before making your next suggestion. If your boss looks at you warily and skeptically when you bring it up, then you'll know to lengthen the string to two months or even three.

Still other power freak bosses, when they have taken possession of your ideas and they have worked, may be more open to your suggestions. You have made them look good, a key to working for any power freak. You don't have to lengthen the frequencies for presenting new ideas. You can research and dream to your heart's content, because your power freak boss is actually looking for you to develop ideas that he can call his own without a whimper from you. If one of the ideas fails badly your recognized competence may continue as long as you take the blame, although your boss may return to his initial hesitancy and skepticism about your future ideas.

And so the game goes.

REACTIVE

Regardless of how proactive you are capable of being, either in generating new, workable ideas, or in your power freak boss's capacity to receive them, you must be consistent in your reactivity.

Power freak bosses demand absolute obedience. If they call you in their office with a directive they want you to carry out, if the idea has any merit at all, your response should be something like those stated previously: "Yes, sir," "Can do," "No problem," "Consider it done." If you can respond in your own words to this effect and mean it, you have succeeded in showing your compliance to your boss's higher status. His or her mind's emotional pleasure system will create positive feelings toward you, at least for the moment.

The challenge that needs to be addressed is when the directive is so flawed you are relatively certain it won't work in its present form. The last thing you want to say is, "Mr. Matson, I don't think this is a good idea." Wham, bam, he would literally want to kill you if he thought he could get a way with it, as the crayfish effect kicks in and feelings of anger, rage, and vindictiveness flood his mind. A power freak boss never wants to be told directly that anything he suggests is flawed. Yet your ultimate responsibility, again, is to the company you work for and so you need to intervene, but in a tangential way.

The best method is to begin by discussing with the boss all of the _positive_ things that may result from his suggestion. Perhaps his flawed idea is to eliminate the company's sales representatives and have all customers call a toll-free number, where lower-cost service personnel can handle orders, service requests, and complaints without the need for travel, expense accounts, and high salaries and/or commissions. Your initial discussion might go like this:

"What you're saying, Mr. Matson, is that we eliminate the entire outside sales force and bring the function inside."

"Exactly. I read an article in _Forbes_ about a company who did exactly that and it was a huge cost-savings, a great success."

"Yes, that would save us a lot of money and might be appropriate for us. What kind of products was that company manufacturing that was described in the _Forbes_ article?"

"I believe it was radar detectors, they sold them to automotive dealerships. Very successful. And they didn't miss a beat when they converted."

"I see, yes . . . but our conversion to this method of selling might be a bit more complicated because we sell commercial water heating systems. We'd have to really train those inside people."

"Of course we'd train them . . . train them thoroughly, but it would still be cheaper." Mr. Matson pauses and smiles. "But remember, they don't travel. Look at the money we'd save right there."

"Yes, this definitely might work. But have you thought about the fact that our two major competitors would still have salesmen on the street, calling on our customers face-to-face, establishing relationships they were unable to do before because our field sales force is considered one of the best?"

"Of course I've thought about it. We'll pick inside people who are real personality types, get to know their customers personally, even though it's over the phone."

You would then continue to raise questions about the details of the boss's proposal. How does he or she see us doing this or doing that? The idea initially is only to create some doubt in the boss's mind. Then you might say, "I tell you what, Mr. Matson, the idea definitely has some strong advantages for us. Why don't I take the next several days to develop the cost savings that the program would generate and list both the strengths and the problems we might have as the program rolls out? Then we can discuss this again."

You would then put the numbers to the program and make judicious inquiries among your sales and marketing colleagues about the problems the program might cause, including the estimated percentage of market share loss that would undoubtedly result, comparing that loss of revenue to the cost savings of the program. Depending on the nature of the company and your relationship to the power freak boss, you might want to attribute the idea not to your boss, but some anonymous board member or higher up. Even in private companies with advisory boards, managers are used to getting poppycock ideas from board members who haven't the vaguest idea of the processes they're suggesting, but do so to justify their board positions.

The point is to be able to come back to your power freak boss with documentation that indicates what the gains might be from his proposal, but also the risks and potential losses to the company. Power freak bosses don't like to lose. If they sense the risks as too great, they'll usually say something like, "Okay, let's give this some further thought." They eventually let the proposal die, without ever saying that it was a bad idea.

The axiom with a suggestion or directive that you perceive as flawed is never to confront the power freak boss directly with your opinion, but as we've described, to question and probe and do the grunt work necessary that in the end will indicate to your boss that the direction is a poor one.

Years ago, I knew a vice president of sales who was up high on the power/status scale, was good at his job, but who, reporting directly to a power freak president, was candid to him. What a combination. The confrontations in staff meetings were embarrassing. The president would bring up an idea, a thought, and the vice president of sales would almost always tell him bluntly that the idea would never work, or that it stunk . . . or that the president should get out in the field and talk to customers before making suggestions like that, and so forth. Eventually, the vice president of sales, despite his effectiveness, was forced into resigning. Direct confrontations with power freak bosses simply won't work.

On the other hand, the axiom when you receive a suggestion or directive from the boss that *appears solid and workable, is to be immediately reactive*. Get right on it and then keep the boss informed of your progress. If he doesn't hear from you about this progress, he may begin to think you're trying to bury the idea, that you inwardly think the project is bad and are therefore not a team player. Send him frequent notes and e-mail that detail your progress. Show your eagerness to be working with him. Show that you respect him as the expert, that you are merely an imple- mentor. If you run into problems with the project, come back and seek his advice on those problems, projecting optimism that they can be over- come.

SUBLIMATION

Is it ever possible to enjoy working for an extreme power freak?

It is, if you have the capacity to sublimate yourself to his or her needs, to direct any resentment or anger you may feel into a calling to work unselfishly for this person.

There is a scene in the motion picture *Patton*, where a new orderly quickly gains the trust of the general by being around to light his cigars and tend to all his needs without being obtrusive. If Patton bounced an idea off of him and he had his own thoughts, he would begin by saying, "May I suggest, General, that . . ." It was obvious that this orderly was truly enjoying his job of being subordinate to a power-hungry and ambi- tious general who frequently exhibited psychopathic traits. It would appear that the orderly's own drive for power, though ostensibly nowhere near as intense as Patton's, was being fulfilled by working in the shadow of a powerful person.

We've seen the same phenomena in the White House, where aides to whoever is president at the time fall all over themselves to be fawning and subordinate in the president's presence, believing that their proximity to this powerful person will raise their own status, which apparently it does. They appear to revel in their role of subordinate, even though outside the Oval Office they may become intimidating to their own staffs and to each other.

In the business world the same phenomenon occurs. There are many people who enjoy working for an extreme power freak. "You know, he is misunderstood," I was once told by an assistant to a power freak departmental manager.

"But I don't know how you can stand his temper tantrums, his constant belittling of people, including you," I replied.

"Oh, that's all for show. You don't see his better side."

"So you like working for him."

"I do. It has been a great experience."

This person never took advantage of his position as a trusted aide of his boss, to intimidate others or feather his own nest. Perhaps he had a relatively low power drive himself, and so found it easy as well as enjoyable to be submissive. Or, he had a high power drive that was fulfilled by the status of working in a center of power.

Still others may not totally enjoy being subordinate to a power freak boss, but they are able to play the part with aplomb. "All I have to do is bury myself in the identity of this man and play the game," they might say.

Sublimation differs from submission in that you are able to mesh your instinctual power/status drives with those of your power freak boss. You are not number one, the alpha, but you are in his or her sphere and you bask in the power, which will be projected to others. Many others, even those in high positions, may need to come to you to get to the "chief." As Joe Torre put it, you are able to accept the "total package," the good with the bad and in the bad moments, you don't let him or her get you down, knowing that the moments will pass.

Sublimation also means becoming comfortable with a power freak boss, actually relishing her company, but knowing innately how far to go with remarks and humor. Those who succeed in sublimation are not hanging their heads in raw submissiveness. On the contrary, they can be more frank in stating their opinions in appraisal of a power freak's ideas or suggestions. "May I suggest, General . . . ," "May I speak frankly, ma'am?" are among the magic words. The power freak boss knows innately that a sublimated subordinate is enjoying the ride and can accept comments from him that they wouldn't tolerate from others.

Sublimation appears to be a form of role playing that takes on a life of its own. Once immersed, we may not be totally aware of the process. It can make life easier, if we can carry it off, but it's obviously not for everyone.

WHEN YOU ARE AT YOUR WITS' END: THE CONFRONTATION

It has been my experience in over forty years of dealing with companies large and small that the extreme power freak manager whose own agenda supercedes that of the company or institution employing her will eventually either be side-tracked or leave. Extreme power freak bosses only endure when they have a core competency that is unique and necessary and the company or department they are running is enormously successful, despite the obviously warped nature of their personalities.

Time and again I have counseled tortured people working for these power freak managers to be patient, to endure the pain, that the overwhelming odds are that it won't last. In some cases they were unable to take it any longer and resigned or worked out a termination package. Then in many instances, only months later, the power freak boss met his or her comeuppance and the people who had left were kicking themselves for not staying.

In many cases, these power freak bosses left for another job. Oddly enough, many of them are sought out by headhunters who are looking for managers with reputations for toughness and intimidation, particularly for jobs with companies who have had problems and need someone tough to come in and clean house. Some companies seek out a hatchet man to do this work, which frequently allows those higher in the organization's hierarchy to project an image of innocence, particularly to veteran managers who may have to be let go.

Or, these bosses might be "sent out to the fringes," as the saying goes in companies that tend to hang on to their managers, even those who are obvious power freaks. They are put into innocuous jobs where they can't cause much trouble. Some actually come to enjoy these jobs, particularly if they are older and only a few years away from retirement. Others frantically look for new positions, while working diligently in their new, innocuous job to assure a paycheck. Remember that power freak bosses, regardless of the amount of havoc they have left in their wake, will never take responsibility for what happened. In interviews for new positions, they will point out reasons why the havoc occurred, "why their hands were tied," when they tried to deal with it. Then they'll spell out exactly what they would have done if it wasn't for the backward people they dealt with, or the backward policies that handcuffed them, even though they were the ones who actually caused the mess. I have frequently been amazed at the new jobs that incompetent power freaks, "Teflon executives," they've been called, have been able to find for themselves after running company after company into the ground. Go figure. The point is that no matter how incompetent you think your power freak boss is— to the point that you believe no other company would ever hire him— there is a reasonable chance that he will leave or be transferred and may be replaced with someone relatively normal.

However, if you are becoming increasingly miserable and are unable to find coping methods for tolerating your power freak boss that your nature will allow, then it may be time for a confrontation. But before you decide on this course of action, you must realize that the odds are that you will be terminated either immediately or in the near future. If the job market is tight and you have a family to support, then use these issues as a legitimate excuse for your own rational mind to delay the confrontation. Take comfort in the fact that you have decided to have a confrontation, that you are prepared to leave the company, but this will be in accordance with your own timetable. If you keep telling the instinctual-emotional side of your mind that you are only biding your time, that you will take action when the time is right, you may be able to feel better about having to deal with your power freak boss in the interim.

When you do decide to have a confrontation with a prototypical power freak boss who reflects psychopathic and other pathological disorders and/or is status-obsessed, don't make it an angry one. That will seal your fate with a certainty. Instead, consider a submissive confrontation as one strategy that may work to improve your relationship with your power freak boss, at least for a short period of time.

Almost all of the books I reviewed about dealing with difficult bosses advise that you practice the confrontation; that you pick the right time for the meeting, when your power freak boss is in a relatively good mood, for example; that you speak from your own point of view and avoid a head-on fight; that you remain calm and professional, and so forth. I would add that you make your confrontation a submissive one.

A friend of mine, "Paul," some years ago told me about a successful confrontation he had with his power freak boss at the time. The following is a brief recollection of Paul's strategy.

"Mr. Ellis," he started out. "I'm at my wit's end, I don't know what to do."

"What are you talking about?" Ellis replied gruffly, shuffling through papers on his desk. "Get to the point."

Paul looked down at his feet submissively, then said, "To be quite frank, Mr. Ellis, I don't think I can do this job correctly, nothing I seem to do pleases you."

"If you want to hear good things, talk to your pastor."

"The thing is, Mr. Ellis, it's the nature of my personality to want to be encouraged, to want to have some positive feedback. I don't really know if you think I'm doing a good job or not. If I'm not, maybe it's time for me to move on."

"Okay, you're doing a good job. Is that enough? I'm busy today."

"No, it's really not, Mr. Ellis. There are a few additional issues I'd like to discuss."

"Oh, for Christ's sake, why don't you just suck on a pacifier?"

Paul then reached into his pocket and pulled out a single sheet of paper and said, "Look, Mr. Ellis, it took me a few weeks to get up the courage to come in and see you about this. Now that I'm here I'd like to let it all hang out. And if you don't mind, I would like to refer to some notes I made."

Ellis groaned, sat back in his chair, rubbed a hand through his hair, then looked at Paul and said, "Okay, but make this quick."

Paul then reviewed about six items he had on the list, including Ellis's sometimes abrupt manner, the fact that he didn't return Paul's proposals and then blamed Paul for not submitting them in staff meetings, and so forth. "I don't even think you're aware of how you act sometimes," Paul said.

According to Paul, Ellis never threatened to fire him. Nor did he change his temperament after the confrontation, except for the fact that he would occasionally and grudgingly mention to Paul that a job was done satisfactorily, if indeed it was. In addition, Ellis appeared to be making a conscious effort to ignore Paul, only dealing with him when absolutely necessary, which was fine with Paul. He knew that his future at this company was limited as long as Ellis was around. He was intent on either outlasting Ellis or biding his time until a better opportunity came along. And so the space that developed between Ellis and him was a welcome respite.

Would this kind of interview have worked with Adolf Hitler and Joseph Stalin? Probably not. Paul would have been lucky to avoid a firing squad. Would it have worked with Al Dunlap at Sunbeam? Probably not. Can everyone who works for a power freak boss act submissive in a confrontation? Absolutely not. Larry Dore, my friend who grew up in an environment where he learned never to "suck up" to an authority figure, a teaching that carried over well into his adult life, would never have been able to carry this off.

But for those of us who are role players, who can come out of meetings like that and laugh about what we had to put ourselves through to stay on the payroll, at the time when there were few alternatives and we had a family to support, it's worth a shot.

Make sure your resume is updated, however.

Dealing with a Peer
Who Is an Extreme Power Freak

"We do not have to visit a madhouse to find disordered minds; our planet is the mental institution of the universe."

Johann von Goethe

The following description I noted earlier in chapter 1 appears most appropriate for portraying a power freak peer:

> Cain [the author's metaphor for a power freak peer] is so driven by ambition that he'll do almost anything to satisfy his lust for success. To get his way, he will use and manipulate others; he will stab an innocent colleague in the back, with no remorse; he will not only mislead those he works with, he will abuse them and make their lives miserable—and he will take pride in doing so.[1]

A peer has been described as someone who doesn't have official authority over you and you don't have official authority over him or her. You might thus be in the environment of an extreme power freak peer not only in the workplace, but among community and religious groups, particularly in their committees. You might also have to deal with peer power freaks among siblings, other relatives, and even parents when you are an adult yourself. Wherever they are, they are capable of destroying the chemistry of the environment you share with them, and can cause almost as much stress and discomfort as the extreme power freak boss. The primary difference between being under the sway of the power freak boss versus dealing with a peer appears to be that the former can create greater levels of fear. He has your livelihood in his hands. Nonetheless, imagine how much stress you might feel if Dave, described on pages 149–50 as an example of a business psychopath, moved into the office next door as your equal.

Dave, as you recall, believes that "fighting and aggression are necessary forces and that people need them to advance in life." As we quoted on page 150, his co-workers are consistent in their descriptions of him; they find him "rude, selfish, immature, self-centered, unreliable and irresponsible." Like most people with psychopathic traits, he "never acknowledges that he has done anything wrong and always acted surprised when given feedback, insisting that he had never been told that he had done anything wrong before." And now there he is, sitting in the office or cubicle next to you. Within the week, when you are both in the same meeting, he says something that totally undermines you.

What do you do?

In reading through the thirty-seven best books I could find on the subject of dealing with difficult people and conflict management, there were no universal suggestions for dealing with the extreme power freak peer (we'll use the term "power freak peer"). I found this surprising since most adults encounter such people numerous times in their lives, some much more frequently than others. This lack of consensus probably centers on a comment made by Sandra A. Crowe, president of a consulting firm that provides advice on dealing with difficult people, in her book *Since Strangling Isn't an Option . . . Dealing with Difficult People— Common Problems and Uncommon Solutions*: "Human behavior is not an exact science. What works in one case may not work in another. In fact, what works right now may not work tomorrow, even with the same person. Be armed with a variety of techniques and try another when your first attempt fails."[2]

We might add to this that the way we react to a Dave sitting in the office next to us, who we know is working hard to undermine and belittle us, also depends on where we stand on the power scale ourselves. Are we a level eight, ready to do battle, or are we a level three, who would find it hard to confront anyone? Or, are we a situational power freak, described in chapter 7, capable of shifting into a power freak mode in a competitive or challenging situation? Recall my friend, described on pages 115–16. He was normally mild mannered, but when he stepped foot on a basketball court, he was transformed into an extreme competitive power freak. He returned to normal as soon as he left the court. How high does our power drive rise when we are thrust into a competitive situation or our status is being challenged by a newly hired and power-crazed peer who tells us the first day that he wants us fired because he can do our job as well as his? Do we become angry, nasty, mean, and confrontational, displaying our own psychopathic traits while we are in the mode? Or is there little or no transformation in our personalities beyond mild stress and discomfort?

Therein lies the primary problem for developing universal answers for dealing with a power freak peer.

At the one extreme are people like Bill Porter, a grizzled veteran of the corporate wars, the author of *Eat or Be Eaten*, who said:

> What do you do when one of them [someone in the office] screams at you? You can do two things. You can curl up your tail between your legs like most others, or you can bare your fangs and let the idiot know that you don't push around easily. I've always operated on the latter premise and it has yet to hurt me. When the screaming is directed at me, I scream back with the same ferocity as the blasts that are directed at me.[3]

Then there is my friend Larry Dore, who I mentioned in the last chapter has been admittedly unable for his own benefit to "suck up" to any superior he had during his more than twenty-five years as the head of sales and marketing for two large companies. If he was unable to play games to mollify a boss, then he certainly was incapable of playing them for a peer. To illustrate, Larry told me about "Dwight," a new vice president of manufacturing, who was brought in not long after Larry took over the job of vice president of sales and marketing at the first company. Dwight was given an office down the hall. Apparently in sizing up the entire executive management team, including the president, Dwight concluded that he was capable of becoming president himself and relatively quickly.

He started by attacking Larry in staff meetings, proclaiming "facts" that were unverified by the financial data. Larry, gradually transforming into a challenged power freak mode at a high level, noisily confronted Dwight both at these meetings and in private. Finally, one day, Larry called a plant manager to learn what was in inventory and the manager said he had been instructed by Dwight never to talk to Larry. Larry had

had enough. He walked into Dwight's office ready to punch him in the nose. A secretary saw what was happening and rushed in, telling Larry he had an important phone call. Larry left Dwight's office. There was no phone call, but fortunately he calmed down enough to put the incident behind him. It turned out that Dwight was incompetent and was terminated within a year. And Larry was finally able to return to being Larry. But like many incompetents in the business world whose backgrounds aren't thoroughly checked and/or who interview exceedingly well, Dwight was hired to head the manufacturing of a company in another state. These people, as noted previously, are frequently referred to as "Teflon executives"—nothing sticks to them. Two years later, Larry bumped into Dwight at a trade show and Dwight acted as if they were long lost friends, asking about Larry's wife and family, apparently wearing the glib and charming mask of the psychopath.

At the other extreme, I remember an office manager, "Ted," who was very competent, but quiet and reserved. A new controller, "Dennis," was hired who was the epitome of a power freak peer. Dennis attempted to mow down everyone in his sight, including Ted, who had no idea how to respond. I saw Ted sitting at his desk one day, his face red as a beet. He told me that Dennis had just confronted him in the hall, berating him loudly in front of others, about the expenses for office supplies that month, which it turned out, were in line with previous months.

I asked him how he replied to Dennis. He said he told him he would look into it and continued down the hall. He told me he couldn't take this much longer and was thinking of quitting, since he was unable to stand up to the man.

This was not his boss. This was an equal down the hall. And yet three months later, Ted did resign.

It turns out that the dozens of experts who deal with the subject of difficult people, or who specialize in the field of conflict management, view the conflicts between peers as what those in the world of athletics call "challenge matches." To determine how we'll meet the challenge of any given power freak peer, they advise, we need a "game plan."

In the field of athletics, a game plan can be relatively simple or complex, depending on the nature of the upcoming match. In professional football, to use one sport as an example, the coaches prepare a game plan that assesses the strengths and weaknesses of their own team as against those of the opponent. They may eliminate some plays or tactics that have been successful against other teams, but which would play into the strengths of their upcoming opponent; they may add tactics that they perceive play into an opponent's weakness. During the actual match, they may deviate from that game plan in the heat of the battle, but they almost always attempt to return to it.

The point of the experts is that when dealing with a power freak peer, we need a game plan to follow. We need a series of strategies and tactics we can put into play in dealing with the challenge of someone who is getting his highs from attempting to intimidate, belittle, and possibly get rid of us. The following are the key elements.

ASSERTING YOUR POSITION

In his book _Coping with Difficult People_, Robert Bramson makes the point of this game plan tactic quite succinctly:

> The first rule of coping with anyone aggressive, hostile or not, is that you stand up to that person. If you let yourself be pushed around by aggressive people, you simply fade in to the scenery for them. That is, they will not see you as someone to whom attention need be paid. . . . Mark raises an idea for consideration only to have Sharon, an aggressive person say something like, "No, no, that won't work at all." Unless Mark does something to stand up for himself, such as saying, "Well, wait a minute, I'm not sure you really heard what I was trying to say," something interesting will happen. Sharon will begin to act as if Mark is not a part of the meeting. She won't look at him, she will speak through him, she will not react to anything he says.[4]

If we assume that Sharon is an extreme power freak and not simply a worker with irritable habits, which, over time, might be smoothed out, then she will be doing everything she can to fight her way up the ladder of her organization. She may possess psychopathic and narcissistic traits or be afflicted with sadistic personality disorder or all three—and thus be incapable of realizing the harm her actions are doing to her peers and to her organization as a whole. If she does know it, lacking any capacity for guilt or remorse, she simply won't care. Further, she probably harbors grandiose illusions about herself and believes that the havoc she is wreaking among the organization is for the ultimate good, that her genius will conquer all.

How do we assert ourselves against such people without additional harm to ourselves or the organization?

If we are like author and corporate veteran Phil Porter, we are tough enough not to take any guff. When we are confronted with arrogant, power-driven peers, we transform ourselves into severe competitive or challenged power freaks, taking on the manifestations of the charging display and we are basically ready to fight it out if that's what it takes to get them off our backs. In his book Porter describes "The Got'cha Game":

1. Find out something bad about another manager's department.

2. Guard this information carefully—don't talk to the responsible manager because if you do he'll be prepared to answer for it when you reveal it in step #3.

3. Reveal the got'cha at a general-manager-level or higher meeting. The result will give the general manager the impression that you're on top of things and the guy you're dropping the got'cha on is not. . . .

I don't recommend you practice this game unless you're secure enough in your position that you can stand retribution, because once you act, it will come.[5]

In that last sentence Porter makes the critical point regarding this tactic. Not only will one's own position in the company be threatened, because he or she no longer will be viewed as a team player with the right chemistry, but the power freak peer will do everything possible to get even. The organization suffers as this process continues.

At the other end of the scale there are some people who are too timid to assert themselves at all. I recall one manager, "Abby," who was quiet and shy, to say the least. She had great difficulties standing up for herself. Then we sent her to a firm of psychologists for one week of "Assertiveness Training." Among other things during the course of this training, instructors would attack the students verbally, while being videotaped. Later, the students would watch their reactions on video with an instructor and be counseled on how to respond better. The process was repeated over and over again. Our contact at the firm called after the course was over and said she thought Abby had made great progress. I didn't see any noticeable difference in Abby when she returned. But about two weeks later in a meeting, one of Abby's peers attacked her about a client proposal she had developed and which he didn't like. Abby replied calmly that the proposal had already been accepted by the client. Then this fellow stood up and started shouting at Abby, stating that he should have seen it first, before it went to the client. "After all, I'm closer to that client than you are." There was an embarrassing pause, after which Abby in her own quiet and timid way, but with a new inner force that was obvious, said, "Stan, get lost." The others at the meeting actually stood up and gave her a round of applause, they were so proud of her. Stan quickly quieted down, looking stunned. With three words, spoken in the right tone at the right time, she was able to inflict a social defeat that Stan's limbic amygdala didn't like at all.

The experts in this field all appear to agree that in dealing with a power freak peer, the key is being *assertive*, not *aggressive*. If Abby was a level nine on the power scale or elevated to that level by an abusive challenge, she might have been tempted to come back with outbursts of vitriol and personal attack in a rage of temper. This aggressiveness would have been viewed negatively. Assertiveness is the key word. Stand up for yourself, and as Charles J. Keating in his book *Dealing with Difficult People*, reminds us, "Don't allow yourself to be discounted."[6] In other words, don't allow anyone to demean your capabilities. You can't be an idle bystander and just let it happen, hoping it will all go away. It won't unless one of you is transferred or leaves the company. The worse you feel, the more you will make the power freak peer's day. She likes to see you suffer. It gives her a high. You need to find a solution that works for you against the specific power freak peer who is creating the problems.

TAKE THE HIGH ROAD

Taking the high road may be easier said than done, of course. It is part of the philosophy of being assertive rather than aggressive.

The issue is how do you take the high road and stick to it, particularly if your tolerance for personal attacks is low? How do you remain assertive rather than aggressive in the heat of battle?

There are some of us who will remain calm in a confrontation, make an assertive statement, and then walk away. But that night in bed, our instinctual-emotional mind, our inner consciousness may begin churning. We dream of what we should have said: unkind, cutting, and vindictive remarks. Then the next day or the day after that we walk into the power freak's office and lash out, getting it off our chest, thinking that we feel better and that we have put the power freak peer down. But that night the power freak is dreaming of ways to get back at you. It's a dead end, the result of an emotional system that calls for throttling the opponent.

Some of us are simply incapable of taking the high road under adverse circumstances. But attempting to do so should be in your game plan. You might slip and fall along the way, you might lash out unwittingly, but get back to where you were. Don't keep sinking further into the mud and use vindictive actions and remarks that will only produce reciprocal, negative, vengeful actions against you. "A-ha," the power freak peer will think. "Now I know she is against me. I've got to find a way to fix her once and for all." Get up, calm yourself down and begin rehearsing the assertive, thwarting, deflecting remarks that you think will work for you. That's all you need to do for starters, and there are a whole list of them beginning on page 229.

In this sense, your game plan should include the demeanor you want to project during the course of a conflict with a peer. If you can, attempt to exude a quiet air of confidence, stay above the fray as much as your emotions will allow, play the part of the quiet hero who is being wronged.

Your plan should also include a go-it-alone strategy. Accept sympathies if necessary from other colleagues who recognize your plight, or who may also be victims of the power freak's intimidations. Work together if you are like-minded in trying to keep the power freak at bay. But don't build formal coalitions per se against the power freak peer, your group of people versus his group of people—those he has succeeded in bringing into his inner circle. Remember that your first obligation is toward the organization. Coalitions with "our" versus "their" mentalities will lead to a muddled work environment. Nothing good can come of this in the long term and your name will be associated with it.

EXPECT AND ACCEPT DISHARMONY

Most of us would prefer to be in harmonious environments, being with people with whom we are chemically attuned. Unfortunately it is practically impossible to achieve harmony with a power freak peer unless we become submissive and do his or her bidding without objection. It's one thing to be submissive to a power freak boss, who holds our livelihood in his or her hands; it is another thing to do this for a peer, who is attempting to make us miserable simply to serve his or her agenda.

Author Muriel Solomon, a specialist in the field, says in her book *Working with Difficult People*; "You're not after 100 percent harmony. You and your Tackler [her term for a power freak] will seldom sing the same tune. You just need to come to some understanding that lets you get on with your work."[7]

She also reiterates the point previously made: "Continue your game plan. Don't be sidelined by a groveling match. Instead, question the Tackler to show that you are determined to do the job without stooping to his level. Elevate the discussion by moving the emphasis away from individuals back to the issue at hand."[8] More importantly, don't spend unnecessary time hoping that your power freak peer will change . . . that once you get to know him you will be able to get him to see the true light and you'll be able to work in a harmonious relationship.

As formerly noted, the only thing that can change the thought patterns of an extreme power freak is a trauma: the death of a loved one, a divorce or separation, a demotion or termination at work. And sometimes the trauma will not make the person kinder and gentler, but nastier. Simply get used to the fact that the work environment that includes the presence of this person will not be harmonious and that as good as you think you might be at conciliation, the odds of your getting the extreme power freak to change are beyond calculation.

DON'T MAKE IT PERSONAL

Not making it personal is easier said than done, of course. But as Alan Axelrod and Jim Haltje, business communications consultants, assert in their book *201 Ways to Deal with Difficult People,* "Don't let disputes and rivalries get personal. Avoid criticizing colleagues on a personal level. Personal affronts escalate a bad situation into something worse. . . . Separate the person from the problem. Then attack the problem rather than the person."[9] The point is to stick with the facts of whatever the issue is at the moment. With a power freak peer, however, the issues may be endless. If a disagreement becomes heated, you need to rationally recollect your game plan, which should be to step away. "Bob, I've got to make a phone call. We'll talk about this again later." Emotional intelligence, in essence, is basically being able to train ourselves to use the will power of our cerebral cortex to override, stifle, discipline, or sidestep whatever negative emotions are capturing our consciousness at a given point in time. The instinctual-emotional side of our mind may have served our best interests when we lived millions of years ago in the wilderness, but in the twenty-first century, it can be our worst enemy. A heated disagreement with a power freak peer will trigger feelings of anger and vindictiveness. Our instinctual-emotional side will want us to lash out with expletives to help us level the playing field, which it still thinks is some primitive cave. Remember, it has no sense of time or awareness or logic. If we allow it to vent against a power freak peer, then those same or more intense feelings of anger and vindictiveness will be aroused in the peer and we will have the beginnings of a feud, which will serve no one's interest.

If we do allow our emotions to get the better of us in a heated debate, if we say something personal and demeaning such as, "Bob, you are the biggest asshole I've ever met. As a matter of fact you may be a world class asshole," then our game plan needs to remind us to apologize as quickly as possible after we calm down and we begin to feel the chemistry of our own remorse. Maybe it will be later that day. Maybe it will be the next day or the day after. Whenever it is, and we need to do it at a point in future time when we feel reasonably sincere about doing it, we need to walk into Bob's office and apologize: "Bob, I don't know what got into me. My emotions simply got the best of me and I want to apologize for those remarks I made. I hope you will accept my apology." He may not get up and hug you. He may hardly acknowledge the fact that you are talking to him. But he knows that you are in front of him and apologizing. And if all he does is nod with a soft grunt, that is enough. Then get out of there as quickly as possible before the issue that triggered your anger is raised again. Come back and face that issue on another day, using a different approach.

DON'T USE E-MAIL AND MEMOS TO MAKE ACCUSATORY STATEMENTS

You come to the office in the morning and go through your e-mail. You spot a message from Bob to another colleague, copying you, which directly or indirectly accuses you of doing something that you either didn't do or misinterprets negatively what you in fact did.

If your boiling point is relatively low that day, you may again be overwhelmed by strong feelings of anger and vindictiveness whereas at another time, you might have let the e-mail roll off your back. You immediately click on the reply button and begin to write a seething note back to Bob. *Stop!* There is something about the impersonal nature and ease of an e-mail message or memo that allows us to vent our worst emotions. We want to let it all fly because there is nothing in our office, cubicle, or room stopping us except the intellectual side of our cerebral cortex that may for the moment be overwhelmed. But this unthinking response is one of the worst things we can do. If we send the e-mail, it will recreate the feudal conditions just described. But worse, all of your irrational thoughts are now on the record. Bob, regardless of his reply to you, can forward them to anyone he pleases, if he thinks that it will make you even more unhappy than you are.

Again, do nothing until you calm down. If it will help you release your anger, write the message out, but don't send it. Delete it. When you have calmed down, meet with Bob on a face-to-face basis with a hard copy of his e-mail in hand and discuss it, asserting what your true position was. If you have difficulties with confronting any peer on an unpleasant manner, then see the suggestions beginning on page 231 on how to handle a confrontation.

Confronting a peer on a disagreement in person is far different than doing so in a written form. She is now in front of you, acting as a monitor on what you say. She may even admit that she misinterpreted your thoughts and may apologize or stand corrected.

The rule of thumb with e-mail needs to be this: Never send angry or accusatory notes. State your point of view in person. The accusatory note that started the whole thing may disappear. All that will be left is a written record of your anger. Even if it was justifiable, no one may know.

DON'T TAKE RIGID, CONFRONTATIONAL POSITIONS

Lucy Gill, an expert on dealing with nonproductive behavior, puts it this way:

> In most conflicts, it's best to not take a rigid, confrontational stance. The one-up position will usually trigger a similar stance from others as they try to get even, either actively or subtly. While tempting, this reaction prolongs the conflict, obscures the problem that needs solving, and leaves residual resentment festering. A more nonconfrontational stance avoids these hazards and can be much more effective.[10]

A power freak peer will usually consider a rigid, "in-your-face" position a challenge to his status. The facts may then become irrelevant in the ensuing discussion as the peer works to demean your ideas and put you down in order to maintain his status.

For example, if you're in a scenario where you are sitting on a committee with Bob and discussing a new position in the human resources department and you say, "Look, case closed. We'll promote Edna, there are no other candidates worth considering," Bob will probably respond with something like, "Edna? Are you crazy? Edna couldn't get to first base with a seeing eye dog." A nonconfrontational approach would begin with something like, "Bob, you've worked with Edna. Do you think we should consider her as a candidate?" You have relinquished status to Bob through this approach, and may have to address the issue from other directions if you feel that strongly for Edna while he opposes her. In the meantime, you will probably avoid a heated discussion, which could kill the issue right then and there.

Rigid, confrontational positions on facts and issues that are ambiguous are the scourge of the business world and probably the world at large. I've been in cars with rigid, status-obsessed, but otherwise highly intellectual people when we're unsure of where we are and the other person will make a definite statement like, "Take a left." I'll ask, "How do you know I should take a left?" and they'll reply, "Look, I know, take a left." If it turns out that they are right, they will look proud as a peacock, part of the crayfish effect. If they are wrong, they will blame the poor street lighting or a new store on the corner, or they might simply slump back in their seat looking defeated and saying nothing more the entire trip. I prefer to be with more balanced people in the car, who might say, "Aren't we supposed to take a left here?" We can then discuss the option rationally. This also applies to family life where power-driven and status-obsessed relatives will say things like, "That dress looks terrible on you," or, "You're eating the wrong foods," or, "Your boyfriend is dumb," or whatever their opinion is on these subjective issues. They are driven to display their power and status with these rigid, opinionated remarks. If you respond to them with similar remarks, a heated argument will almost always follow, making their company even more unpleasant than it already is.

In the business world, rigid stances can tie up decisions on important issues as one side attacks another without thought of compromise. Human relations consultant Charles J. Keating points out that in intense business atmospheres, competitive instincts may impede the need for cooperation: "[C]ompetition is the soil in which difficult people grow. Hostility builds, we view our side only positively and the other side as only negative, members of either side accept even dictatorial leadership for the sake of unity, compromise is seen as treason and concessions are perceived as sell-outs."[11]

The more balanced of us have a great advantage. We are not delusional about ourselves, which is half the battle. We can use our intellectual capacity to deal with power freak peers who have been placed in our midst, without getting into confrontational battles that may unfortunately wind up as "our side" versus "their side," pitting one group against another. We can create a game plan for dealing with them, for as long as we have to deal with them and for whenever they are in our presence, which should be as little as possible. It won't be fun, but neither is taking out the garbage. It is something we have to do. And being careful about how we talk to them, how we raise ideas and opinions, how we respond to their suggestions, how we work to reach effective compromises that encompass the best aspects of their position and ours is simply part of the game plan battle.

CONTINUALLY ENHANCE YOUR KNOWLEDGE, YOUR COMPETENCE

A solid knowledge of the facts that lie within our competence is one of the greatest weapons for fending off power freak peers, many of whom believe that they can do your job better than you can. Remember, they think they can do any job better than any person, given the proper tools.

One of their favorite strategies is to pick up a piece of information in your area of authority, perhaps in a trade magazine or on a visit to a single customer, and turn that one piece of knowledge into a truism that they have uncovered after a "lot of hard digging." And they can be compelling in a meeting.

"Joe," I recall a power-driven colleague saying to a vice president of sales of a company making electrical products, "I don't know why we give all these scholarships to the high school children of journeymen who work for electrical contractors. How many of our circuit-breaker systems can these people order without their boss's authorization?"

Joe immediately left the room and returned with a recent electrical contractor customer survey. It showed extremely high satisfaction with the company, including the fact that it went out of its way to support their industry, particularly the journeymen who go into homes and institutional establishments and do the work.

The best managers I know continually try to expand their knowledge. On airplanes and in other spare moments they are reading trade publications and other reference material, clipping out data to keep on file. At conventions they are out in the aisles talking to people, working to soak up the latest information in a world where the business climate can change within a week. They understand the need to absorb wide swaths of information so that they can weigh and measure conflicting points of view.

In this sense, they are open to any ideas, including one that might not have worked last year because the business climate was different then. The most competent managers are open to any suggestion, any idea. You'll never hear them say, "Well, we tried that one time and it never worked." They will probe for more information, and through expert questioning, as noted in the previous chapter about dealing with power freak bosses, will bring out the flaws in any suggestion that is indeed flawed, including those made by power freak peers who are "just trying to be helpful." And they will grab onto any suggestion that has potential, even those offered by power freak peers. They will study it and dutifully report back a recommendation.

These managers are team players who submerge their own personal agenda into that of the company as a whole. They are not rigid. They are not confrontational. They will treat the power freak boss or peer with quiet competence, which is the ultimate weapon if it's in your arsenal. But it may not be enough for some of us, and so we continue.

IF YOU HAVE A GOOD SENSE OF HUMOR, USE IT

A handful of the experts in dealing with difficult people suggest the use of humor as a deflecting tool during abrasive discussions. I would add that you should do this only if you have a good sense of humor and a wit, which you can recognize by the simple fact that people sometimes laugh at what you say when you want them to laugh. If you don't have this capacity, forget using humor. What you say might make things worse.

The humor, when you do use it, should almost always be *self-deprecating*, a form of humor the more balanced of us can employ, since we know we don't have all the answers. The following are some suggestions on how humor might be used:

* *Change the subject.* In the middle of a heated discussion, break in with something like, "Bob, you've got a point and I had a point to make that I can't remember. But more importantly, when do we all think we can break for lunch?"
* *Change the pace.* "You know, Bob, my mother always told me there would be tension-packed days like this. Do you have any Valium on you?"

- ❀ *Point up a weakness.* "Bob, this is much too complicated for my little brain. Can you send me a memo on it?"
- ❀ *Break the tension.* After Bob finishes with a very long and serious diatribe, say something like, "So Bob, I take it you're serious about this?"
- ❀ *Concede a victory.* "The reason I can't sit still, Bob, is because my behind hurts from that beating you gave me in the meeting yesterday."

Most power freak peers enjoy a joke as long as the joke is primarily on you, never on them. Self-deprecating humor is the way to go, if this is part of your arsenal of personality traits.

MAINTAIN AN OPEN CHANNEL OF COMMUNICATION

Les Parrott III said the following in his book *Control Freaks*: "Keep controlling coworkers informed. Let them know what's going on. If they are in the know, they may just drop their guard and become true peers."[12]

Many of us who have been pained by the offensive remarks of a power freak peer may ponder for days ways of getting even without compromising ourselves, the high road be damned. One day a piece of information comes across our desk that we know would be useful to the power freak peer in carrying out her duties. We decide not to send it on and perhaps take some smug satisfaction in withholding the information. But we may be hurting ourselves in the process because cutting off appropriate communications with this peer makes us smaller and over time can diminish the efficiency of our organization and ultimately blow up on us later.

I recall many years ago knowing "Dan," a vice president of a company, who was one of five vice presidents reporting to the president. One of his colleagues was at least a level eight on the power scale. It was well known that this colleague would do practically anything to advance his career, and had his eye on the presidency. Everyone who worked with him gave him a wide berth, except for Dan. Dan was quiet, polite, modest, but yet extremely competent and resolute in his work. He never talked about his colleagues negatively, never played politics, and treated his power freak peer with the same kindness and courtesy with which he treated everyone else. But more to the point, he kept his lines of communication open to this man, no matter how derisive and obnoxious he was in meetings. Dan would dutifully walk into this man's office at least once a week and bring him up to date on matters he thought important to him. He was the only one of the group of vice presidents to do so.

Much to the chagrin of the power freak, when the presidency did open up, Dan got the job, one more testimony to the fact that nice guys can finish first if they have the competency and the skills required to get the job done.

Knowledge is a source of power and when you pass knowledge about matters of importance to a power freak peer they may begin to view you as the lesser of their adversaries and perhaps make your life easier. It may be that they perceive the act of keeping them informed as a conviction on your part that they are going far and that you want to hang onto their coattails. If this is what they think, so be it. If we have to work with them, we have to know and accept their delusions.

Keeping channels of communication open is something you need to do even in the most difficult of situations. It is part of taking the high road. As Charles J. Keating put it, "keep the channels of communication open, even in the face of discount or insult. . . . [K]eep your own goals and objectives in mind; don't be diverted."[13]

It won't be easy.

ATTEMPT TO REACH OUT

If you find that you are successful in attempting to do the right thing for the organization in dealing with power freak peers, then you might also have success in reaching out to them. Not all of us can do this, particularly when a peer appears to enjoy attacking us at every opportunity. Instead of reaching out, depending on where we ourselves stand on the power/status scale, our instincts may be to defend our turf, to create a me-versus-him position, to maintain only as much communication as is absolutely necessary, and to do everything in our power to make this peer's job more difficult. We are not members of a diplomatic corps, we may say to ourselves, we are not being paid to coddle those who think themselves all-powerful. Further, we might have made previous attempts to reach out to this peer, only to have been stung in the process.

So why continue to make any effort at all?

Because it can't harm your position in the long run and at some point, what you attempt to do in reaching out may help to lessen the intensity of the conflict between you.

The experts in the field appear to agree that an attempt to reach out should include the following strategies.

Give Them Whatever Recognition They Deserve

If they do something well, suck it up and congratulate them. If you can do it at a meeting in front of others, all the better. At the very minimum, send them a note. The natural instincts for many of us would be to say nothing to them, to actually feel uncomfortable that they have done something well. This is not at all what we have counted on, we may say to ourselves. We would prefer to see them fail and forced to leave the company, to get out of our sight all together. Goodbye, so long. Congratulate them, give them recognition for something they have achieved in areas in which they have excelled? Yes, do it if they deserve it and do it sincerely, as if you mean it, because if they have done something well, you should mean it. Don't contrive compliments. They'll smell a rat and it will probably make your relationship worse. On the other hand, when they give you a compliment, take it with a grain of salt. They may have some plan up their sleeves, which could be to your detriment.

Seek Out Areas in Which You Can Agree

There has to be subject matter on which you can agree, particularly in meetings where the power freak peer is on the attack. "Hold on a minute, Bob, let's step back and see where we agree, before we go any further." Or, you seek out agreement on something that has to do with an action that is outside your individual purviews. You both might agree that the human resources department needs to be expanded, for example, or that something needs to be done to upgrade the conference room. It may have something to do with benefits or it may be an area outside the company all together. If you are both fans of the same sports team, you can commiserate over a loss or congratulate each other over a win. Perhaps you both have children in a little league or other sports program and you can discuss that, looking for something on which you can agree. The idea is to reflect that you are not a total contrarian or adversary to the power freak peer, that you can ally yourself with him or her when you genuinely agree on a subject or course of action.

On the other hand, be careful and don't go overboard. Remember that you are dealing with a person who finds it easy to discard those around him who are the most loyal to him, and feel good about it because it shows how ruthless he can be.

So ally with him when it is in the best interests of the company, but don't think you have made a friend. Dinner is probably out.

Let Them Share in the Credit, When Appropriate

Harry S. Truman is one of a number of successful people to whom the following quote is attributed: "It's amazing what you can accomplish if you don't care who gets the credit." I thought Brandon Toporov hit the mark in his book when he said, "A good many difficult colleagues remain in 'fact-finding' mode not because they're concerned an initiative will fail, but because they're afraid it will succeed, thereby elevating someone else's reputation or prestige within the organization."[14] The way to get around this roadblock is to share the credit, or if circumstances are appropriate, give power freak peers the credit for the idea all together, just as you might with a power freak boss. As Toporov points out, "Every once in a while, be willing to be that person who stops worrying about who gets all the credit."[15]

On the other hand, getting credit for a successful idea is like mother's milk to an extreme power freak peer. They will do everything they can to bask in the limelight of a successful program. If you let them take sole credit for a successful program that was primarily your doing, it may whet their appetite to steal program ideas from you in the future and frame them as their own before you are aware of what's happening. It is better to allow them to "share" in the credit, whenever it is appropriate, when they have made even a minor contribution. Always proceed with caution.

Ask for Their Advice

Asking power freak peers for advice on how to handle a problem you are having in your own area of authority or expertise will make their day, particularly if they feel they have some expertise on the subject. For one thing, you may be the only colleague of this person who has asked for advice. And if he does have some expertise in the area, then perhaps his thoughts can be useful to you. Remember that the idea of reaching out in general is to keep the power freak peer from being consistently adversarial with you, which may hinder you from doing your job. In this sense, you can also put the power freak peer on the defensive by asking for advice after he has been critical of what you have just done, or plan to do.

I recall "Harry," a purchasing manager, who kept a small, blue-covered paper tablet in his shirt pocket. Whenever someone he thought didn't know anything about his field of expertise criticized him for something he did, he would sit the person down, take out the tablet and ask the person for all the suggestions he or she might have about solving that specific problem. He didn't get many takers.

This is better than saying with gritted teeth, "Okay smart alec, tell me what you would do."

Calmly Acknowledge the Truth of Some Criticism

In her book *Difficult People: How to Deal with Impossible Clients, Bosses and Employees*, Roberta Cava makes the point that when a competitive and critical co-worker criticizes you unfairly and inappropriately, you can disarm him by calmly acknowledging that some aspect of the criticism may be true: "Calmly acknowledge to your critic that there may be some truth in what he or she says. This allows you to receive criticism comfortably, without becoming anxious or defensive, and gives no reward to those using the manipulative criticism."[16] This technique has been one of my personal favorites for meeting criticisms from power freaks of all types. Usually what happens when you receive what you consider unfair criticism is that your blood starts to boil, and your first reaction may be to come back with a hard retort. But if you can pause long enough to get some self-deprecation to kick in temporarily, it is amazing how quickly this disarms the critics. Some of my favorites are these:

"That book you wrote, _Brain Tricks_, I couldn't get past the first chapter."

"Yeah, I know, I have trouble reading the book myself."

"That was some stupid hire you made. The person left in less than three months."

"I made a mistake, what can I tell you? We'll try to get it right the next time."

"This ad concept sucks."

"To tell you the truth, I don't like it either. We're already developing alternatives."

For some reason, admitting that we were wrong or made a mistake is one of the most difficult things for many of us to do. We instinctually feel admitting we are wrong lowers our status. But in fact, just the opposite happens. By saying or implying "I screwed up," we are wielding the power in the situation, particularly if we follow it up with a plan of action that includes detail on how the mistake won't happen again. We are back in charge, our status is saved, and we will feel fine as the tension in the situation is released.

Go into a room at home, look into a mirror and practice, "Yeah, you're right, I screwed this up. But here's what I think we ought to do now . . ." Then, if you have an understanding spouse, hit the mirror with a hammer. That might help as well.

In the field of corporate public relations, one of the first axioms is to admit to a mistake, if a mistake was indeed made. I recall Dan Rather, of CBS News, who had just written a book, being interviewed by Bill O'Reilly of Fox News, on his nighttime show, _The O'Reilly Factor_. O'Reilly has made his mark by asking hard questions and editorializing on issues on which he takes hard stands. He likes to pick on the "elite media," which would include CBS News, and so Rather had to be courageous to come on the show at all. Both are apparently power-driven men and O'Reilly immediately went on the attack, criticizing Rather for a number of well publicized mistakes he had made over his career.

Rather, in his own quiet way, immediately admitted to the mistakes, including speaking at a Democratic party fund-raiser hosted by his daughter. (News anchors are expected to maintain a demeanor of neutrality in politics.) It appeared that these frank admissions of error, one after another, caught O'Reilly by surprise, and he was unable to follow up each of the subjects with his usual volley of piercing commentary and penetrating questions. He seemed to let down his guard when Rather admitted that the higher-ups at CBS might have something to do with the content of the news show. O'Reilly said that would never happen on his show and Rather came back with a comment that was perfect for young ears, but we all knew had some fire behind it. It was something like, "Feather dusters," an apparent euphemism for bullshit, that seemed, momentarily, to take the breath out of O'Reilly.[17]

There is great power to be wielded when a mistake is properly admitted.

Don't Become the Problem

I don't know how many times I've had lunch or dinner with a business friend who was in a rivalry with a power freak peer in which almost the entire conversation was dominated by how my friend was being wronged. Even when he appeared to be correct about his stand in the conflict with this peer, the conflict itself appeared to be working to impair his judgment. If you can avoid it, try not to become obsessed about your conflict with a peer, don't let it become an all-consuming passion even though it seems to be a constant companion in your mind.

If you can't control it, your normal peers and subordinates who have to keep hearing this will begin to feel great discomfort when they are with you. It is best to share the problem with colleagues and friends quickly and concisely from time to time, and then ask them how they are doing. Turn the conversation to them. In addition, it is best not to feed the fire by spreading stories throughout the organization about the power freak peer. Eventually, this will reflect poorly on you.

Believe it or not, there is life beyond this peer.

DEFLECTING RETORTS

Most of the best books dealing with difficult people who are co-workers, colleagues, and peers suggest deflective retorts that those of us who are less confrontational can memorize and use at the most appropriate time. I'm sure that Phil Porter, author of *Eat or Be Eaten*, wouldn't need a list of retorts. When power freaks scream at him, he screams right back at them. Case closed. However, people like Abby, described earlier in this chapter, who was extremely competent but mild and retiring in her temperament, needed assertiveness training before she could finally react to a power freak peer who was all over her back with the simple deflective retort, "Stan, get lost."

Following is a short listing of some of the best retorts I could find combing through books touching on the subject of dealing with difficult colleagues.

❖   Sandra W. Crowe, *Since Strangling Isn't an Option:*

> Tell him your assessment of the situation, and be careful to put it into those terms. "The way I see it . . ." "It seems to me . . ." "I'm getting the impression . . ." "Do we really have a problem?" "Let's talk about that . . ." "[Can we] discuss our options?"[18]

❖   Muriel Solomon, *Working with Difficult People:*
   1. Rehearse retorts at home.
   2. Force yourself to appear poised and calm.
   3. Psych yourself (put emotional space and physical space between you and your intimidator).
   4. Know when to laugh it off.

A few quick replies to the intimidator:
   (Laughing it off) "You're not really serious are you?"
   (Buying time) "Don't rush me, I'm weighing what you said."
   (Being selective) "I don't feel totally comfortable with that."[19]

❖   Leonard Felder, *Does Someone at Work Treat You Badly?: Finding the Vulnerable Spot:*

To protect yourself and not get intimidated by an Angry Screamer, you can find and focus your attention on the most humorous spot of this person's appearance. . . . Simply catch a glimpse and then think about the physical characteristic you find most vulnerable and awkward about this supposedly fearless person.[20]

Felder's three favorite comeback lines are these:
1. "Stop! I don't appreciate being talked to like this!"
2. "Time out! I want to hear what you're saying, but I've got to ask you to slow down a bit."
3. "Let's talk about this. You go first and I won't interrupt. Then when you're done, I'll see if I have any questions."[21]

※ William Lundin and Kathleen Lundin, in *Working with Difficult People*, suggest that you *think* the following during confrontations:
1. "If I let someone like you push me around and frighten me away with your crazy antics, loud noises and crazy faces, what respect can I have for myself?"
2. "I may be uptight, but I'm not stupid. If you think I'm going to stand still and be eaten alive, you've picked the wrong person."[22]

And, say the following:

"I appreciate all your help and advice. Let me do it my way. You wouldn't want me to be all over your back. Relax. We'll get more done."[23]

Rick Brinkman and Rick Kirschner, *Dealing with People You Can't Stand:*

[Say] "From my point of view . . . ," or "The way I see it . . ." If you've been accused of being behind on a project, the retort would be, . . . "I understand that you think the project ought to be finished already. From my point of view, the time I'm investing in it now will save time and money in the future."[24]

※ Lucy Gill, in *How to Work with Just about Anyone*, recommends that you encourage someone to attack you more. Gill uses the example of

"Jeanette," who was repeatedly attacked and intimidated by Gwen at meetings, until she tried something different:

> She pointed out to Gwen that their boss seemed to view Jeanette's work much more sympathetically when Gwen attacked it and so she would appreciate Gwen's continuing her criticism. At the very next meeting, when Gwen launched into her usual tirade about Jeanette's work, Jeanette sat quietly. Then, after the meeting, Jeanette thanked her for the help and walked away, leaving Gwen standing in the hall looking puzzled.[25]

My own personal and favorite retort to a power freak peer who was attacking unjustly was simply, "Get the fuck off my back." However, I now realize that this was the wrong thing to say.

THE STRUCTURED CONFRONTATION

Following are the elements of a structured confrontation, as suggested by the experts in the field as noted.

Creating the Right Climate for a Confrontation

Consider the timing first. As Lucy Gill points out, "If your colleague is rushing to leave the office early on Friday, you're not likely to find her receptive to your message." Pick the right day and time for the confrontation is the advice here. Gill adds, "Consider the staging. Your place or hers? Will the other person be more willing to listen to if you meet in her office or yours? Perhaps neutral territory would be best."[26] Sandra Crowe suggests, "Get him in a place where you can talk to him alone. Don't attempt this conversation in the middle of a staff meeting or in an elevator."[27] Charles J. Keating adds, "We need to ask ourselves whether emotions are too high to confront at the moment."[28] If you've just had a heated argument, in other words, wait until you've both calmed down. That takes some will power because you'll probably feel driven to get this off your chest.

Most of the experts agree that it is best to have your confrontation when you are both seated. Richard Bramson suggests, "Since most people behave less aggressively when seated, it's worth a try. Point to a chair and say, 'Look, if we're going to argue we might as well be comfortable.' Start to sit down yourself, but . . . if he or she doesn't sit, remain standing yourself."[29]

Prepare and Rehearse Yourself

Consider this similar to a public debate. If you've ever been on a debate team, then you know the drill. If not, you need to make notes on the points you want to make in the confrontation and to assume what retorts the power freak peer will make to you. Then you need to think out countering facts to those. It is perfectly proper to have a tablet in front of you to remind you of all the points to make. Remember that you will be speaking with someone who may have psychopathic traits and who may be delusional in their points of view. You will not be coming out with an agreement on a joint position unless a miracle takes place. What you want to do is come out of the meeting with at least a tentative truce in your conflict. You need to couch your comments as diplomatically as possible, so as to prevent a heated argument that will leave you where you were before the meeting started. Stay calm. If the meeting does lapse into a heated argument, call a halt and suggest you meet again the following week. Get out of there.

Structuring the Meeting

It would be easiest to find a neutral room, close the door, sit down, and, being polite, ask your power freak peer to begin with his or her complaints about you. You will probably sit there red-faced, wishing you had a quarter to throw against the wall, as he or she harangues you about your shortcomings. It is only with the greatest self-control that you'll be able to get through his or her speech, making notes and promising to make your retorts after he or she has finished, which you then proceed to do, practically as you had them rehearsed.

Now he is sitting there red-faced, listening to your retorts, which, because they disagree with his perception of things, will threaten his status. You both may have stacks of files before you, ready to pull out implicating documents to make or rebut a point. It will be a miracle if anything is resolved.

There is another method you might think about, told to me by an expert I know in the field of conflict resolution. He suggests that the conflict be treated objectively by both of you, and then you get to the core of the problem using the same methods you would use if these were larger corporate problems concerning your department or the company at large. Such problems are never resolved at one meeting. Rather, a series of meetings takes place, each focusing in more narrowly and objectively on the subject matter.

This expert recommends that you suggest this structure to your power freak peer as being more tried and true because these tactics are aimed at making the face-to-face discussions as objective and substantive as possible. You could remind your peer that it would be best if you could iron out your differences just between the two of you, rather than having the mediation handled by your boss, the results of which would be uncertain for both of you. Mention also that this structure will help both of you keep your heads while you delve through the subject matter. If your peer agrees, develop a subject agenda for a series of three meetings of twenty to thirty minutes each, and then try to stick to three meetings, even if it turns out that on some issues you have less to talk about and a meeting runs short.

The First Meeting

Begin this meeting by suggesting that you determine the three most *annoying methods of communicating* with each other. Let your peer list his first, if he agrees. He may not, telling you that this is all a waste of time, that there is no problem. If this happens, then simply proceed, using a marker and a bulletin board to list yours. Is it being interrupted rudely at meetings? Is it the feeling of being demeaned by his attitude in general? Is it the fact that you feel it's wrong for him to be taking full credit for the efforts of many people? Is it an implication that you are incompetent in your job? Is it jokes that he makes at your expense?

With just three points to discuss, you will have a focus. However, your peer might look at you as if you are the one who is irrational, denying that he has any such outlooks. If so, make the point that he may not feel this way at all, but this is the way he is being perceived. Don't get into an argument. Suggest that he simply think about this and agree to a time and date for a second meeting. This could be a very short meeting.

The Second Meeting

Begin by rewriting on the bulletin board the list of three annoying communications that you resent the most and are making you unhappy. He will either continue to deny the problem or rationalize it in some way. "This is how I am." "I need to be aggressive to get the job done." "Business isn't for softies, it's the equivalent of war." "I'm not doing anything other people aren't doing." "I can't help it if you have a problem." If on the other hand, he denies there is any problem, bring up actual examples of his behavior at meetings or otherwise. Be specific. Now is the time to assert to him that you are not going to roll over and play dead, that it is best if you can both adjust your behavior and try to get along even it's in the form of an armed truce, that it would be foolish to continue having open battles. Suggest he think about it again and come to a third meeting with some ideas for making small adjustments in his behavior to help make your relationship workable . . . that you are willing to make adjustments in your own behavior in response. He may refuse to continue, insisting that there is nothing wrong. If so, once again warn him in a quiet, succinct, and calm manner that you are not going to be his dartboard, that you will strike back, if and when necessary, and that both of you will be harmed by this behavior. Do not make this sound like a threat, just a detached matter of fact. If he agrees to think of some minor adjustments he might make—"Okay, I'll think about it if that will make you happy, but this is all stupid"—then schedule a third meeting.

The Third Meeting

Devote this last meeting to hearing his ideas about what might be done, if he has any. If he has at least one that makes sense, you can congratulate yourself on a breakthrough. There is possibly some hope. Discuss his suggestion, telling him how you might respond to him with adjustments of your own. Then try to get his agreement to meet privately in the future to settle future differences. If he has no ideas for improving your relationship, no suggestions, then the handwriting is on the wall. You might try to have your boss mediate the dispute as we'll describe shortly, but you're going to have to accept the fact that this person is in your life and it's not going to be a lot of fun. You can attempt to avoid him as much as you can, as per the suggestions in the next chapter, but when you are in his presence and he demeans you, you must remain assertive. Keep in mind while you are doing so that being in the front lines during World War II would have been much worse.

Don't Win the Battle and Lose the War

If at any point your meetings degenerate into a pitched battle in which you actually come out on top, don't get giddy. "My God, I beat this jerk back," you might think. You might have won the battle and lost the war. So after a brief respite, be prepared for future misery because your temporarily defeated peer is going to get even with you. If at any time during any of the meetings the discussion degenerates into a pitched battle, even if you can sense you're winning, use your emotional intelligence to gain control of your emotions and call for a recess. Agree to set a date and time to resume the meeting and then get out of there.

CONFRONTING THE STEALTH POWER FREAK PEER

At some point you will learn who this person is and how he is attempting to undermine you. He may be using his staff to do the actual dirty work while he remains behind the scenes, acting innocent and charming. Or he may be doing things himself behind your back that may be difficult to detect. When these acts of cunning add up to indisputable evidence that the peer is acting against you, you need to react with a structured confrontation.

One meeting will probably do it, because this type of power freak peer likely won't admit to anything or even attempt to rationalize his actions. In all probability he will deny that any act was purposefully designed to hurt you. "If I did hurt you in any way, if any of my staff hurt you in any way, I can assure you that this was not our intent." If this peer has psychopathic traits and is using a veneer of innocence to hide his true nature, then part of that veneer will include pathological lying. You need to be suspicious of anything he has to say, including what the temperature is outside.

At your first meeting, use the bulletin board and a marker to list at least five incidents that you have reason to believe were instigated by this peer. He will deny or attempt to explain them away, but the fact that they are listed on the board will make him understand that you are on to him. Be assertive, not aggressive in discussing the incidents. Simply relate the facts as you understand them. *Being calm and detached is essential.* This peer must not be led to believe that you are threatening him. All you want him to understand is that you are on to his game.

You may say something like, "Ed, I don't really know if you caused all of this or not, everything seems to point to it. Now you are a likable person and we don't want to create any mess that may be to your detriment or to mine. We both want to do the best we possibly can in our jobs. And so the next time something like this happens, I hope you don't mind if we get together again privately to straighten it out."

He'll probably reply, "Of course not. I am really upset that you think I am behind all of this. Anytime anything like this comes to your attention, I'll be happy to meet with you to straighten it out."

All you will have achieved at this meeting is probably a little more caution on the part of this peer. He may say to his people the next time an opportunity arises to undermine you, "Look, we have to be more careful, he may be on to us." Or, "Let's give this a pass until a more opportune time." In other words, your confrontation in all probability is not going to stop the peer from undermining you, but may slow him down. Perhaps at some point, he'll decide he needs to pick on someone else. Or better yet, top management will find him out, decide that the havoc he is causing internally isn't worth the benefits he offers, and will terminate him.

To get a better perspective of the problem, think of yourself as a colleague of Adolf Hitler during the 1920s when he was attempting to rise to power and was working behind the scenes to subvert your position. Do you think a confrontation would have stopped him? Do you think writing evidence of what he did against you on a blackboard would have worried him? The confrontation might only have made him think that you were more incisive than he thought . . . that he would have to be more careful in the future. You would need to remain on guard.

Dealing with these people is never easy.

ASKING YOUR BOSS FOR MEDIATION

Conflict resolution has become its own management field. A growing number of conflict resolution consultants are now thriving in the corporate world. These are professionals in the field. The average boss to whom you will appeal your case is probably not a conflict resolution specialist. As a matter of fact, the last thing the average boss wants to hear about is a personal conflict between two of his managers. First one, then the other is walking into his office, obsessed with the incompetencies and oversights of each other. He hears the same story over and over, hoping against hope that the managers will settle it themselves. Worse, on one day he may agree with one of the peers and take some action on her behalf, while on the next day, under the influential sway of the second peer, he feels that his prior action was unjustified. This was one of the criticisms of Bill Clinton: He would believe whatever the last expert in his office said to him. The most seasoned and successful managers, who are placed in a position of mediation, eventually learn to take all the input they are getting from compelled subordinates with a grain of salt, do some background work on their own, and form their own opinion.

Further, while you may be absolutely convinced of the correctness of your stand, that is no guarantee that faced with two opposing views, the boss is going to decide in your favor. Basically, who you have facing you is a "Judge Judy," who is going to try to make a valiant decision based on the facts, but whose decision may go against you.

When it comes to substantive issues affecting the success of the organization or department, the best managers want to hear the pros and cons no matter how serious the conflicts may be among his or her subordinates. The problem comes when the boss must resolve personal conflicts: how your power freak peer treats you in meetings, how he demeans you in front of others, his low opinion of your competence, and how you are simply unable to work together. As we've noted, in many organization environments, high ambition, aggressiveness, and ruthlessness in reaching goals are perceived as attributes. If the boss is fond of the power freak peer because he gets results, your position will be weakened. He may ask you to leave the room for five minutes while he talks in private to this peer, commiserating with him for having to deal with weaker people, but suggesting that he make some adjustments to his behavior "to maintain organizational chemistry." It is less than a slap on the wrist. He then gets the peer to agree to a few changes, calls you back in the room and asks the peer to tell you what he has agreed to do. The next week, this peer may be all over you again, because he knows he wasn't really punished for his transgressions. And threat of punishment is the only thing that may restrain people who are psychopathic or exhibit psychopathic traits.

CHAPTER 13

The Last Gasp Solution
Calculated Avoidance

Status obsessed? The board of a posh Upper East Side co-op apartment building in New York City tried to stop a well known medical practitioner from buying a unit in their building because the credit report they had drawn on him showed that he carried a J.C. Penney card.[1]

In the fields of psychology and interpersonal relationships, the strategy of avoidance is sometimes called "avoidant coping style" or "setting boundaries." Basically, it means what it says. You avoid as much as humanly practical the people in your lives whose presence causes you pain because of their intimidating and abusive behavior toward you. They may be your boss, a peer, a parent, a child, a relative, a neighbor, someone you're forced to work with at your children's school or on a church or synagogue committee, or whatever.

The idea is to set boundaries protecting yourself from them, without causing them to feel unduly rejected or worse, retaliatory. Mental health counselor Anne Katherine advises in her book *Where to Draw the Line: How to Set Boundaries Everyday*,

> Boundaries can be used in two ways—by limiting the actions of the people who have hurt you, and by including the people who have shown themselves to be trustworthy. . . . With boundaries you can protect yourself in specific and mindful ways instead of walking around armed to the hilt. You can limit your exposure to uncaring people and nourish contacts with the people who have the potential to become dear.[2]

For the purposes of this book, I prefer the term "calculated avoidance" because we are dealing with people we want to keep away from us at specified, calculated, and comfortable distances.

The greatest example of calculated avoidance that I have ever witnessed was a hilarious scene in a stage play, later adapted in 1955 into a Josh Logan and Tom Heggen movie called *Mr. Roberts*. The scene struck such a strong note with audiences that shortly after the movie was released, it was recreated by the actors on a Sunday night *Ed Sullivan Show*.

The entire movie takes place on the small cargo ship *Reluctant*, which plied the South Seas during all of World War II, delivering cargo from one port to another. It is a little ship with only sixty-two crew members. The scene involves three characters, Captain Morton, performed by James Cagney; Ensign Pulver, performed by a young Jack Lemmon; and Lieutenant Roberts, performed by Henry Fonda. The following is how the scene played out:

Captain Morton is on the deck, dressing down Lieutenant Roberts for allowing the crew to unload cargo in the broiling, South Pacific sun with their shirts off. His standing order had been that shirts must be worn at all times. Captain Morton typifies an extreme power freak. Throughout the movie he is shown taking sadistic pleasure in causing Lieutenant Roberts and the rest of the crew to suffer through his unreasonable demands. If those demands aren't carried out to the letter, he hands out punishments such as cancelling shore excursions or movie nights or confining officers and crew to their cabins or bunks. He takes particular pleasure in punishing Lieutenant Roberts, because Roberts wants to get off the *Reluctant* and onto a fighting ship. If Captain Morton could have been a sea captain during the late 1700s, the time of *Mutiny on the Bounty*'s Captain Bligh, when thrashing seamen tied to a pole was allowed, he undoubtedly would have had every man on the ship thrashed at some point during their time at sea, including the officers. Captain Morton ate all his meals in his cabin.

As Morton is dressing down Roberts, he hears a noise, turns around and is surprised to see Ensign Pulver coming down the stairs from the ship's bridge. Pulver stops in front of the captain, looks Morton briefly in the eye, spins around, and runs back up the stairs.

The captain does a double take and says "Who's that?" Then he shouts to Pulver who is walking swiftly away on the bridge, "You boy, come here." Pulver, stops, hesitates, points to himself as if saying "Me?" then comes slowly down the stairs and stops in front of the captain, who says in surprise:

"Are you one of my officers?"

"Yes, sir," Pulver replies softly.

"What was your name again?"

"Ensign Pulver . . . sir," he replies, saluting.

The captain turns slightly to address himself to Mr. Roberts, who is standing to one side.

"Well, I'm pleased to see that someone aboard this vessel knows how to salute."

The captain then turns back to Pulver and says, "How is it I don't see you around more, Pulver?"

"Well, I've often wondered about the same thing myself, sir."

"What's your job, Pulver?"

"Officer in charge of laundry and morale, sir."

"How long have you been aboard, Pulver?"

After a long pause, Pulver replies timidly, "fourteen months, sir."

A look of shock crosses the captain's face. *Fourteen months?*" he blares in disbelief, looking around at Roberts, who has his back turned and is using a hand to hold back his laughter.

"Yes, sir."

The captain thinks for a moment. "Oh, I see," he says settling down. "You spend most of your time in the laundry."

Pulver replies in relief. "Most of my time, yes, sir . . . down. . . ."

"Well, you do a very fine job, Pulver."

"Well, thank you, sir."

"Except for one thing."

"Sir"?

"I don't like starch in my pajamas. You'll watch that won't you?"

"Yes, sir."

"You must come to my cabin sometime . . . have dinner."

Pulver pauses and then simply salutes. The captain walks away.[3]

How many of us in an organization of fewer than sixty-five people could have pulled off what Pulver did, being able to avoid being in the presence of a power freak boss for as long as fourteen months? The idea is appealing, because if we don't have to deal with the power freak directly, if we can avoid being in his presence, we deflect the mental pain he inflicts. How can we do it?

AVOIDING THE POWER FREAK BOSS

Perhaps the operative terms are "distancing ourselves" and "tuning out." There are workers who need to be in the presence of their boss, power freak or not, to maintain their status. Under the strategy of calculated avoidance, the idea is to do just the opposite: to distance yourself. If you have to be in staff meetings when the power freak is present, take a seat as far away from him as you can. If you are asked a question or for a report, be as brief and to the point as you can. Make yourself as small in his presence as you possibly can. If he begins to berate you, try to tune out, simply nod your head in agreement, thinking, "That's what you believe, fine. I'm working on my resume, anyway." You might have tried some of the strategies in dealing with a power freak boss listed in chapter 11, but still found that none of them worked for you. Then calculated avoidance may be your best approach. This person is a jerk you are either trying to outlast or you are waiting for a better opportunity in another department or at another company.

I've never seen anyone as good as Ensign Pulver when it comes to avoiding a power freak boss, but I've seen a few who came close. For example, "Marty," an old friend of mine, was vice president of manufacturing for a client, a division of a multibillion dollar corporation. Each year Marty had to participate in a planning conference at the corporation's headquarters. He had to give an annual presentation that would be lambasted at the end by the CEO, who would literally scream questions and rebukes at Marty. Marty may have been a quiet and retiring person by nature, but he was an effective leader in his own right. He would work hard to avoid the CEO when he visited the division, shaking hands and then sauntering to the area of the room farthest from the CEO. Before his presentation at the annual planning conference, he would understandably begin to get nervous and anxious. When he presented his report, he got through it as quickly as he could, grasping the lectern at the end with whitened fingers as he prepared to endure the profane deprecations of the CEO, running out of the room as soon as it was over.

This happened every year for several years, until the year of Marty's retirement. As he finished his presentation, and was waiting for the usual lambasting from the CEO, he noticed that the CEO was distracted for an instant, talking to someone next to him. Marty took advantage of the lull and literally ran off the stage, out the room, and over to the coffee table in the outside corridor. The president of the division, Marty's immediate boss, soon came out and said, "Marty, you've got to come back, the CEO wants to talk to you."

"Not on your life," Marty said. "You can put a gun to my head, but I'm not going to go back in there."

"But he wants to say something nice to you."

And so Marty went back into the room, unbelieving, as the CEO actually paid him some compliments.

Another manager I knew, an inventory control manager, always worked with his office door closed, primarily because he was scared to death of his vitriolic boss. You hardly ever saw him. He would appear to sneak out to go to the bathroom when absolutely necessary. We never saw him eat lunch, so we assumed he brought something from home and ate behind closed doors. He did his job well, issuing reports on time, and nobody ever bothered him. He was called "The Phantom."

Of course, if you're working for a small company or your power freak boss has an office nearby, calculated avoidance may not be possible. Maybe you can ask to work from home.

AVOIDING THE POWER FREAK PEER

In his book *The Eight Essential Steps to Conflict Resolution*, specialist Dudley Weeks makes the following points:

- Avoidance merely postpones dealing with the conflict and usually allows it to worsen.

❦ Frustrations are usually exacerbated by avoidance and misperceptions go unclarified.

❦ Avoidance denies parties in conflict the opportunity of using their differences to clarify their relationship and to open their minds to the possibility of improvement.[4]

Another specialist, Daniel Dana, calls avoidance "Walk-Aways," which includes avoidance to the point that you don't even talk to each other. Like Weeks, he also recommends against this strategy.[5]

They are both generally correct in their viewpoints. But we are assuming that at this point in your relationship with an extreme power freak peer you have done everything practical, as suggested in the previous chapter, to try to make the relationship work. She is still making you miserable. It is only at this point that you might attempt the strategy of calculated avoidance, since you have little to lose. Calculated avoidance is not the total avoidance of an Ensign Pulver. This may be impossible in a close working environment of colleagues. Further, it is beneficial to employ the strategy in such a way that the power freak peer is unaware of it. You don't walk by him in the hall and not say hello, for example. As a matter of fact if you can, you stop, exchange greetings and some small talk, and then move on. You need to maintain a demeanor of acceptance and cooperation. On the other hand, when you do have contact and she belittles you, or orders you or your staff to do something that is outside of her authority, you need to assert your position. This has particular relevance with a power freak peer. You need to stand your ground and deflect her with assertive rather than aggressive remarks as described in the previous chapter: "Bob, time out. I don't appreciate your attitude," or "Bob, we need to talk about this." "Bob, if you think I'm going to stand still and be eaten alive, you're mistaken." But that is it. You want this person on the fringes of your "boundaries." You no longer, at this point, attempt to reach out, ask for advice, allow her to take credit for your ideas or give her undue recognition. If you know she is going to be at a gathering and you can avoid it, do so. If it is a company social event and you think you should be there, find other people to talk with. But make sure that at some point you encounter the power freak peer, exchange greetings and small talk, and then move on. In meetings that you need to attend where these peers are present, remain concise in any discussion you need to have with them, asserting yourself only when necessary.

If the power freak peer begins to believe that you are deliberately ignoring her, she may conclude in her paranoia that you are working behind the scenes to threaten her position, and you don't want that. You simply want a neutral position, to be perceived as simply disinterested, but with a clear understanding that she won't be able to cow you, to bring you under the sway of her control and power. However, if the peer continues to pursue you, to belittle you, to attack you, to seek you out to the point that your efforts to avoid her aren't effective, even after a series of last-gasp confrontational meetings and mediation with the boss, then you have to weigh whether it is best to stay on and endure the torment, hoping you'll outlast this person, ask for a transfer to another department, or begin looking for opportunities elsewhere.

AVOIDING OTHER POWER FREAKS IN YOUR LIVES

Calculated avoidance may also be the ultimate solution with other extreme power freaks in your lives, whose controlling, manipulating, rejecting, and intimidating personalities are making you uncomfortable. It may be one or both of your parents or one or more of your children. It may be your in-laws or the entire family of your spouse; it may be a sibling or another relative. It may be someone in a civic or church group, who is in charge of a committee on which you sit.

Avoidance per se becomes more difficult the closer the person is to you. An extreme power freak parent may be difficult to avoid without feelings of remorse and guilt, even if the parent is at the edges of psychopathy. "Mom, Dad," some children will plead, "can't you tell me you love me? Can't you tell me you're proud of me?" The trauma of intimidation and/or rejection by a parent to a son or daughter can be intense, well beyond childhood and adolescence. Sons and daughters, in their thirties, forties, and fifties with parents who remain rejecting and/or intimidating, may continue to suffer. Phone calls and visits home can create deep anxieties. If these adult offspring are high on the nurturance scale discussed on pages 51–53, they can rarely get over the pain. Yet they find that avoiding their parents to any calculable extent is extremely difficult because they don't want their parents to feel hurt. The same phenomena can occur when one or both parents are abusive alcoholics. On the other hand, adult children who are capable of putting significant space between themselves and their parents find over time that it can be a great relief. Their love and attachment for their parents may have been significantly diminished by years of hostility.

We have also read about parents who have cut off adult children who have become abusive to them, particularly those who are alcoholic and/or exhibit such psychopathic traits that they become intimidating and demeaning to their parents, even to the point of stealing from them. And so the parents, if they are well balanced themselves, undergo severe mental anguish when they cut these children out of their lives. On the other hand, if the parents are incapable of feeling remorse or guilt themselves, then the separation can be relatively painless. We have seen the same phenomenon among siblings, who may cut each other out of their lives for even relatively small slights that have been exaggerated to the point of delusion.

Maybe you have an in-law in your life who is an extreme power freak. If your spouse remains close to that person, you can't entirely ignore him or her. You need to negotiate a boundary line with your spouse. I know one person who is quiet and refined, but who can't stand to be in the company of her spouse's family because they are loud, gregarious back-slappers. And so she simply doesn't go to his family functions, a boundary she was able to negotiate with her husband and that he was willing to accept.

Some years ago I knew a man who couldn't stand to be in the company of his father-in-law, who even though in his seventies, continued to rule the family with an iron hand. And so this man told his wife that he would see her father only on Father's Day, on Thanksgiving, on Christmas Day, and on his birthday. Other family functions where her father was present she would go to alone. He told me that he managed to get through the hours with his father-in-law at the required functions by greeting his father-in-law warmly, making small talk for a few minutes, and then finding others to talk to, and getting them into deep, involved conversations so that his father-in-law wouldn't think he was avoiding him.

"The only problem with this method," he told me, "is that you have to pick your conversation partners carefully. At one family function, a guy was there who looked like an ideal partner for a conversation. But it turned out that he was a hypochondriac and I had to listen for two hours about every little pain he had—and he had them everywhere. He wouldn't let me get away. During the last twenty minutes I was praying for a chance to talk to my father-in-law, just for a change of pace in my misery."

In her book, Anne Katherine has an interesting chart that indicates how far into our lives most of us will allow each of four relationships: "acquaintances," "neighbors," "comrades," and "intimates." She lists the activities. For example, she says that most of us will "give or get a ride to an airport," with all four of these relationships, as well as "help them move," "touch hands when sad," and "invite to Thanksgiving dinner." On the other hand, we will only "cuddle," with an "intimate [not necessarily a spouse or lover]," but might "hug spontaneously" both a comrade and an intimate.

I'm not sure that I would help anybody move, even an intimate, but she points out that, "Different people have different styles, so just because it can be appropriate to cuddle with an intimate friend doesn't mean all intimate friends would be comfortable with it."[6] She's probably right. I don't think I could cuddle with my tennis partner, Joe Farago.

Most of us innately establish boundaries with the annoying, quirkish, peripheral people in our lives without giving it a second thought, particularly neighbors, church and civic group members, acquaintances, and so on, with whom we feel uncomfortable. We avoid them as much as possible and when they cross the line, we say or do something that sends them a message. For example, as Anne Katherine suggests, "If someone hugs you and it doesn't feel right, that's all you need to know. Pull out of the hug immediately and say something like, 'Please don't. I'm not comfortable with hugging yet.'"[7]

I intend to save that last line for Joe Farago if he ever tries to hug me.

These people are but relatively insignificant annoyances when compared to extreme power freaks, who may not want us out of their lives because we are easy targets for their attacks and intimidation. We make their day. They can even make it miserable for us to avoid them, using whatever charm they have to remind us of all that they have done for us up to and including, if they are a parent, changing our diapers.

But do we want them in our lives? If they are out of our lives altogether, will the guilt and remorse we feel be worse than the depression, despondency, and sadness we feel when they are in our lives? Can we establish a boundary line that calls for only limited contact? Can we live with that? Can they honor this type of commitment? These are all tough calls.

I remember many years ago after my first divorce I found a list of advice attributed to a sixteenth-century monk on what we can do to achieve contentment in life. I pasted that list on my refrigerator and looked at it often. I have since lost the list, but one item has always remained clear in my memory: "Avoid vexatious people."

Wonderful advice.

Afterword

Charles T. Snowdon, chair of the University of Wisconsin's Department of Psychology and, as previously noted, one of the world's leading primatologists, pointed out to me that alpha chimpanzees will frequently groom and be conciliatory to the lower ranks in their groups in order to gain their help or support. He also pointed to the work of another primatologist and author Fran de Waals, quoted on page 99, who focuses on the power politics of chimpanzee groups, an important part of which is their use of reconciliation gestures.

It may be that the human extreme power freak who is demeaning and tyrannical to his subordinates rather than supportive and conciliatory is some form of evolutionary regression. If you are suffering under the pressure of an extreme power freak in your life and a friend says, "I feel your pain," you can thus safely tell him that what you feel is a lot more than he can possibly appreciate.

If the extreme power freak is your boss or another authority figure, each time you are in his or her presence you, in all probability, begin to feel like the slumping, losing crayfish because you know, whether words are said or not, that he or she is intent on demeaning your status. If the extreme power freak is a peer, you are never sure when the next blow might come. Each time he or she strikes, the pain may be intense and become cumulatively worse.

When an extreme power freak is ruthless in putting us down, the painful feelings of humiliation, anxiety, despair, and even torment can last for months or longer, because the power freak remains in our presence, a constant reminder that some level of terrorization may happen at any moment. We come to dread going to work or going home, wherever the extreme power freak lurks.

Many years ago, we had a retiree who came back to work for us after his wife passed away. He only wanted to come in the office three times a week, for half days, which was fine with us. At the time, we had a window office available temporarily, so we put him there. A few months later we needed the office and so on his day off, we moved him to a nearby office across the hall. It never dawned on us that he would be offended, because of the few hours he put in every week and the fact that he was just happy to have a place to hang his hat. But he became so depressed when he saw where his desk was now that he could hardly speak to any of us. Worse, he couldn't get any work done. He told me over lunch that he hadn't felt such pain since his wife passed away and that he was actually embarrassed about it. Finally, we moved him back to a window office and he was fine.

It would appear that the pain we might feel from the loss of status, even a minor loss of status, can be completely disproportionate to the event that provoked it. It's as if nature really went overboard with punishing feelings when it designed this emotional reaction, perhaps because status and the dominance hierarchy of which it is part were so critical to our ultimate survival when we were primitives living in caves.

We observed in chapter 3 the pain felt by Michael Jordan when his young Chicago Bulls team lost its first run at a championship to the Detroit Pistons. His status was drastically demeaned. He was inconsolable. But as the days passed, he snapped out of it. There were new challenges ahead. Those working or living in the presence of an extreme power freak, as just noted, may not snap out of it. The pain can endure. Even other victories in our lives may begin to ring hollow.

How we handle ourselves, if we are unable to leave for more collegial surroundings, is serious business. If we sustain the battering long enough, and we are vulnerable to it, we may be pushed into a mood or personality disorder of our own. At the very least, we're probably not going to be pleasant company.

Unless we have that blessed capacity for allowing the vitriol directed at us to roll off our backs, we need to work hard to develop coping solutions—a game plan for dealing with this person who is basically beyond reason. As we've observed, there are no universal answers. We each have to find our own way and we have to keep working at it.

In a sense, we are working two jobs at the same time. The first is the one we are being paid for. The second may be an even tougher job of positioning ourselves to avoid or deflect as much as we can, while maintaining our base level of self-esteem, the demeaning venom that the extreme power freak *enjoys* aiming our way. Every little step we take toward achieving this position can be considered a significant victory.

Whenever you feel you've made some progress in attaining this goal, you deserve to stop for a moment and pat yourself on the back. If you get to a point where you can co-exist with some level of comfort in the presence of this nutcase, you will have truly done a mighty thing.

Notes

INTRODUCTION

1. David G. Winter, *The Power Motive* (New York: Macmillan, 1973), p. xvii.
2. Ibid, p. 5.

CHAPTER 1. WHO ARE THESE PEOPLE?

1. David McCullough, *John Adams* (New York: Simon & Schuster, 2001), p. 170.
2. Sam Smith, *The Jordan Rules* (New York: Simon & Schuster, 1992), pp. 25, 63, 82, 111.
3. Ron Rapoport, "Knight, Texas Tech: Match Made in Hell," *Chicago Sun-Times*, March 21, 2001, p. 157.
4. Joel Stein, "Bosses from Hell. They Don't Want to Be Your Friend. You Don't Want to Be Their Enemy," *Time*, December 7, 1998, p. 100.
5. Herbert P. Bix, *Hirohito and the Making of Modern Japan* (New York: HarperCollins, 2000), p. 547.
6. Gerry Lange and Todd Domke, *Cain & Abel at Work: How to Overcome Office Politics and the People Who Stand between You and Success* (New York: Broadway Books, 2001), p. 4.
7. Doris Kearns Goodwin, *No Ordinary Time: Franklin and Eleanor Roosevelt: The Home Front in World War II* (New York: Simon & Schuster, 1994), p. 209.

CHAPTER 2. HOW DOES A POWER FREAK THINK?

1. Story based on actual experience as reported on the Internet site: www. employeesurveys.com/bosses/badboss22.htm, accessed January 10, 2001.

2. John Bowlby, *Attachment* (New York: BasicBooks, 1982), pp. 207–208.

3. Craig Nakken, *The Addictive Personality* (Center City, Minn.: Hazelden, 1988), p. 35.

4. Jim Sidanius and Felicia Pratto, *Social Dominance* (Cambridge: Cambridge University Press, 1999), p. 5.

5. Norman Doidge, "Appetitive Pleasure States: A Biopsychoanalytic Model of the Pleasure Threshold, Mental 'Representation and Defense,' " in *Pleasure Beyond the Pleasure Principle: The Role of Affect in Motivation Development and Adaptation*, ed. Robert A. Glick and Stanley Bone (New Haven, Conn.: Yale University Press, 1990), p. 163.

6. Edward O. Wilson, *Concilience: The Unity of Knowledge* (New York: Knopf, 1998), p. 97.

7. Donald W. Black, *Bad Boys, Bad Men: Confronting Antisocial Personality Disorder* (New York: Oxford University Press, 1999), p. 109.

8. Steven Levy, "Dr. Edelman's Brain," *New Yorker*, May 2, 1994, pp. 66–68.

9. Paul McLean, *A Triune Concept of the Brain and Behavior* (Toronto: University of Toronto Press, 1973), pp. 8–12.

10. "Mapping Similarities between Humans and Chimpanzees," Genome News Network, http://gnn.tigr.org/articles/01_02/Human_chimpanzees.shtml, accessed January 4, 2002.

11. L. Sprague de Camp, *The Ape-Man Within* (Amherst, N.Y.: Prometheus Books, 1995).

12. Joseph E. LeDoux, *The Emotional Brain: The Mysterious Underpinnings of Emotional Life* (New York: Simon & Schuster, 1996), pp. 186–89.

13. David L. Weiner with Gilbert M. Hefter, *Battling the Inner Dummy: The Craziness of Apparently Normal People* (Amherst, N.Y.: Prometheus Books, 1999), p. 65.

14. Information taken from a *Biography* documentary on the A&E Channel, March 2001.

15. Black, *Bad Boys, Bad Men*, p. 60.

16. Daniel Goleman, *Emotional Intelligence* (New York: Bantam, 1995), pp. 13–14.

CHAPTER 3. THE POWER FREAK AS CAVEMAN

1. William Lundin and Kathleen Lundin, *When Smart People Work for Dumb Bosses: How to Survive in a Crazy and Dysfunctional Worplace* (New York: McGraw-Hill, 1998), pp. 15–16.

2. John Cartwright, *Evolution and Human Behavior* (Cambridge, Mass.: The MIT Press, 2000), p. 282.

3. Personal written communication with Charles T. Snowdon.

4. Cartwright, *Evolution and Human Behavior*, p. 282.

5. Terry Burnham and Jay Phelan, *Mean Genes: From Sex to Money to Food: Taming Our Primal Instincts* (Cambridge, Mass.: Perseus Publishing, 2000), pp. 37–38.

6. Steven Pinker, *How the Mind Works* (New York: Norton, 1997), p. 388.

7. Ibid., p. 386.

8. I watched this subject covered on a segment of the CBS television show *60 Minutes*, during February 2001.

9. David M. Buss, *Evolutionary Psychology* (Needham Heights, Mass.: Allyn & Bacon, 1999), p. 321.

10. Francis H. C. Crick, *The Astonishing Hypothesis: The Scientific Search for the Soul* (New York: Macmillan, 1994), p. 21.

11. "The Book of Humankind," *National Post*, February 12, 2001, p. A01.

12. David L. Weiner with Gilbert M. Hefter, *Battling the Inner Dummy: The Craziness of Apparently Normal People* (Amherst, N.Y.: Prometheus Books, 1999), p. 76.

13. David G. Winter, *The Power Motive* (London: The Free Press, 1973), p. 7.

14. Buss, *Evolutionary Psychology*, p. 345.

15. Patricia R. Barchas and M. Hamit Fisek, "Hierarchal Differentiation in Newly Formed Groups of Rhesu and Humans," in *Social Hierarchies: Essays toward a Sociophysiological Perspective*, ed. Patricia R. Barchas (Westport, Conn.: Greenwood Publishing Group, 1984), p. 41.

16. I worked with one company where the chairman had one of the smallest offices on the floor. I've worked with Japanese companies where the CEO and president occupied the same, relatively small, office space so that they would know what each other was doing.

17. Robert Ardrey, *The Territorial Imperative: A Personal Inquiry into the Animal Origins of Property and Nations* (New York: Kodansha International, 1966), p. 10.

18. John Madden with Dave Anderson, *One Size Doesn't Fit All* (New York: Jove Books, 1988), p. 14.

19. David Gergen, *Eyewitness to Power: The Essence of Leadership* (New York: Simon & Schuster, 2000), p. 91.

20. Richard N. Ostling, "Researcher Tabulates World's Believers," Associated Press, May 19, 2001. He quoted from the World Christian Encyclopedia, published by Oxford University Press, which also noted that there are 33,830 separate Christian denominations.

CHAPTER 4. THE POWER FREAK FACTOR IN ALL OF US

1. Adapted from a story in Russell Wilde, *Games Bosses Play* (New York: McGraw-Hill, 1997), p. 33.

2. David C. McClelland, *Human Motivation* (Cambridge: Cambridge University Press, 1987), p. 35.

3. Jack Panksepp, *Affective Neuroscience: The Foundations of Human and Animal Emotions* (Oxford: Oxford University Press, 1998), p. 145.

4. Michael Eysenck, *Psychology: An Integrated Approach* (Essex, England: Longman, 1998), p. 457.

5. One of the best compendiums on the subject is *Pleasure beyond the Pleasure Principle: The Role of Affect in Motivation Development and Adaptation*, ed. Robert A. Glick and Stanley Bone (New Haven, Conn.: Yale University Press, 1990).

6. Tony Helm, "Hitler a 'Friendly, Easygoing' Boss," *Chicago Sun-Times*, February 5, 2002, p. 23.

7. Sam Smith, *The Jordan Rules* (New York: Pocket Books, 1992), p. 63.

8. Ibid., pp. 217–18.

9. Stefan Fatsis, "All Mac, All the Time," *Wall Street Journal*, August 24, 2001, p. W6.

10. Norman Doidge, "Appetitive Pleasure States: A Biopsychoanalytic Model of the Pleasure Threshold, Mental 'Representation and Defense,' " in Glick and Bone, *Pleasure beyond the Pleasure Principle*, p. 155.

11. Sandra Blakeslee, "Scientists Examine How 'Social Rewards' Can Hijack the Brain's Circuits," Science Times, *New York Times*, February 19, 2002, pp. D1, D5.

12. Ibid.

13. Otto F. Kernberg, "Hatred as Pleasure," in Glick and Bone, *Pleasure beyond the Pleasure Principle*, pp. 195–96.

14. Judith R. Harris, *The Nurture Assumption: Why Children Turn Out the Way They Do* (New York: Simon & Schuster, 1998), pp. 352–53.

15. Suellen Fried and Paula Fried, *Bullies and Victims: Helping Your Child Survive the Schoolyard Battlefield* (New York: M. Evans & Co., 1998).

16. Peter Randall, *Adult Bullying: Perpetrators and Victims* (London: Routledge, 1997), p. 39.

17. Joel Stein, "Bosses from Hell. They Don't Want to Be Your Friend. You Don't Want Them to Be Your Enemy," *Time* (special issue), December 7, 1998, p. 181.

18. Doidge, "Appetitive Pleasure States," pp. 163–65.

19. David Gergen, *Eyewitness to Power: The Essence of Leadership* (New York: Simon & Schuster, 2000), p. 181.

CHAPTER 5. THE POWER FREAK AS MENTALLY DISORDERED

1. Rick Brinkman and Rick Kirschner, *Dealing with People You Can't Stand: How to Bring Out the Best in People at Their Worst* (New York: McGraw-Hill, 1994), pp. 4–5.

2. V. Mark Durand and David H. Barlow, *Abnormal Psychology: An Introduction* (Pacific Grove, Calif.: Brooks/Cole Publishing Co., 1997), p. 375.

3. Robert D. Hare, David J. Cooke and Stephen D. Hart, "Psychopathy and Sadistic Personality Disorder," in *Oxford Textbook of Psychopathology*, ed. Theodore Millon, Paul H. Blaney, and Roger D. Davis (Oxford: Oxford University Press, 1999), p. 555.

4. Quoted from *60 Minutes II*, "Dr. Park Dietz: Spotting Psychos on the Payroll," broadcast January 16, 2001.

5. Remi J. Cadoret, "Epidemiology of Antisocial Personality," in *Unmasking the Psychopath*, ed. William H. Reid, Darwin Door, John I. Walker, and Jack W. Bonner III (New York: Norton, 1986), p. 29.

6. Durand and Barlow, *Abnormal Psychology*, p. 374.

7. Harvey Cleckley, *The Mask of Sanity* (Augusta, Ga.: Emily S. Cleckley, 1988), p. viii.

8. Robert D. Hare, *Without Conscience: The Disturbing World of the Psychopaths among Us* (New York: The Guilford Press, 1999), p. 24.

9. Ibid., p. 113.

10. Cleckley, *The Mask of Sanity*, p. 208–17; quoted in Hare, *Without Conscience*, p. 64.

11. Hare, *Without Conscience*, p. 59.

12. Cleckley, *The Mask of Sanity*, p. 339.

13. Ibid., pp. 192, 195.

14. Donald W. Black, *Bad Boys, Bad Men: Confronting Antisocial Personality Disorder* (New York: Oxford University Press, 1999), pp. 109, pp. 162–65.

15. I saw this woman interviewed in a documentary about Hitler on the History Channel in the spring of 2001.

16. Aaron T. Beck, Arthur Freeman, and Associates, *Cognitive Therapy of Personality Disorders* (New York: The Guilford Press, 1990), p. 154.

17. HBO interview with Bob Costas, week of March 12, 2001.

18. Cited by Carl Sherman, "Treatment for Psychopaths Is Likely to Make Them Worse," *Clinical Psychiatry News* 28, no. 5 (2000): 38.

19. James Morrison, *DSM-IV Made Easy: The Clinician's Guide to Diagnosis* (New York: The Guilford Press, 1995), p. 5.

20. Black, *Bad Boys, Bad Men,* p. 169.

21. Theodore Millon and Roger B. Davis, "Ten Subtypes of Psychopathy," in *Psychopathy: Antisocial, Criminal and Violent Behavior,* ed. Theodore Millon, Erik Simonsen, Morten Birket-Smith, and Roger B. Davis (New York: The Guilford Press, 1998), pp. 162–70.

22. Hare, "Psychopathy and Sadistic Personality Disorder," pp. 572–73.

23. Sadistic Personality Disorder was included in DSM-III, but deleted from DSM-IV. Here are the reasons for the deletion, as described by Hare in "Psychopathy and Sadistic Personality Disorder":

A range of considerations influenced the complete removal of the disorder from DSM-IV. The primary consideration was the lack of a coherent body of research concerning the validity and utility of the concept. In addition, it was thought that enshrining the disorder in DSM-IV—thereby providing it with official status—could lead to misuse of the diagnosis in forensic settings. Further, it is conceivable that those suffering from the disorder might endeavor to use the diagnosis to mitigate their responsibility for their violence against women. . . . Nonetheless, it has been argued forcefully that the deletion of the SPD from the nomenclature of personality disorders is a major error underpinned by political rather than scientific considerations. Many diagnostic categories can be misused in forensic settings, yet this is not a good reason to obscure their existence and inhibit their study. It is the responsibility of the legal system—not those endeavoring to describe, measure, and understand the disorder—to determine the influence that expert testimony has on such issues as responsibility and risk." (p. 575)

24. Hare, "Psychopathy and Sadistic Personality Disorder," pp. 572–74.

25. Durand and Barlow, *Abnormal Psychology*, p. 396.

26. Robert D. Hare and Stephen D. Hart, "Association between Psychopathy and Narcissism," in *Disorders of Narcissism: Diagnostic, Clinical, and Empirical Implications*, ed. Elsa F. Ronningstam (Washington, D.C.: American Psychiatric Press, Inc., 1998), p. 324.

27. American Psychiatric Association, *Diagnostic and Statistical Manual of Mental Disorders: DSM-IV* (Washington, D.C.: American Psychiatric Association, 1994), p. 661.

28. Theodore Millon with Roger Davis, *Disorders of Personality: DSM-IV and Beyond* (New York: Wiley, 1996), p. 410.

29. American Psychiatric Association, DSM-IV, p. 637.

30. Roy F. Baumester, "Violent Pride: Do People Turn Violent Because of Self-Hate or Self-Love?" *Scientific American*, April 2001, p. 100.

31. Lauren Slater, "The Trouble with Self-Esteem," *New York Times Magazine*, February 3, 2002, pp. 44–47.

CHAPTER 6. THE POWER FREAK AS STATUS-OBSESSED

1. Dennis Mack Smith, *Mussolini: A Biography* (New York: Vintage Books, 1982), p. 202.

2. Jerome H. Barkow, "Beneath New Culture Is Old Psychology: Gossip and Social Stratification," in *The Adapted Mind: Evolutionary Psychology and the Generation of Culture*, ed. Jerome H. Barkown, Leda Cosmides, and John Tooby (Oxford: Oxford University Press, 1992), pp. 633–34.

3. Carl Sagan and Ann Druyan, *Shadows of Forgotten Ancestors: A Search for Who We Are* (New York: Ballantine Books, 1992), pp. 210–11.

4. Ibid., p. 207.

5. David M. Buss, *Evolutionary Psychology* (Needham Heights, Mass.: Allyn & Bacon, 1999), p. 346.

6. Ibid., p. 347.

7. Frans De Waal, *The Ape and the Sushi Master: Cultural Reflections of a Primatologist* (New York: Basic Books, 2001), p. 304.

8. Doreen Carvaal, "Still Around the Neighborhood," *New York Times*, April 10, 2001, p. B1.

9. Richard Severo, "Perry Como, Relaxed and Elegant Troubadour of Recordings and TV, Is Dead at 88," *New York Times*, May 15, 2001, p. 39.

10. I saw the story about bed linen on a 1999 PBS documentary about the duke of Windsor, written by Prince Edward. The duke was Prince Edward's great-uncle.

11. Ray Mosely, "Remarks Causing a Royal Headache," *Chicago Tribune*, April 7, 2001, Section 1, p. 3.

12. Jim Sidanius and Felicia Pratto, *Social Dominance: An Intergroup Theory of Social Hierarchy and Oppression* (Cambridge: Cambridge University Press, 1999), p. 37.

13. Ibid., p. 33.

14. Ibid., p. 35.

15. Boye De Mente, *Japanese Etiquette & Ethics in Business* (Chicago: Passport Books, 1987), p. 26.

16. Marler named Bernhardt et al.'s study (published in *Physiological Behavior* 65 [1998]: 59–62) regarding testosterone among sports fans.

17. One of the characteristics of antisocial personality disorder, which is synonymous with psychopathy, as listed in the DSM-IV in "Evidence of Conduct Disorder with onset before age 15 years." American Psychiatric Association, *Diagnostic and Statistical Manual of Mental Disorders: DSM-IV* (Washington, D.C.: American Psychiatric Association, 1994), p. 650.

CHAPTER 7. SITUATIONAL POWER FREAKS

1. Bob Rosner, *Working Wounded: Advice That Adds Insight to Injury* (New York: Warner Books, 1998), p. 64.

2. Jane Goodall, *In the Shadow of Man* (Boston: Houghton Mifflin, 1971), pp. 116–17.

3. Ibid., p. 115.

4. Michael Moss, *Palace Coup* (New York: Doubleday, 1989), p. 111.

5. Randolph M. Neese, "Evolutionary Explanations of Emotions," *Human Nature* 1, no. 3 (1990): 277.

6. Peter Randall, *Adult Bullying, Perpetrators and Victims* (London: Routledge, 1997), p. 8.

CHAPTER 8. DIRECTIONAL POWER FREAKS

1. Harvey A. Hornstein, *Brutal Bosses and Their Prey: How to Identify and Overcome Abuse in the Workplace* (New York: Riverhead Books, 1996), p. 17.

2. From the song "A Puzzlement," *The King and I*, Richard Rodgers and Oscar Hammerstein, 1951.

3. Les Parrott III, *The Control Freak: Coping with Those Around You, Taming the One Within* (Wheaton, Ill.: Tyndale House Publishers, 2000), p. 59.

4. W. D. Parker and K. K. Adkins, "Perfectionism and the Gifted," *Roeper Review* (1994): 173.

5. Sidney J. Blatt, "The Destructiveness of Perfectionism: Implications for the Treatment of Depression," *American Psychologist*, 49, no. 12: 1003–20.

6. Aaron T. Beck, Arthur Freeman, et al., *Cognitive Therapy of Personality Disorders* (New York: The Guilford Press, 1990), p. 318.

7. Jim Sidanius and Felicia Pratto, *Social Dominance* (Cambridge: Cambridge University Press, 1999), p. 56.

8. David M. Buss, *Evolutionary Psychology* (Needham Heights, Mass.: Allyn & Bacon, 1999), p. 356.

9. "The Book of Humankind," *National Post*, February 12, 2001, p. A01.

10. Eric Sorensen, "'Race Gene Does Not Exist,' Say Scientists. Skin Color Tied to Small Genetic Site," *Seattle Times*, February 11, 2001, p. A1.

11. Jane Golden, seattletimes.com, November 22, 1998, pp. 1–4.

12. Boomers International Newsletter Online, www.boomersint.org, April 24, 2001.

13. Natalie Angier, "Cell Phone or Pheromone? New Props for the Mating Game" *New York Times*, November 7, 2000.

14. Robert Pedone and Rosaria Conte, "Dynamics of Status Symbols & Social Complexity," National Research Council, Institute of Psychology, http://agent2000.anl.gov/abstracts/pedoneConteStatus.pdf, accessed March 10, 2001.

15. Christopher Loch, Michael Yaziji, and Christian Langen, "The Fight for the Alpha Position: Channeling State Competition in Organizations," Working Research Papers, INSEAD, Institut Europeen d'Administration des Affaires, www.lib.purdue.edu/mel/workingpapers/1469.html, updated January 12, 2001.

CHAPTER 9. STEALTH POWER FREAKS: MANIPULATING WHILE UNDERCOVER

1. I heard this story told some years ago on a PBS radio show. I noted it and have finally found a use for it.

2. Harvey Cleckley, *The Mask of Sanity* (Augusta, Ga.: Emily S. Cleckley, 1988), p. 4.

3. Stanley Bing, *What Would Machiavelli Do?: The Ends Justify the Meanness* (New York: HarperBusiness, 2000), pp. vii–ix.

4. Michael Moss, *Palace Coup: The Inside Story of Harry & Leona Helmsley* (New York: Doubleday, 1989), p. 111.

CHAPTER 10. THE POWER FREAK FACTOR: CAN WE MEASURE OURSELVES?

1. Adapted from an anonymous experience related on www.working-wounded.com/msgboards, accessed May 25, 2001.

2. Paul Babiak, "When Psychopaths Go to Work: A Case Study of an Industrial Psychopath," *Applied Psychology: An International Review* 45, no. 2 (1995): 171–88.

3. Robert Slater, *Get Better or Get Beaten: 29 Leadership Secrets from GE's Jack Welch* (New York: McGraw-Hill, 2001), pp 34–35.

4. Bob Rosner, Allan Halcrow, and Alan Levins, *The Boss's Survival Guide: Everything You Need to Know about Getting through (and Getting the Most Out of) Every Day* (New York: McGraw-Hill, 2001), p. 315.

5. Joseph Epstein, *Ambition: The Secret Passion* (Chicago: Elephant Paperback, 1980), p. 6.

6. Gilbert Brim, *Ambition: How We Manage Success and Failure throughout Our Lives* (Lincoln, Neb.: Authors Guild Backinprint.com, 1992), p. 16.

7. Kenneth S. Davis, *FDR: The War President: 1940–1943* (New York: Random House, 2000), p. 392.

8. Test available at http://www.imsa.edu/~durman/psych/manxiety2.html, accessed June 20, 2001.

9. David G. Winter, *The Power Motive* (New York: MacMillan, 1973), pp. 247–355.

10. Ibid., p. 265.

11. David L. Weiner, *Brain Tricks: Coping with your Defective Brain* (Amherst, N.Y.: Prometheus Books, 1995), pp. 327–28.

12. David L. Weiner with Gilbert M. Hefter, *Battling the Inner Dummy: The Craziness of Apparently Normal People* (Amherst, N.Y.: Prometheus Books, 1999), pp. 106–108.

13. Roman Modrowski, *Chicago Sun-Times*, December 3, 2001, p. 74.

14. Weiner, *Battling the Inner Dummy*, p. 109.

15. Background on this crime can be found at www.crimelibrary.com/loeb/loeb/loebarrest.htm. accessed July 7, 2001.

CHAPTER 11. DEALING WITH THE EXTREME POWER FREAK BOSS

1. U. Yodyinguad, D. De La Riva, D. H. Abbott, J. Herbert, and E. B. Keverne, "Relationship between Dominance Hierarchy, Cerebrospinal Fluid Levels of Amine Transmitter Metabolites (5-Hydroxyindole) Acetic Acid and Homovanillic Acid) and Plasma Cortisol in Monkeys," *Neuroscience* no. 4 (1985): 851–58.

2. Kenneth S. Davis, *FDR: The War President: 1940–1943* (New York: Random House, 2000), p. 8.

3. Brandon Toropov, *The Complete Idiot's Guide to Getting Along with Difficult People* (New York: Alpha Books, 1997), p. 89.

4. Jerry Useem, "A Manager for All Seasons," *Fortune*, April 30, 2001, pp. 66–72.

5. Frans de Waal, *The Ape and the Sushi Master: Cultural Reflections of a Primatologist* (New York: Basic Books, 2001), p. 310.

6. Les Parrott III, *The Control Freak: Coping with Those Around You, Taming the One Within* (Wheaton, Ill.: Tynsdale House, 2000), p. 60.

7. Robert M. Bramson, *Coping with Difficult People* (New York: Dell, 1981), p. 127.

8. Brian Tracy, *Advanced Selling Strategies* (New York: Simon & Schuster, 1995), pp. 244–45.

9. Toropov, *The Complete Idiot's Guide*, p. 85.

10. Ibid., pp. 86–87.

11. Albert J. Bernstein and Sydney Craft Rozen, *Neanderthals at Work: How People and Politics Can Drive You Crazy . . . And What You Can Do about Them*, (New York: Ballatine Books, 1992), pp. 166, 187, 203, 218, 217, 224–28.

12. William Lundin and Kathleen Lundin, *Working with Difficult People* (New York: American Management Association, 1995), p. 13.

CHAPTER 12. DEALING WITH A PEER WHO IS AN EXTREME POWER FREAK

1. Gerry Lange and Todd Domke, *Cain & Abel at Work: How to Overcome Office Politics and the People Who Stand between You and Success* (New York: Broadway Books, 2001), p. 4.

2. Sandra A. Crowe, *Since Strangling Isn't an Option . . . Dealing with Difficult People—Common Problems and Uncommon Solutions* (New York: Perigee, 1999), p. 143.

3. Phil Porter, *Eat or Be Eaten: Jungle Warfare for the Master Corporate Politician* (Paramus, N.J.: Prentice Hall, 2000), p. 37.

4. Robert M. Bramson, *Coping with Difficult People* (New York: Dell, 1981), pp. 14–15.

5. Porter, *Eat or Be Eaten*, pp. 23–24.

6. Charles J. Keating, *Dealing with Difficult People: How You Can Come Out on Top in Personality Conflicts* (Mahwah, N.J.: Paulist Press, 1984), p. 115.

7. Muriel Solomon, *Working with Difficult People* (Paramus, N.J.: Prentice Hall, 1990), p. 15.

8. Ibid., p. 14.

9. Alan Axelrod and Jim Holtje, *210 Ways to Deal with Difficult People* (New York: McGraw-Hill, 1997), p. 23.

10. Lucy Gill, *How to Work with Just about Anyone: A 3-Step Solution for Getting Difficult People to Change* (New York: Fireside, 1999), p. 119.

11. Keating, *Dealing with Difficult People*, p. 120.

12. Les Parrott III, *The Control Freak: Coping with Those Around You, Taming the One Within* (Wheaton, Ill.: Tynsdale House, 2000), p. 78.

13. Keating, *Dealing with Difficult People*, p. 121.

14. Brandon Toropov, *Complete Idiot's Guide to Getting Along with Difficult People* (New York: Alpha Books, 1997), p. 74.

15. Ibid.

16. Roberta Cava, *Difficult People: How to Deal with Impossible Clients, Bosses and Employees* (Buffalo, N.Y.: Firefly Books, 1997), p. 133.

17. Dan Rather appeared on *The O'Reilly Factor* primarily to promote his new book, *The American Dream*, during the late summer of 2001.

18. Crowe, *Since Strangling Isn't an Option*, p. 117.

19. Solomon, *Working with Difficult People*, pp. 18–19.

20. Leonard Felder, *Does Someone at Work Treat You Badly?: How to Handle Brutal Bosses, Crazy Coworkers . . . and Anyone Else Who Drives You Nuts* (New York: Berkley, 1993), pp. 57–58.

21. Ibid., pp. 64–69.

22. William Lundin and Kathleen Lundin, *Working with Difficult People* (New York: American Management Association, 1995), p. 119.

23. Ibid., p. 75.

24. Rick Brinkman and Rick Kirschner, *Dealing with People You Can't Stand: How to Bring Out the Best in People at Their Worst* (New York: McGraw-Hill, 1997), p. 76.

25. Gill, *How to Work with Just about Anyone*, p. 102.

26. Ibid., p. 126.

27. Crowe, *Since Strangling Isn't an Option*, p. 84.

28. Keating, *Dealing with Difficult People*, p. 179.

29. Bramson, *Coping with Difficult People*, p. 17.

CHAPTER 13. THE LAST GASP SOLUTION: CALCULATED AVOIDANCE

1. Neal Travis, "Co-op Board Horror Stories," *New York Post*, November 15, 2001, p. 11.

2. Anne Katherine, *Where to Draw the Line: How to Set Boundaries Every Day* (New York: Simon & Schuster, 2000), pp. 38–39.

3. Josh Logan and Thomas Heggen, *Mr. Roberts*, Warner Bros., 1955.

4. Dudley Weeks, *The Eight Essential Steps to Conflict Resolution: Preserving Relationships at Work, at Home and in the Community* (New York: Penguin Putnam, 1992), p. 22.

5. Daniel Dana, *Conflict Resolution: Mediation Tools for Everyday Worklife* (New York: McGraw-Hill, 2001), p. 51.

6. Katherine, *Where to Draw the Line*, pp. 118–20.

7. Ibid., p. 119.

Bibliography

Aggleton, John P. *The Amygdala: A Functional Analysis.* Oxford: Oxford University Press, 2000.

American Psychiatric Association. *Diagnostic and Statistical Manual of Mental Disorders: DSM-IV.* Washington, D.C.: American Psychiatric Association, 1994.

Angier, Natalie. "Cell Phone or Pheromone? New Props for the Mating Game," *New York Times,* November 7, 2000.

Ardrey, Robert. *The Territorial Imperative: A Personal Inquiry into the Animal Origins of Property and Nations.* New York: Kodansha International, 1996.

Aron, Elaine N. *The Highly Sensitive Person.* New York: Broadway Books, 1996.

Axelrod, Alan, and Jim Holtje. *210 Ways to Deal with Difficult People.* New York: McGraw-Hill, 1997.

Babiak, Paul. "When Psychopaths Go to Work: A Case Study of an Industrial Psychopath," *Applied Psychology: An International Review* 45, no. 2 (1995): 171–88.

Baker, Robin R., and Mark A. Bellis. *Human Sperm Competition: Copulation, Masturbation and Infidelity.* London: Chapman & Hall, 1995.

Barchas, Patricia R., and M. Hamit Fisek. "Hierarchal Differentiation in Newly Formed Groups of Rhesu and Humans." In *Social Hierarchies: Essays Toward a Sociophysiological Perspective,* ed. Patricia R. Barchas. Westport, Conn.: Greenwood Publishing Group, 1984.

Barkow, Jerome H. "Beneath New Culture Is Old Psychology: Gossip and Social Stratification." In *The Adapted Mind: Evolutionary Psychology and the Generation of Culture,* ed. Jerome H. Barkown, Leda Cosmides, and John Tooby. Oxford: Oxford University Press, 1992.

Baumester, Roy F. "Violent Pride: Do People Turn Violent Because of Self-hate or Self-love?" *Scientific American* (April 2001): 96–101.

Beck, Aaron T., and Gary Emery with Ruth L. Greenberg. *Anxiety Disorders and Phobias: A Cognitive Perspective*. New York: Basic Books, 1985.

Beck, Aaron T., Arthur Freeman, and associates. *Cognitive Therapy of Personality Disorders*. New York: The Guilford Press, 1990.

Bell, Arthur H., and Dayle M. Smith. *Winning with Difficult People*. New York: Barron's Educational Series, Inc., 1997.

Bennett-Goleman, Tara. *Emotional Alchemy: How the Mind Can Heal the Heart*. New York: Harmony Books, 2001.

Bernstein, Albert J., and Sydney Craft Rozen. *Neanderthals at Work: How People and Politics Can Drive You Crazy . . . And What You Can Do about Them*. New York: Ballatine Books, 1992.

Bing, Stanley. *What Would Machiavelli Do?: The Ends Justify the Meanness*. New York: HarperBusiness, 2000.

Birkhead, Tim. *Promiscuity: An Evolutionary History of Sperm Competition*. Cambridge, Mass.: Harvard University Press, 2000.

Bix, Herbert P. *Hirohito and the Making of Modern Japan*. New York: HarperCollins, 2000.

Black, Donald W. *Bad Boys, Bad Men: Confronting Antisocial Personality Disorder*. New York: Oxford University Press, 1999.

Blakeslee, Sandra. "Scientists Examine How 'Social Rewards' Can Hijack the Brain's Circuits," *New York Times*, February 19, 2002, pp. D1, D5.

Blatt, Sidney J. "The Destructiveness of Perfectionism: Implications for the Treatment of Depression," *American Psychologist* 49, no. 12: 1003–20.

Bowlby, John. *Attachment*. New York: Basic Books, 1982.

Bramson, Robert M. *Coping with Difficult People*. New York: Dell, 1981.

———. *What Your Boss Doesn't Tell You until It's Too Late*. New York: Simon & Schuster, 1996.

Breitman, Patti, and Connie Hatch. *How to Say No without Feeling Guilty*. New York: Broadway Books, 2000.

Brim, Gilbert. *Ambition: How We Manage Success and Failure throughout Our Lives*. Lincoln, Neb.: Authors Guild Backinprint.com, 1992.

Brinkman, Rick, and Rick Kirschner. *Dealing with People You Can't Stand: How to Bring Out the Best in People at Their Worst*. New York: McGraw-Hill, 1994.

Burnham, Terry, and Jay Phelan. *Mean Genes: From Sex to Money to Food: Taming Our Primal Instincts*. Cambridge, Mass.: Perseus Publishing, 2000.

Buss, David M. *Evolutionary Psychology*. Needham Heights, Mass.: Allyn & Bacon, 1999.

Byrne, John A. *Chainsaw: The Notorious Career of Al Dunlap in the Era of Profit-at-Any-Price*. New York: HarperBusiness, 1999.

Cadoret, Remi J. "Epidemiology of Antisocial Personality." In *Unmasking the Psychopath*, ed. William H. Reid, Darwin Door, John I. Walker, and Jack W. Bonner III. New York: Norton, 1986.

Cartwright, John. *Evolution and Human Behavior*. Cambridge, Mass.: The MIT Press, 2000.

Carvaal, Doreen. "Still Around the Neighborhood," *New York Times*, April 10, 2001, p. B1.

Cava, Roberta. *Difficult People: How to Deal with Impossible Clients, Bosses and Employees*. Buffalo, N.Y.: Firefly Books, 1997.

Chang, Iris. *The Rape of Nanking: The Forgotten Holocaust of World War II*. New York: Basic Books, 1997.

Changeux, Jean-Pierre. *Neuronal Man: The Biology of Man*. New York: Pantheon Books, 1995.

Christie, Richard, and Florence L. Geis. *Studies in Machiavellianism*. New York: Academic Press, 1970.

Cleckley, Harvey. *The Mask of Sanity*. Augusta, Ga.: Emily S. Cleckley, 1988.

Coppinger, Raymond, and Lorna Coppinger. *Dogs: A Startling New Understanding of Canine Origin, Behavior & Evolution*. New York: Scribner, 2001.

Crick, Francis H. C. *The Astonishing Hypothesis: The Scientific Search for the Soul*. New York: Macmillan, 1994.

Crowe, Sandra A. *Since Strangling Isn't an Option . . . Dealing with Difficult People—Common Problems and Uncommon Solutions*. New York: Perigee, 1999.

Curry, Patrick, and Oscar Zarate. *Introducing Machiavelli*. New York: Totem Books, 1996.

Dana, Daniel. *Conflict Resolution: Mediation Tools for Everyday Worklife*. New York: McGraw-Hill, 2001.

Davenport, Noa, Ruth Distler Schwartz, and Gail Pursell Elliott. *Mobbing: Emotional Abuse in the American Workplace*. Ames, Iowa: Civil Society Publishing, 1999.

Davis, Joel. *Mapping the Mind: The Secrets of the Human Brain & How It Works*. Secaucus, N.J.: Carol Publishing Group, 1997.

Davis, Kenneth S. *FDR: The War President: 1940–1943*. New York: Random House, 2000.

Dawkins, Richard. *The Selfish Gene*. Oxford: Oxford University Press, 1989.

de Camp, Sprague L. *The Ape-Man Within*. Amherst, N.Y.: Prometheus Books, 1995.

de Lisser, Peter. *Be Your Own Executive Coach*. Worcester, Mass.: Chandler House Press, 1999.

De Mente, Boye. *Japanese Etiquette & Ethics in Business*. Chicago: Passport Books, 1987.

Dennett, Daniel C. *Consciousness Explained*. Boston: Little, Brown & Co., 1991.

de Waal, Frans. *The Ape and the Sushi Master: Cultural Reflections of a Primatologist*. New York: Basic Books, 2001.

Diamond, Jared. *The Third Chimpanzee: The Evolution and Future of the Human Animal*. New York: HarperPerennial, 1992.

Doidge, Norman. "Appetitive Pleasure States: A Biopsychoanalytic Model of the Pleasure Threshold, Mental 'Representation and Defense.'" In *Pleasure Beyond the Pleasure Principle: The Role of Affect in Motivation Development and Adaptation*, ed. Robert A. Glick and Stanley Bone. New Haven, Conn.: Yale University Press, 1990.

Durand, Mark V., and David H. Barlow. *Abnormal Psychology: An Introduction*. Pacific Grove, Calif.: Brooks/Cole Publishing Co., 1997.

Early, Emmett. *The Raven's Return: The Influence of Psychological Trauma on Individuals and Culture*. Wilmette, Ill.: Chiron Publications, 1993.

Edelman, Gerald M., and Jean-Pierre Changeux. *The Brain*. New Brunswick, N.J.: Transaction Publishers, 2001.

Engel, Freman. *Taming the Beast: Getting Violence out of the Work Place*. Montreal: Ashwell Books, 1998.

Epstein, Joseph. *Ambition: The Secret Passion*. Chicago: Elephant Paperback, 1980.

Eysenck, Michael, ed. *Psychology: An Integrated Approach*. Essex, England: Addison-Wesley Longman, 1998.

Fatsis, Stefan. "All Mac, All the Time," *Wall Street Journal*, August 24, 2001, p. W6.

Felder, Leonard. *Does Someone at Work Treat You Badly?: How to Handle Brutal Bosses, Crazy Coworkers . . . and Anyone Else Who Drives You Nuts*. New York: Berkley, 1993.

Fossey, Dian. *Gorillas in the Mist*. Boston: Houghton Mifflin, 1983.

Freud, Sigmund. *The Ego and the Id*. New York: Norton, 1960.

Gay, Peter, ed. *The Freud Reader*. New York: Norton, 1989.

Gergen, David. *Eyewitness to Power: The Essence of Leadership*. New York: Simon & Schuster, 2000.

Gerth, H. H., and C. Wright Mills. *From Max Weber: Essays in Sociology*. New York: Oxford University Press, 1946.

Gill, Lucy. *How to Work with Just about Anyone: A 3-Step Solution for Getting Difficult People to Change*. New York: Fireside, 1999.

Gladwell, Malcolm. *The Tipping Point: How Little Things Can Make a Big Difference*. New York: Little, Brown & Co., 2000.

Goleman, Daniel. *Emotional Intelligence*: New York: Bantam, 1995.

Goodall, Jane. *In the Shadow of Man*. Boston: Houghton Mifflin, 1988.

Goodwin, Doris Kearns. *No Ordinary Time: Franklin and Eleanor Roosevelt: The Home Front in World War II*. New York: Simon & Schuster, 1994.

Griffiths, Paul E. *What Emotions Really Are: The Problem of Psychological Categories*. Chicago: University of Chicago Press, 1997.

Hare, Robert D. *Without Conscience: The Disturbing World of the Psychopaths among Us*. New York: The Guilford Press, 1999.

Hare, Robert D., David J. Cooke, and Stephen D. Hart. "Psychopathy and Sadistic Personality Disorder." In *Oxford Textbook of Psychopathology*, ed. Theodore Millon, Paul H. Blaney, and Roger D. Davis. Oxford: Oxford University Press, 1999.

Hare, Robert D., and Stephen D. Hart, "Association between Psychopathy and Narcissism." In *Disorders of Narcissism: Diagnostic, Clinical, and Empirical Implications*, ed. Elsa F. Ronningstam. Washington, D.C.: American Psychiatric Press, Inc., 1998.

Harris, Judith R. *The Nurture Assumption: Why Children Turn Out the Way They Do*. New York: Simon & Schuster, 1998.

Hazan, Cindy, and Phillip Shaver. "Romantic Love Conceptualized as an Attachment Process," *Journal of Personality and Social Psychology* 52, no. 3 (1987): 511–24.

Hornstein, Harvey A. *Brutal Bosses and Their Prey: How to Identify and Overcome Abuse in the Workplace*. New York: Riverhead Books, 1996.

Johnson, Gerald L. *Bad Bosses, Bad Jobs, Fight Back*. Cheyenne, Wyo.: Western Star Publishing, 1994.

Katherine, Anne. *Where to Draw the Line: How to Set Healthy Boundaries Every Day*. New York: Simon & Schuster, 2000.

Keating, Charles J. *Dealing with Difficult People: How You Can Come Out on Top in Personality Conflicts*. Mahwah, N.J.: Paulist Press, 1984.

Kernberg, Otto F. "Hatred as Pleasure." In *Pleasure beyond the Pleasure Principle: The Role of Affect in Motivation, Development and Adaptation*, ed. Robert A. Glick and Stanley Bone. New Haven, Conn.: Yale University Press, 1990.

Koopmans, Judith R., et al. "A Multivariate Genetic Analysis of Sensation Seeking," *Behavior Genetics* 25, no. 4 (1995): 349–56.

Kotulak, Ronald. *Inside the Brain: Revolutionary Discoveries of How the Mind Works*. Kansas City, Mo.: Andrews and McMeel, 1996.

Kroll, Jerome. *The Challenge of the Borderline Patient: Competency in Diagnosis and Treatment*. New York: Norton, 1988.

Lange, Gerry, and Todd Domke. *Cain & Abel at Work: How to Overcome Office*

Politics and the People Who Stand between You and Success. New York: Broadway Books, 2001.

LeDoux, Joseph E. *The Emotional Brain: The Mysterious Underpinnings of Emotional Life*. New York: Simon & Schuster, 1996.

Ledeen, Michael A. *Machiavelli on Modern Leadership*. New York: Truman Talley Books, 1999.

Levine, Daniel S. *Disgruntled: The Darker Side of the World of Work*. New York: Berkley Boulevard Books, 1998.

Levy, Steven. "Dr. Edelman's Brain," *New Yorker*, May 2, 1994, pp. 66–68.

Lewis, Dorothy O. *Guilty by Reason of Insanity: A Psychiatrist Explores the Minds of Killers*. New York: Ballantine, 1998.

Lewis, Gerald W., and Nancy C. Zare. *Myth and Reality: Workplace Hostility*. Philadelphia: Accelerated Development, 1999.

Lewis, Michael, and Jeanette M. Haviland, eds. *Handbook of Emotions*. New York: The Guilford Press, 1993.

Lichtenberg, Ronna, with Gene Stone. *Work Would Be Great If It Weren't for the People: Ronna and Her Evil Twin's Guide to Making Office Politics Work for You*. New York: Hyperion, 1998.

Littauer, Florence. *How to Get Along with Difficult People*. Eugene, Ore.: Harvest House Publishing, 1999.

Loch, Christopher, Michael Yaziji, and Christian Langen. "The Fight for the Alpha Position: Channeling State Competition in Organizations," Working Research Papers, INSEAD, Institut Europeen d'Administration des Affaires, www.lib.purdue.edu/mel/workingpapers/1469.html [accessed January 12, 2001].

Lundin, William, and Kathleen Lundin. *When Smart People Work for Dumb Bosses: How to Survive in a Crazy and Dysfunctional Workplace*. New York: McGraw-Hill, 1998.

———. *Working with Difficult People*. New York: American Management Association, 1995.

Luria, A. R. *The Working Brain: An Introduction to Neuropsychology*. New York: Basic Books, 1973.

Machiavelli, Niccolo. *The Prince*. New York: Bantam Books, 1966.

Madden, John, with Dave Anderson. *One Size Doesn't Fit All*. New York: Jove Books, 1988.

"Mapping Similarities between Humans and Chimpanzees," Genome News Network, http://gnn.tigr.org/articles/01_02/Human_chimpanzees.shtml [accessed January 4, 2002].

Markham, Ursula. *How to Deal with Difficult People*. London: Thorsons, 1993.

McClelland, David C. *Human Motivation*. Cambridge: Cambridge University Press, 1987.

McCullough, David. *John Adams*. New York: Simon & Schuster, 2001.

McLean, Paul. *A Triune Concept of the Brain and Behavior*. Toronto: University of Toronto Press, 1973.

Meloy, J. Reid. *Violent Attachments*. Northvale, N.J.: Jason Aronson, Inc., 1997.

Miall, Hugh, Oliver Ramsbotham, and Tom Woodhouse. *Contemporary Conflict Resolution*. Cambridge: Polity Press, 1999.

Miller, Joy. *Addictive Relationships: Reclaiming Your Boundaries*. Deerfield Beach, Fla.: Health Communications, 1989.

Millon, Theodore, and Roger B. Davis. "Ten Subtypes of Psychopathy." In *Psychopathy: Antisocial, Criminal and Violent Behavior*, ed. Theodore Millon, Erik Simonsen, Morten Birket-Smith, and Roger B. Davis. New York: The Guilford Press, 1998.

————. *Disorders of Personality DSM IV and Beyond*, 2d ed. New York: Wiley, 1996.

Montgomery, Sy. *Walking with the Great Apes: Jane Goodall, Dian Fossey, Birute' Galdikas*. Boston: Houghton Mifflin, 1991.

Moss, Michael. *Palace Coup: The Inside Story of Harry & Leona Helmsley*. New York: Doubleday, 1989.

Morrison, James. *DSM-IV Made Easy: The Clinician's Guide to Diagnosis*. New York: The Guilford Press, 1995.

Nakken, Craig. *The Addictive Personality*. Center City, Minn.: Hazelden, 1988.

Namie, Gary, and Ruth Namie. *The Bully at Work*. Naperville, Ill.: Source Books, 2000.

Neese, Randolph M. "Evolutionary Explanations of Emotions," *Human Nature* 1, no. 3 (1990): 277.

Noyes, John K. *The Mastery of Submission Inventions of Masochism*. New York: Cornell University Press, 1997.

Ostling, Richard N. "Researcher Tabulates World's Believers," *Associated Press*, May 19, 2001.

Page, George. *Inside the Animal Mind*. New York: Broadway Books, 1999.

Panksepp, Jack. *Affective Neuroscience: The Foundations of Human and Animal Emotions*. Oxford: Oxford University Press, 1998.

Parker, W. D., and K. K. Adkins. "Perfectionism and the Gifted," *Roeper Review* (1994): 173.

Parrott, Les III. *The Control Freak: Coping with Those Around You, Taming the One Within*. Wheaton, Ill.: Tynsdale House, 2000.

Pedone, Robert, and Rosaria Conte. "Dynamics of Status Symbols & Social

Complexity," National Research Council, Institute of Psychology, http:// agent2000.anl.gov/abstracts/pedoneConteStatus.pdf, [accessed March 10, 2001].

Pert, Candice B. *Molecules of Emotion: Why You Feel The Way You Feel.* New York: Scribner, 1997.

Pinker, Steven. *How the Mind Works.* New York: Norton, 1997.

Porter, Phil. *Eat or Be Eaten: Jungle Warfare for the Master Corporate Politician.* Paramus, N.J.: Prentice Hall, 2000.

Ramachandran, V. S. and Sandra Blakeslee. *Phantoms in the Brain: Probing the Mysteries of the Human Mind.* New York: Morrow, 1998.

Randall, Peter. *Adult Bullying: Perpetrators and Victims.* London: Routledge, 1997.

Rapoport, Ron. "Knight, Texas Tech: Match Made in Hell." *Chicago Sun-Times,* March 21, 2001, p. 157.

Reardon, Kathleen Kelley. *The Secret Handshake: Mastering the Politics of the Business Inner Circle.* New York: Random House, 2000.

Richmond, Virginia P., and James C. McCroskey. *Organizational Communications for Survival.* Englewood Cliffs, N.J.: Prentice Hall, 1992.

Ridley, Matt. *The Origins of Virtue: Human Instincts and the Evolution of Cooperation.* New York: Penguin, 1997.

Rosner, Bob. *Working Wounded: Advice That Adds Insight to Injury.* New York: Warner Books, 1998.

Rosner, Bob, Allan Halcrow, and Alan Levins. *The Boss's Survival Guide: Everything You Need to Know about Getting through (and Getting the Most Out of) Every Day.* New York: McGraw-Hill, 2001.

Sagan, Carl, and Ann Druyan. *Shadows of Forgotten Ancestors: A Search for Who We Are.* New York: Ballantine Books, 1992.

Samerow, Stanton. *Inside the Criminal Mind.* New York: Times Books, 1984.

Sanday, Peggy R. *Female Power and Male Dominance: On the Origins of Sexual Inequality.* Cambridge: Cambridge University Press, 1981.

Savage-Rumbaugh, Sue, and Roger Lewin. *Kanzi: The Ape at the Brink of the Human Mind.* New York: John Wiley & Sons, Inc., 1994.

Schaef, Anne Wilson. *When Society Becomes an Addict.* New York: Harper-Collins, 1987.

Schaef, Anne Wilson, and Diane Fassel. *The Addictive Organization.* New York: HarperCollins, 1988.

Schechter, Harriet. *Conquering Chaos at Work: Strategies for Managing Disorganization and the People Who Cause It.* New York: Fireside, 2000.

Severo, Richard. "Perry Como, Relaxed and Elegant Troubador of Recordings and TV, Is Dead at 88." *New York Times,* May 15, 2001, p. 39.

Sherman, Carl. "Treatment for Psychopaths Is Likely to Make Them Worse." *Clinical Psychiatry News* 28, 5 (2000): 38.

Sidanius, Jim, and Felicia Pratto. *Social Dominance.* Cambridge: Cambridge University Press, 1999.

Simmel, Georg. *On Individuality and Social Forms.* Chicago, Ill.: University of Chicago Press, 1971.

Siu, R. G. H. *The Craft of Power.* Malabar, Fla.: Krieger Publishing Co., 1979.

Slater, Lauren. "The Trouble with Self-Esteem," *New York Times Magazine,* February 3, 2002, pp. 44–47.

Slater, Robert. *Get Better or Get Beaten: 29 Leadership Secrets from GE's Jack Welch.* New York: McGraw-Hill, 2001.

Smith, Dennis Mack. *Mussolini: A Biography.* New York: Vintage Books, 1982.

Smith, Sam. *The Jordan Rules.* New York: Simon & Schuster, 1992.

Solomon, Muriel. *Working with Difficult People.* Paramus, N.J.: Prentice Hall, 1990.

Sorensen, Eric. " 'Race Gene Does Not Exist,' Say Scientists. Skin Color Tied to Small Genetic Site," *Seattle Times,* February 11, 2001.

Steen, R. Grant. *DNA and Destiny: Nature and Nurture in Human Behavior.* New York: Plenum Press, 1996.

Stein, Joel. "Bosses from Hell. They Don't Want to Be Your Friend. You Don't Want to Be Their Enemy," *Time,* December 7, 1998, p. 181.

Stekel, Wilhelm. *Sadism and Masochism: The Psychology of Hatred and Cruelty.* New York: Liveright Publishing Co., 1929.

Temple, Christine. *The Brain: An Introduction to the Psychology of the Human Brain and Behaviour.* New York: Penguin, 1993.

Te Paske, Bradley A. *Rape and Ritual: A Psychology Study.* Toronto: Inner City Books, 1982.

"The Book of Humankind," *National Post,* February 12, 2001, p. A1.

Toropov, Brandon. *Manager's Guide to Dealing with Difficult People.* Paramus, N.J.: Prentice Hall, 1997.

Tracy, Brian. *Advanced Selling Strategies.* New York: Simon & Schuster, 1995.

Travis, Neal. "Co-op Board Horror Stories." *New York Post,* November 15, 2001, p. 11.

Useem, Jerry. "A Manager for All Seasons," *Fortune* (April 30, 2001): 66–72.

Washton, Arnold, and Donna Boundy. *Willpower's Not Enough: Recovering from Addictions of Every Kind.* New York: Harper & Row, 1989.

Weiner, David L., with Gilbert M. Hefter. *Battling the Inner Dummy: The Craziness of Apparently Normal People.* Amherst, N.Y.: Prometheus Books, 1999.

———. *Brain Tricks: Coping with Your Defective Brain.* Amherst, N.Y.: Prometheus Books, 1995.

Weiner, Jonathan. *The Beak of the Finch*. New York: Vintage Books, 1994.

Weinstein, Bob. *I Hate My Boss: How to Survive and Get Ahead When Your Boss Is a Tyrant, Control Freak, or Just Plain NUTS*. New York: McGraw-Hill, 1998.

Weeks, Dudley. *The Eight Essential Steps to Conflict Resolution: Preserving Relationships at Work, at Home and in the Community*. New York: Penguin Putnam, 1992.

Whitaker, Todd, and Douglas J. Fiore. *Dealing with Difficult Parents: And with Parents in Difficult Situations*. Larchmont, N.Y.: Eye on Education, 2001.

Whybrow, Peter C. *A Mood Apart: The Thinker's Guide to Emotion and Its Disorders*. New York: HarperPerennial, 1997.

Wild, Russell. *Games Bosses Play*. Lincolnwood, Ill.: Contemporary Books, 1997.

Wilson, Edward O. *Concilience: The Unity of Knowledge*. New York: Knopf, 1998.

———. *Sociobiology*. Cambridge, Mass.: The Belknap Press of Harvard University Press, 1980.

Winter, David G. *The Power Motive*. London: The Free Press, 1973.

Wood, Karen Ginsburg. *Don't Sabotage Your Success: Make Office Politics Work*. Oakland, Calif.: Enlightened Concepts, 2001.

Wolman, Benjamin B. *Antisocial Behavior: Personality Disorders from Hostility to Homicide*. Amherst, N.Y.: Prometheus Books, 1999.

Wright, Lawrence. *Twins: And What They Tell Us about Who We Are*. New York: Wiley, 1997.

Wright, William. *Born That Way: Genes Behavior Personality*. New York: Knopf, 1998.

Yodyinguad, U., D. De La Riva, D. H. Abbott, J. Herbert, and E. B. Keverne. "Relationship between Dominance Hierarchy, Cerebrospinal Fluid Levels of Amine Transmitter Metabolites (5-Hydroxyindole) Acetic Acid and Homovanillic Acid and Plasma Cortisol in Monkeys," *Neuroscience*, no. 4 (1985): 851–58.

Yunker, Teresa. "Yard Rage: Protecting Your Turf Is a Basic Instinct, but It's Best to Try Friendly Persuasion when Tempers Flare over Real or Imagined Space Violations," *Los Angeles Times*, March 1, 1998, p. K1.

Zimbardo, Philip G. *Shyness: What It Is, What to Do about It*. Reading, Mass.: Addison-Wesley Publishing, 1977.

Zuckerman, Marvin, Monte S. Buchsbaum, and Dennis L. Murphy. "Sensation Seeking and Its Biological Correlates," *Psychological Bulletin* 88, no. 1 (1980): 187–214.

Index

David L. Weiner author of *Battling the Inner Dummy: The Craziness of Apparently Normal People* and *Brain Tricks: Coping with Your Defective Brain*, is on the board of advisers of the HealthEmotions Research Institute of the University of Wisconsin. He is also the founder and CEO of Marketing Support, Inc., a marketing agency with a variety of Fortune 500 and other clients.

Foreword by Robert E. Lefton, Ph.D:
Robert E. Lefton is co-founder, President and CEO of Psychological Associates, Inc., one of the nation's largest business behavioral science firms, serving many Fortune 500 companies. It has offices in London, Paris, Mexico, Spain, Greece, Italy and Canada. Dr. Lefton serves on many business boards, is a noted speaker, co-author of four books and author of many business journal articles.